NEIL
YOUNG
The *Rolling Stone* Files

Other Books in the ROLLING STONE Series
U2: The ROLLING STONE Files

NEIL YOUNG

The *Rolling Stone* Files

The Ultimate Compendium
of Interviews, Articles, Facts
and Opinions
from the Files of Rolling Stone

BY

T H E   E D I T O R S

O F

Rolling Stone

INTRODUCTION BY HOLLY GEORGE-WARREN

HYPERION

NEW YORK

Library of Congress Cataloging-In-Publication Data
Neil Young, the Rolling stone files : the ultimate compendium of interviews, articles, facts and opinions from the files of Rolling stone / by the editors of Rolling stone ; introduction by Holly George-Warren. — 1st ed.
    p. cm.
    Includes discography and videography.
    ISBN 0-7868-8043-0
    1. Young, Neil—Criticism and interpretation. 2. Rock music—History and criticism. I. Rolling stone (New York, N.Y.)
    ML420.Y75N45 1994
    782.42166'092—dc20
    [B]
94-11012
CIP
MN

Design by ROBERT BULL DESIGN
First Edition
10 9 8 7 6 5 4 3 2 1

CONTENTS

FOREWORD

THUMBING THROUGH BACK issues of ROLLING STONE to put together *Neil Young: The* ROLLING STONE *Files* was like getting a mini-history lesson of the magazine. Stories on Young's career appear almost from the beginning—the third issue of ROLLING STONE (December 14, 1967). So, while reading pieces on Young and his ever-changing output, you can't help but notice the magazine's editorial evolution as well. In the early days, ROLLING STONE's take on Young (and his colleagues in the Buffalo Springfield and Crosby, Stills, Nash and Young) was very personal; for example, the magazine ran an item heralding the fact that CSNY members had relocated from Los Angeles to the San Francisco area, ROLLING STONE's then-hometown.

At the time notoriously media-shy, Young tried to avoid the spotlight, and frequently complained about all the hoopla, particularly anything concerning his ups and downs with CSNY. "The music press writes the weirdest shit about us," he told ROLLING STONE's Cameron Crowe. "I've read so much gossip in ROLLING STONE alone. . . . Ann Landers would blanch."

Yet when the groundbreaking album *Tonight's the Night* was released in 1975, Young chose ROLLING STONE as the vehicle for his first-ever comprehensive interview. After years of refusing all Q&A requests (with the response that he had nothing to say), Young spent several weeks with Cameron Crowe in 1975 and again in 1979, for two landmark cover stories. Their in-depth conversations, detailed in "So Hard to Make Arrangements for Yourself" (August 14, 1975) and "Neil Young: The Last American Hero" (February 8, 1979), are still part of any longtime Young-lorist's vocabulary (and are reprinted here in their entirety). In addition, Young later gave lengthy interviews to ROLLING STONE's James Henke and Alan Light in 1988 and 1993, respectively.

A word about the organization of *Neil Young: The* ROLLING STONE *Files*. For the most part, the book is arranged chronologically, with each piece appearing in the order that it ran in the magazine. There are a few exceptions, however. In 1987 and 1992, in celebration of the magazine's twentieth and twenty-fifth anniversaries, special issues honored certain milestones of rock & roll: the best albums, the greatest singles, breakthrough live concerts and so on. Neil Young's work, not surprisingly, was chosen for each special feature. Here, we've positioned these critiques within the time frame of the subject's original release, so the reader can compare the hindsight review with the one published at the time of its issue (quite a wide margin of opinion in some cases).

For information on Young's early career (prior to Buffalo Springfield) discussed in the introduction, most helpful was John Einarson's *Neil Young: Don't Be Denied/The Canadian Years,* published in 1992 by Canada's Quarry Press. Young's own opinions of his work, annotated on the 1978 retrospective *Decade,* was also of great interest.

For this endeavor, many people lent a helping hand, particularly Shawn Dahl and Anthony DeCurtis. We also owe thanks to ROLLING STONE's Jann S. Wenner, Kent Brownridge, John Lagana and Fred Woodward, and at Hyperion, Mary Ann Naples, Laura Chittenden, Bob Miller and Victor Weaver. In addition, we're grateful to Sarah Lazin, Laura Nolan, Laura Whiteley, Mark Krzos, Joseph Tristano, Carrie Klein and Alison Kalfus. To George Usher and Charles Leland, the men with the hard-to-find music, a million thanks. Our appreciation also goes to Bob Merlis and Ken Phillips at Warner Bros., Patti Conte and her staff at Atlantic, Thanh-Thanh at Geffen, Laura Fagin at Rondor Music, Bob Hilderley at Quarry Press and Ben Berry at InBook.

We offer a deafening round of applause to all the writers—close to fifty—who have written about Neil Young in the pages of ROLLING STONE; add to that countless "Random Notes" reporters and un-bylined news writers over twenty-five-plus years.

And, of course, the most thanks of all goes to Neil Young himself, whose music is a true inspiration for any writer struggling to put things down on paper.

H.G-W
Rolling Stone Press
February 1994

INTRODUCTION

I REMEMBER THE FIRST time Neil Young really surprised me. It was the fall of 1978 and I was driving the twenty-five miles home from seeing one of the few punk bands that existed in North Carolina at the time. Possessed by the sounds of the Clash, Ramones, Pistols, Vibrators, Television and Richard Hell, I, at twenty-one, still had a soft spot for Neil Young. After all, I'd been hooked on Young's music since I was twelve or thirteen. One of the first 45s I ever bought at my small-town record shop was "Only Love Can Break Your Heart," from *After the Gold Rush,* Young's third album, in 1970. But, before that, I'd loved the few songs of his that got radio airplay—"Mr. Soul" with Buffalo Springfield, "Helpless" and "Ohio" from his Crosby, Stills, Nash and Young days, "Cinnamon Girl" with Crazy Horse. But it was that brokenhearted single that inspired me to save my babysitting money to get all three Neil Young albums.

By the late Seventies, I'd continued to buy each new Neil Young release, and somehow, through all the changes—his, mine and the music's—they always seemed somehow right. Young, alone among my old heroes, still made music that I wanted to listen to. And, believe me, becoming a punk rocker in 1977–78 meant packing away all vestiges of hippie-dippiness.

Then, even down South, word got out that Young had embraced punk rock as much as I had. In concert, he'd been playing a sort of tribute to Johnny Rotten called "Rust Never Sleeps," which had all the jagged edges and desperate-sounding vocals—"it's better to burn out than it is to rust"— of my new favorite bands.

To my horror—and surprise—this autumn eve the local FM DJ gleefully announced a preview of Young's upcoming "country-folk album." I had been hoping for feedback and shrieking guitars; instead I heard pedal steel and strings, as the soft sounds of *Comes a Time* came purring out of my VW Beetle's tiny speakers.

More than fifteen years later, I've grown to appreciate that album—and I've also become quite accustomed to the Young Surprise Factor. Though there have been constants—Young's emotive vocals, impassioned guitar playing and prodigious songwriting—he has zigzagged all over the musical map. From nostalgic romantic to cynical misanthrope, from acoustic folkie to techno wiz, mellow country rocker to abrasive feedback king, Young has veered to each end of the spectrum. The only place he has seemed really uncomfortable has been, as he's put it, "in the middle of the road."

Young's unpredictability has, in fact, been a staple of his creative endeavors since he left his native Canada for the States in 1966. Beginning in 1967, when his career was first chronicled in ROLLING STONE, critics have continually applauded or castigated Young for embarking on the latest leg of his musical journey. And fans—of all ages—have either gone along for the ride or disembarked, waiting around for the next trip.

Indeed, throughout his long, near thirty-year career, Young has defied categorization; his songwriting has ricocheted from the personal to the political, from the straightforward to the obtuse. Dipping into almost every musical genre (rock, pop, soul, country, folk, jazz, blues, rockabilly, punk, technopop, grunge), rather than merely "do" a certain kind of music, Young has grabbed it, shaken it upside down and turned it into his own unique style—sometimes with uneven results. Throughout, Young has committed himself to stretching limits, taking risks. The result: Unlike any other artist, Young has traveled the often treacherous road from the Sixties to the Nineties without ramming into a dead end, arriving battle-scarred but vibrant, with a compelling body of work.

PERHAPS YOUNG'S RESTLESS AND persistent creative drive is due to the fact that since childhood, he *knew* that he wanted to be a musician. There was never a doubt. This strong belief in himself and his desire to make music grew out of a difficult adolescence. Born in Toronto, on November 12, 1945, to a vivacious mother (Rassy) and a journalist father (Scott), Young spent his early years in rural Omemee, a small community in northern Ontario. When he was six, he fell victim to a polio epidemic sweeping Canada, and had to be hospitalized in Toronto. He recovered successfully, with the only aftereffect being fatigue. A short time later, Young received his first instrument, a plastic ukulele; a Harmony Monterey acoustic guitar soon followed.

Nineteen-sixty was a traumatic year for Young: His father left the family, so Young, his brother and mother packed up and moved to Winnipeg, Manitoba. A ninth-grader, Young didn't fit in easily at his new school, fighting with local toughs and seeking refuge in his guitar, to which he added an electric pickup. Years later he described his obsession to then-ROLLING STONE reporter Cameron Crowe: "All of a sudden I wanted a guitar and that was it. I felt it. I couldn't stop thinking about it."

Young began DJ'ing sock-hops at local community centers. Then, at fourteen, he assembled his first band, the Jades, which soon fell apart, but led to a succession of other groups—the Esquires, the Stardusters, the Classics, and finally, in early 1963, the Squires. Though Young had initially been inspired by seeing Elvis on TV, his new musical role models were guitarist Duane Eddy and guitar-slinging instrumental bands such as England's Shadows (led by ax-master Hank B. Marvin), Johnny and the Hurricanes and the Ventures. Young's local guitar hero was Randy Bachman (then playing with Chad Allan and the Reflections), who would later form the Guess Who with another small-town garage-band vet, Burton Cummings.

Though the Squires mostly did covers, Young began writing instrumentals around this time, soon adding them to the combo's repertoire. By the end of '64, the band was accomplished enough to record a single at a local radio station. "The Sultan" b/w "Aurora," both Young originals, came out on the tiny V Records label. As Young continued to hone his guitar technique, he also began testing his voice. That same year, he'd gotten up the nerve to sing with the band, but his high, quavery pitch met with derision—creating a self-consciousness he would take some time to overcome.

Smitten with the Beatles and Dylan, Young also started writing lyrics to his own songs. Spending every spare minute on music, Young flunked the tenth grade, repeated it, then failed eleventh grade. Farewell to school days: rather than repeat his junior year, he quit, becoming at eighteen a full-time musician, the only occupation he would ever have.

Though rock & roll still ruled Canada in 1964, folk music boomed as well. Young begun hanging out at local coffeehouses where he met touring folk singers, including Joni Mitchell and Stephen Stills. The driving force behind the Squires, Young started booking out-of-town gigs for the group, frequently in nearby Fort William. To haul the band's equipment, Young saved up and bought a 1948 Buick Roadmaster hearse, which he named Mortimer Hearseburg (affectionately known as "Mort"), marking the start of his continuing love of vintage cars.

The Squires became quite popular in Fort William, and Young eventually relocated there with the band. He crashed in a cramped room at the Victoria Hotel, where, on his nineteenth birthday, he wrote "Sugar Mountain," his wistful ode to innocence lost, a subject to which he would repeatedly return. His Squires material also began to take on folk shadings. Throughout his career, Young would draw equally upon both the loud-fast-rules ethic of rock & roll and the acoustic, lyric-driven aspect of folk.

After a series of misadventures trying to drive Mort across Canada, Young ended up abandoning the car—as well as his band mates back in Fort

William (a pattern he would repeat many times in the years to come)—and hitching a ride to Toronto. There he struck out on his own to break into the burgeoning coffeehouse scene in that town's boho Yorkville district. Without much success getting engagements, he nonetheless wrote constantly, including one song called "Nowadays Clancy Can't Even Sing," inspired by a Winnipeg classmate. Young briefly searched for greener pastures in New York, checking out the Village folk scene and trying to find Stills, who'd been living there but who had split for Los Angeles before Young arrived. Stills' ex-roommate, Richie Furay, jammed with Young, who taught him "Clancy." Young also recorded some demos in New York for Elektra Records, which rejected the tapes.

BACK IN TORONTO, YOUNG'S next step was to try to put together another band, an endeavor that led to his meeting bassist Bruce Palmer. The two landed spots in an R&B outfit called Ricky James and the Mynah Birds, ready-made with a Motown record deal and an American lead singer, who later shortened his name to Rick James. With all new equipment purchased by the band's manager, Young played guitar and Palmer bass in a Detroit recording session in early 1966. Unfortunately, James, who was AWOL from the navy, got busted while in the Motor City, spelling the end for the Mynah Birds. Back home, Palmer and Young pawned the band's equipment, bought a 1953 Pontiac hearse and took off for L.A. in search of Stills—and a shot at the big time. Arriving in Los Angeles—without a clue to Stills' whereabouts—the two were about to give up after a week and head for San Francisco. While stuck in a traffic jam, their hearse (with Ontario plates) was spotted by none other than Stills, in a car with Furay, who'd also moved West a few months earlier. The four had a reunion in the middle of Sunset Boulevard. "I was happy to see fucking *anybody* I knew," Young later recalled to Cameron Crowe. "And it seemed very logical to us that we form a band."

To round things out, they also enlisted drummer Dewey Martin, of the Dillards, a bluegrass outfit. Furay had already taught Stills "Clancy," and when the group spotted a steamroller emblazoned with the sign BUFFALO SPRINGFIELD, they had a name too. The quintet came up with a sound that mixed folk, country and rock & roll, as well as three distinctive vocal styles: Stills' bluesy tenor, Furay's dulcet croon and Young's high, lonesome wail.

The band soon embarked on a Southern California tour opening for the Byrds, followed by a now-legendary six-week stint at Hollywood's Whisky-A-Go-Go. The Springfield was an incendiary live act, with Young, on lead guitar, playing cat and mouse with Stills' riffs; Furay would trade off on vocals with Stills, while Young sang harmony and the occasional lead. Martin and Palmer held down a supple rhythm section. After only a few months, the band signed with Atco/Atlantic, but by the time they began recording, internal strife had already reared its head. To Young's discomfort, the trappings of celebrity began to envelop the band, and he wrote "Out of My Mind" for *Buffalo Springfield* (1966), the group's debut album, to express his feelings on the subject: "Left behind / By myself and what I'm living for / All I hear are screams / From outside the limousine / That are taking me / Out of my mind."

Young also experienced his first grand mal seizure related to epilepsy, which had been diagnosed back in Canada, during this period. For the most part, medication kept the seizures under control, though Young would occasionally have an epileptic episode over the years. He told Crowe, in 1975, "Sometimes when I get really high, it's a very psychedelic experience to have a seizure. . . . The only scary thing about it is . . . realizing you're totally comfortable in this . . . *void.*"

Buffalo Springfield showcased Young's songwriting; five of the twelve tracks were his (the others were Stills'), though he sang lead on only two ("Burned" and "Out of My Mind"). Not long after the album's release, however, Young quit the band. He rejoined for the band's second effort, *Buffalo Springfield Again* (1967), which, with the addition of Furay compositions, seemed even more than the previous album a platform for the individual members' talents. During recording, Palmer was deported after a marijuana bust, his third. Reviewing in ROLLING STONE (December 14, 1967), an uncredited critic pointed out: "This album sounds as if every member of the group is satisfying his own musical needs. Each of them has produced songs in his own bag. Together there is no blend, only a rather obvious alienation among the compositions."

Young's contributions included the rocker "Mr. Soul" and the experimental sound montages "Expecting to Fly" and "Broken Arrow," a despondent description of the downside of being a rock & roll star. On his 1978 retrospective *Decade,* Young said of "Broken Arrow": "I wrote this after quitting the group in '67 due to one of many identity crises. Joined up again soon enough to cut this one though. Took over 100 takes to get it." While Young was hiding out, the band enlisted ex-Byrd David Crosby for its gig at the historic Monterey Pop Festival in June 1967. Though Young returned, a news story in an April 1968 issue of ROLLING STONE reported his impending departure—again—as well as a misdemeanor pot bust involving Young, Furay, Jim Messina (who'd replaced Palmer on bass) and Eric Clapton. Young later described those times to Crowe: "I just couldn't handle it toward the end. My nerves couldn't handle the trip. It wasn't me scheming on a solo career, it wasn't anything but my nerves. I was going crazy, you know, joining and quitting and joining again. . . . I needed more space. . . . So I'd quit, then I'd come back 'cause it sounded so good." Young's stint with the Springfield fully set the pattern for his conflicted on-again/off-again involvement with all future group efforts.

For the third and final Springfield album, *Last Time Around* (1968), Young's presence was minimal. His contributions included a kind of sequel to "Sugar Mountain" (which was still unrecorded at that point), entitled "I Am a Child," and a farewell to the Springfield, "On the Way Home" (with Furay singing lead).

A FTER THE SPRINGFIELD'S IMPLOSION, Young headed to the hills of Topanga Canyon where he bought a house and started building a recording studio. By 1969 he'd married his first wife, Susan, whom he'd met at a Topanga café, and he'd signed a solo deal with Warner/Reprise. His solo debut, *Neil Young* (1969), was to some degree an extention of "Broken Arrow" and "Expecting to Fly," including collaborations with pianist/composer Jack Nitzsche. Along with lushly orchestrated lonesome ballads and western-styled instrumentals, the album also included the stripped-down surrealistic narrative "Last Trip to Tulsa." Young later described the recording as "overdub city."

After *Neil Young*'s initial release, it was remixed to bring the vocals more to the fore, then re-released, but it didn't make much of a commercial dent. Already on to other things, Young was busy jamming with a band of transplanted Easterners, the Rockets, whom he'd met during the Springfield days. Renamed Crazy Horse, the group joined Young in his new studio, and guitarist Danny Whitten, bassist Billy Talbot and drummer Ralph Molina clicked with Young like soul mates, eliciting extraordinarily expressive guitar work from him. The combustible *Everybody Knows This Is Nowhere* (1969) was the result.

Young wrote several of the album's most enduring tracks, "Cinnamon Girl," "Down by the River" and "Cowgirl in the Sand," in one afternoon while whacked out with the flu, he later said. A feverish quality also came across in Young's unrestrained vocals. After the record's release, he explained the change in his approach to ROLLING STONE: "When I was with the Springfield, I held back. I was paranoid about my voice. So on my own first LP I buried my voice intentionally. The second LP I brought it up more. I had more confidence. That's what working with Crazy Horse has done."

In the meantime, Young had patched things up with Stills, who'd invited him to join the newly formed Crosby, Stills and Nash. With one album recorded, the trio realized they needed a lead guitarist for live performances, so Stills pushed for Young. Their Atlantic Records contract allowed each member complete autonomy, which satisfied Young's maverick sensibility.

After recording *Nowhere,* Young hit the road with the renamed Crosby, Stills, Nash and Young, heading for New York's Fillmore East. The following weekend the group played Woodstock, with CSN doing an acoustic set, followed by an electrified raveup with Young, bassist Greg Reeves, and drummer Dallas Taylor joining in. (Young refused to give permission to be filmed, so only footage of the acoustic trio exists in the Woodstock movie.) Reviewing the festival for ROLLING STONE, Greil Marcus wrote of their set, "Visually they are one of the most exciting bands I have seen, the six of them. . . . Their performance was scary, brilliant proof of the magnificence of music. . . ." In its annual recap of the year, ROLLING STONE named CSNY "Best New Group of 1969."

For the first time, Young's stage charisma had become evident to a large audience. Langdon Winner described it in ROLLING STONE: "Young's voice, guitar, compositions and stage presence added elements of darkness and mystery to songs that had previously dripped a kind of saccharine sweetness." The performances were so successful, in fact, that Young's role grew and the entire band headed into the studio to record *Déjà Vu* (1970), to which Young contributed the mournful "Helpless" and the elaborate three-part saga "Country Girl." At the time, Stills told ROLLING STONE's Ben Fong-Torres: "We may shape the album, but Neil'll come along and give us that extra thing."

Throughout, Young insisted to ROLLING STONE reporters that he would continue as a solo artist. In fact, he took to the highway with Crazy Horse right after *Déjà Vu*'s completion; that tour segued into one with CSNY. While Young was doing double duty, *Déjà Vu* became the biggest-selling album of 1970. But by May, rumors escalated of the band's imminent breakup. That same month, Young, horrified by the killing of four students by National Guard troops at Kent State, dashed off the devastating protest song "Ohio," and CSNY returned immediately to the studio to record it. Atlantic rush-released the single, which, though controversial, got significant airplay, peaking at Number Fourteen. In 1988, ROLLING STONE editors chose the song as one of the Top 100 singles of the past twenty-five years; Young's comment: "It was really like the folk process at work. You know, that was really like music as news."

By the end of 1970, friction persisted within CSNY, but the group continued touring, eventually recording the live double album *4 Way Street* (1971). During the summer, Young released a live version of "Sugar Mountain" as a single, with "Cinnamon Girl" on the flip side. Near the year's end came *After the Gold Rush,* an album darkly colored by Young's most plaintive high-octave singing yet. A toned-down Crazy Horse joined him on the mostly acoustic recording, as did Stills and a seventeen-year-old guitarist/pianist named Nils Lofgren. The exception to the album's hushed tone, "Southern Man," an electrified thrasher punctuated by Young's wrecked shrieks, actually outdid "Ohio" in vitriol. The album's single "Only Love Can Break Your Heart" hit Number Thirty-three, bringing the solo Young a wider audience.

ROLLING STONE's Langdon Winner, who had also panned *Déjà Vu,* was not impressed, however, and ended his negative review with, "To the seventy or eighty people who wrote to ROLLING STONE in total rage that I could be anything but 100 percent delighted with *Déjà Vu,* I will simply say: This record picks up where *Déjà Vu* leaves off." ROLLING STONE editors disagreed, though, later naming *Gold Rush* "Album of the Year" and, in 1987, included it among rock's Top 100 LPs (declaring it "one of Young's most moving, satisfying and wide-ranging albums").

Following on the heels of CSNY's triumphs, this album, which peaked at Number Eight, set Young up to become a superstar. Young later said of the album: *"After the Gold Rush* was the spirit of Topanga Canyon. It seemed like I realized that I'd gotten somewhere."

Not long after the album's release, Young began experiencing painful back trouble, first while doing a solo acoustic tour of small halls, and again in a Nashville recording studio. He later recalled that time to Crowe: "I was in and out of hospitals for the two years between *After the Gold Rush* and *Harvest.* I have one weak side and all the muscles slipped on me. My discs slipped. I couldn't hold my guitar up. . . . I couldn't move around too well, so I laid low for a long time on the ranch and just didn't have any contact. . . . I wore a brace. . . . I could only stand up four hours a day. . . . The doctors were starting to talk about wheelchairs and shit, so I had some discs removed. But for the most part, I spent two years flat on my back. I had a lot of time to think about what had happened to me."

By 1971, Young's marriage had dissolved and he'd become involved with actress Carrie Snodgress, who had just been nominated for an Oscar for her performance in the 1970 film *Diary of a Mad Housewife.* Young and Snodgress settled down on Young's newly purchased Broken Arrow Ranch in Northern California, south of San Francisco. There, he began writing the songs for the album that would make his name a household word.

The lushly countrified *Harvest* (which included "A Man Needs a Maid," a track about Snodgress featuring the London Symphony Orchestra) became the biggest-selling album of 1972; it included the Number One single "Heart of Gold." With the very-hummable song wafting out of every radio all summer long, Young's music was finally unanimously embraced by the public; the critics responded, however, less than favorably.

Young explained the album's genesis to Crowe: "I recorded most of *Harvest* in the brace. That's a lot of the reason it's such a mellow album. I couldn't physically play an electric guitar. 'Are You Ready for the Country,' 'Alabama' and 'Words' were all done after I had the operation." ROLLING STONE's John Mendelssohn slagged the album as being a shallow sellout, and Young himself described "Heart of Gold," on *Decade,* as the song that "put me in the middle of the road." Indeed, the placid backing of the Stray Gators, including steel player Ben Keith, and the harmony vocals of James Taylor, Linda Ronstadt, Crosby, Stills and Nash, smoothed out all the wrinkles that had made Young's previous albums so prickly and unpredictable.

IN ADDITION TO OVERWHELMING commercial success, 1972 brought many other changes for Young. Snodgress gave birth to a son, Zeke, in September, and Crazy Horse guitarist Danny Whitten (for whom Young had written "The Needle and the Damage Done" on *Harvest*) overdosed on heroin in November, a few days after Young had fired him for being too drug-addled to play. Young submerged himself in a massive tour, which was marred with problems, including a threatened mutiny by the band over wages. ROLLING STONE's Jon Landau reviewed one of the tour's earliest shows, at Carnegie Hall: "Young was not especially well received, all things considered. The performance was too short and he barely won an encore. Just the same, the morning after, I found myself admiring him as much as a person as I did him as a musician. In 'Don't Be Denied,' he offers one of the few attacks on the star system that a rock musician has made credible. And he makes it so because his performance and style seem free of any taint of cynicism."

Young included the new songs performed during the tour on his first live solo album, *Time Fades Away* (1973). The title song, as well as "Don't Be Denied," set the tone for an anarchic document that seemed to relish capturing all the warts of live performance, such as missed notes and garbled lyrics—rather than slick versions of established favorites.

Around that time, he also focused his energy on *Journey Through the Past,* a disjointed piece of *cinéma vérité* "starring" Young. Since 1968, when he began experimenting with an 8mm camera, Young had exhibited an interest in filmmaking. (In fact, *After the Gold Rush* was inspired by a movie of the same name, which never materialized, written by his friend, actor Dean Stockwell.) Young concocted a film that included music from his days in the Springfield and CSNY, as well as bits from Handel's *Messiah.* Young later told Crowe, "I wanted to express a visual picture of what I was singing about." For all future cinematic endeavors, Young would use a directorial alias, Bernard Shakey.

The film was panned, as was the double album soundtrack, which Young claimed was released against his wishes by his record label (the film's intended distributor). *Time Fades Away,* which followed on *Journey*'s heels, only reached Number Twenty-two, but was praised with some reservations by ROLLING STONE's Bud Scoppa: *"Time Fades Away* has its virtues when taken on its own terms and not as the latest major work of a major artist. . . . If it isn't a resounding success, the album is still a revealing self-portrait by an always fascinating man." As Young wrote on *Decade* about his sojourn in the "middle of the road," during the *Harvest* period, "it soon became a bore, so I headed for the ditch. A rougher ride but I saw more interesting people there."

Young next did the opposite of what one might expect: He rejoined CSNY in 1974 for a massive reunion tour. Having grown more reclusive and distrustful of the press, he was the sole member not to grant ROLLING STONE's Ben Fong-Torres an interview. During the tour, Young played songs that would soon appear on his own albums, the despairing "For the Turnstiles" and the hopeful "Long May You Run," which he said he'd written about his hearse. Amid criticism that the CSNY tour was merely intended to cash in on the group's former success (only Young's solo recordings had sold as well as CSNY's), it nonetheless scored with audiences.

Contrasting greatly with CSNY's sweet sounds, Young's next release was to be his most pessimistic yet. *On the Beach* (1974) seemed cynical and paranoid. With a stripped-down, metallic sound, the album featured some of Young's most gloom-ridden lyrics, particularly the long narratives "Revolution Blues" and "Ambulance Blues," the latter sung in an ominous deeper register than usual. Young, who had relocated to Southern California's Zuma Beach, just north of Malibu, enlisted neighbors Rick Danko and Levon Helm, the Band's bassist and drummer, for some tracks, as well as Crazy Horse's Ralph Molina and Billy Talbot, Stray Gator Ben Keith and Cajun fiddler Rusty Kershaw. In a positive review for ROLLING STONE, critic Stephen Holden called the album "a bitter testament from one who has come through the fire and gone back into it."

FOLLOWING *ON THE BEACH* was a recording so harrowing that Young had shelved it for two years before releasing it. *Tonight's the Night* (1975) could be classified as one of the first true punk albums, if only for its off-the-cuff intensity, reckless and ragged playing, shattered, pain-filled vocals, and live-for-the-moment lyrics. Back in '73 Young had returned to the studio with Crazy Horse for the first time since Whitten's death. Guzzling tequila during all-night sessions, the band recorded nine sloppily played songs—making up in conviction what they lacked in precision—to pay tribute to Whitten and CSNY roadie Bruce Berry, who had also died of a heroin overdose. In 1975, Young decided to release the recordings after listening to them back-to-back against a mellow set, to be called *Home-grown*, intended as his next issue. He and manager Elliot Roberts added three songs to the *Tonight's the Night* batch from previous Crazy Horse sessions, including "Come On Baby Let's Go Downtown," recorded with Whitten singing lead at the Fillmore East four years earlier.

Though Young, again, lost a chunk of his mainstream audience, critics have since lauded the work, and thrash-rockers have pointed to it as a major influence. At the time, a measured Dave Marsh wrote in ROLLING STONE, "Young's whole career may have been spent in pursuit of this story . . . but it is only now that he has found a way to tell the tale so directly." In 1987 ROLLING STONE editors chose the album as Number Twenty-six in their list of rock's 100 greatest recordings, calling it Young's "most personal, stirring work."

Upon the album's release, Young gave his first-ever comprehensive interview, to ROLLING STONE's Cameron Crowe. Having just split from Snodgress, Young seemed to be relishing his newfound bachelorhood, relocation to Southern California and frequent jam sessions with Crazy Horse. "I'm really turned on by the new music I'm making now, back with Crazy Horse," he told Crowe. "Today, even as I'm talking, the songs are running through my head. . . . I think everything I've done is valid or else I wouldn't have released it, but I do realize the last three albums have been a certain way. . . . Somehow I feel like I've surfaced out of some kind of murk. . . . *Tonight's the Night* . . . is the final chapter of a period I went through."

Throughout the interview, Young excitedly described his next project, mostly recorded with Crazy Horse. *Zuma* (1975), praised by ROLLING STONE's Bud Scoppa as "by far the best album he's made," mixed up rollicking electrified numbers—featuring the Horse's new guitarist Frank Sampedro—with acoustic and electric ballads. The album's climax was the masterful "Cortez the Killer," a lengthy narrative punctuated by a whirling, swirling guitar sound. The song has since become a highlight of Young and Crazy Horse's concerts. Ending the album, "Through My Sails" reunited CSNY, foreshadowing Young's next move.

In May of '76, word got out that CSNY were working on a new album. Whatever the plan may have been, the album turned into a Stills-Young joint venture, named after Young's "Long May You Run."

Recorded in Miami, the album (consisting of five Young songs and four by Stills) sounded as if it had been inspired by relaxing on sailboats and slurping piña coladas—in other words, more Jimmy Buffett than Buffalo Springfield. Stills had been down on his luck the past few years, most of his solo albums and work with Manassas having been dismissed by critics and increasingly ignored by the public. Young, perhaps, was repaying an old debt to an early mentor; in fact, in interviews at the time, Young bent over backward to emphasize Stills' singing, playing and songwriting prowess. The reality, though, was that the album sounded lackadaisical, as did the uninspired performances that followed its release.

At North Carolina's Greensboro Coliseum, in 1976, I saw a rather droopy Young and a flat-out boring Stills, both of whom seemed to be going through the motions. Indeed, Young threw in the towel after a few more shows, claiming throat problems (the year before, Young did, in fact, undergo throat surgery, to remove a benign growth), and bringing the tour to an abrupt halt. Reportedly, Young's farewell to Stills was a telegram sent to his hotel room, just prior to an aborted Atlanta performance, that read, "Dear Stephen, Funny how some things that start spontaneously, end that way. Eat a Peach, Neil."

ROLLING STONE's reviews of the Stills/Young duo were mixed: Crowe described a Boston show that "teetered on the edge of magic," while Marsh witnessed a Long Island performance he labeled "a bad idea gone wrong." Young returned to his ranch to lick his wounds and rest his throat, eventually showing up in Santa Cruz, California, bars jamming with a garage band called the Ducks.

YOUNG'S NEXT ALBUM BROUGHT him back into the critics' embrace. Mixing electric and acoustic material, *American Stars 'n Bars* (1977) sounded like a cross between a honky-tonk roadhouse and a barn-dance hoedown. The most upbeat of any Young LP to date, the album's highlight was the anthemic "Like a Hurricane," with its sing-along hook fueled by fluid, soulful guitar solos. ROLLING STONE's Paul Nelson applauded the album, ending his review with the prediction that "Neil Young has a very good chance to be the most important American rock & roll artist in the Seventies. . . . I don't know anyone who goes after the essences with as much daring as Young."

In 1978 came the three-disc retrospective, *Decade,* for which Young personally chose the tracks, annotating each one. Included were cuts spanning his career from Springfield to "Hurricane," as well as a few unreleased gems. And finally, on September 18, in Clarkston, Michigan, Young's "Rust Never Sleeps" tour exploded. On a stage crowded with humongously oversized amps and mikes, a seemingly lilliputian Young opened the show with "Sugar Mountain" and "I Am a Child," both reveries to naiveté. Following thirty minutes of acoustic numbers, he was joined by Crazy Horse for a bone-rattling set of nonstop rockers. Throughout, taped recordings from Woodstock (including "brown acid" warnings) were interspersed with robed "road-eyes" scurrying about, looking like *Star Wars* Jawas with red glowing eyes. Young himself employed a wireless mike—a novelty at the time. Highlights included the song for which the tour was named, performed acoustically ("My My, Hey Hey [Out of the Blue]") and electrically ("Hey Hey, My My [Into the Black]").

Though ROLLING STONE reviewer John Rockwell found the surreal stage setup "silly and self-conscious," he conceded that the Madison Square Garden performance (one of two sold-out shows there) contained "enough subtlety, sophistication and haunting emotionality in the acoustic material, and enough biting passion in the best of the electric songs, to reaffirm Young's permanent place in the past decade of rock & roll."

Thus it was to my—and to many others'—surprise, that, in the midst of this tour, *Comes a Time* (1978) was issued. As it turned out, the album, recorded with the twenty-two-piece Gone With the Wind Orchestra and featuring singer Nicolette Larson, was more than a year old and its release had been delayed due to pressing problems. Young had already moved on to other things, he told Cameron Crowe in 1979, during their second comprehensive interview. Calling *Comes a Time* "in the middle of a soft place," Young remarked, "I hear it on the radio now and it sounds nice. . . . But I'm somewhere else now. I'm into rock & roll."

As for *Comes a Time,* it did reap Young more commercial success than he'd had in a while—peaking at Number Seven. He was back in the Top Ten for the first time since *Harvest*. ROLLING STONE's Greil Marcus found the album disappointing, though, calling it "neither a knockout punch like last year's *American Stars 'n Bars* nor a wildly idiosyncratic, cracked triumph/disaster like *Zuma* or *On the Beach*. It's a pleasing, clearly commercial piece of work that's defended from slickness by Young's insistence on playing out of tune, skewing the levels of the vocals . . . and singing without much affectation."

NINETEEN-SEVENTY-NINE BROUGHT the album I had been waiting for. With basic tracks recorded during the *Rust Never Sleeps* tour, the album by the same name delivered the goods. Like the tour, it was half acoustic, half electric, including both versions of the title song. As a whole, it seemed the true zenith of Young's career, featuring his most consistently vital songwriting in nearly a decade. ROLLING STONE's Paul Nelson rhapsodized, "For anyone still passionately in love with rock & roll, Neil Young has made a record that defines the territory. Defines it, expands it, explodes it. Burns it to the ground." For those who couldn't see the concert, Young released *Live Rust,* which vividly captured the tour, as did the companion film (directed by Bernard Shakey, of course). *Rust Never Sleeps* hit Number Eight, followed by *Live Rust* at Number Fifteen; the *Village Voice* named Young "Artist of the Decade."

Ending the Seventies with a one-two punch, Young started the Eighties somewhat tentatively with another acoustic/electric split, the quirky *Hawks & Doves.* Though the album was somewhat overlooked by the public (it only reached Number Thirty), several songs—particularly, the eerie "Homestead" (recorded in '75) and the forceful "Captain Kennedy"—were among Young's best. The electric tunes were good-time country-rockers on the surface, but upon closer listening, the lyrics seemed edgy and dark. The album also had political overtones; Young would soon shock fans and friends alike by endorsing Reagan's military buildup policies.

Perhaps Young's new militaristic viewpoint inspired the ballistic sounds of 1981's *Re-ac-tor,* which portrayed a shell-shocked Young shrieking the words to the frightening "Shots." An exercise in hard rock, the fairly brief LP also contained the mindless "T-Bone" jam, as well as the chillingly comic "Surfer Joe and Moe the Sleaze" and the churning "Southern Pacific," all backed by Crazy Horse at its most propellent.

Young jumped the Reprise ship in 1982, joining the stable of his old buddy David Geffen. His first release on his new label was his biggest shocker thus far—surprising probably no one more than the president of Geffen Records. Young's latest experiment came from electronic vocal manipulations and synthesizer-driven melody lines. Following the techno lead of the German group Kraftwerk, much of *Trans* featured Young's distinctive voice disguised via Vocoders and octave dividers. Young somehow didn't sound quite convincing in this guise, and, overwhelmed, most listeners overlooked the album's more traditional fare, such as "Little Thing Called Love," which did manage to chart at Number Seventy-one, and the visionary "Like an Inca."

The *Trans* tour gave Young the opportunity to continue his experiment. Though he pleased the crowd with acoustic versions of old favorites, he baffled them when he put on his techno-mask, his shade-wearing visage projected onto a gigantic video monitor. In retrospect, the video antics of Young-as-android now seem a primitive predecessor to U2's Zoo TV production. But back in 1983, I, for one, found Young's innovations more jarring than engaging.

Because of *Trans,* Young was immediately at odds with Geffen, who insisted that he do a "rock & roll record." Young did exactly that, offering

the label an album recorded by yet another new persona, a coiffed rockabilly dude, accompanied by a combo called the Shocking Pinks. *Everybody's Rockin'* (1983), a pastiche of classic rock & roll, mixed covers and
originals, including the laconic "Wonderin' " and the cynical "Payola
Blues." In return, Geffen slapped Young with a lawsuit for making albums
"not commercial in nature and musically uncharacteristic of Young's previous records." ROLLING STONE's David Fricke gave the album the thumbs-
up, however, saying, "You have to admire *Everybody's Rockin'* for its nerve,
and eventually you'll come to love it for its frenzied sound and playful
humor."

At the time, Young's home life was anything but humorous. He described the early 1980s to ROLLING STONE's James Henke, in 1989, as the
most difficult period of his life. He and his bride, Pegi, had spent those years
desperately working with their son, Ben, who'd been born in 1979 with a
severely disabling form of cerebral palsy. (Zeke, Young's son with Snodgress, also has a mild, more treatable, form of cerebral palsy.) The quadriplegic youngster required twelve-hour-a-day, seven-days-a-week therapy
with both parents, according to specialists with whom the Youngs confer-
red. After two years, the Youngs determined the therapy was destroying
their lives rather than helping their son, so they tried other, less physically
demanding techniques. To help children like Ben, Pegi Young subsequently started the Bridge School in San Francisco, for which Young has
since organized several benefit concerts, featuring artists ranging from Bruce
Springsteen to Sonic Youth.

Young's personal life, not surprisingly, had a huge effect on his artistic
output—just as it had in the past. Only, this time, the results mostly baffled
his fans, rather than drawing them in. But, for Young, his musical experiments were the only means of making it through: hence, his interest in
computers (which aided in his son's ability to communicate) evident on
Trans; the escapism inherent in *Everybody's Rockin';* and perhaps the coun-
try-kinship of Young's next release, *Old Ways* (1985). Further aggravating
Geffen, Young softened that album's C&W sounds with strings, particularly
on "The Wayward Wind" (originally a 1956 hit for both Tex Ritter and
Gogi Grant). Many of the album's songs featured the vocals of Nashville
outlaws Willie Nelson and Waylon Jennings. Standouts included the
bouncy "Get Back to the Country" and nostalgic "Are There Any More
Real Cowboys?," duets with Jennings and Nelson, respectively.

While finishing *Old Ways,* Young was inspired by a Nelson comment
about the plight of America's farmers and got the idea for Farm Aid.
Enlisting Nelson's help, Young kicked off the first annual concert in Iowa,
featuring performances by country and rock & roll artists.

Young then toured the country with his old-timey string band, the

International Harvesters, who were frequently joined onstage by Jennings. Vowing to stick with country music, Young told ROLLING STONE's Steve Pond, "It seems like rock & roll has gotten more concerned with fashion and image lately. I miss the feeling of community that rock had in the Sixties. But I got back that feeling when I started hanging out with country guys."

YOUNG, OF COURSE, DEVIATED from his stated plan. Instead, he enlisted session musicians Steve Jordan and Danny Kortchmar to make the crisp "modern rock" of *Landing on Water* (1986). Though Young and his combo grooved with a funky beat, the songs' intensity was diluted by the mechanized sound of the synthesizers and the restrained rhythms. In the lyrics, Young depicted the world as a harsh, heartless place, but saved his most venomous digs for his ex-band mate David Crosby, who'd sunk into drug addiction ("Hippie Dream").

Perhaps *Water*'s restraint got to Young, since he then embarked on a massive tour with his most reckless colleagues—Crazy Horse—for the first time since "Rust Never Sleeps." Using some of the same oversized props, but adding things found in real-life garages (like a giant lawn mower), the revitalized band called its outing "Neil Young and Crazy Horse in a Rusted-Out Garage." The conceit was taken to the hilt, with complaining neighbors, cops and a harried mom. ROLLING STONE's David Fricke described the show as "an ingenious, earnest and often hilarious theatrical tribute to the eternal struggle of garage bands everywhere."

Young's next release, *Life* (1987), elaborated on *Water*'s themes. This time, though, Young backed up his horrified worldview with the muscle of a slightly subdued Crazy Horse. (Though still audible, synthesizers are mostly used as sound effects.) In addition to songs about international political unrest, *Life* was rounded out by four compositions of a more personal nature; another South American mythic saga, "Inca Queen"; and the jubilant paean to garageland, "Prisoners of Rock 'n' Roll"—a highlight of the Rusted-Out Garage tour.

Though Young had been at it more than two decades, he still had plenty of surprises up his sleeve. In 1987, after performing with CSN for a Greenpeace benefit, Young announced plans to rejoin the group for an album and tour, partially because Crosby had kicked drugs and been released from prison. Geffen, however, would not permit Young to rejoin unless the label could release the album by CSNY, who were contractually still committed to Atlantic. By the end of '88, Young, much to his delight, had been released from Geffen and returned to the studio with his ex-band mates. In addition, he'd spent the early part of the year playing clubs with a jazzy blues band, the Bluenotes. Back on Warner/Reprise, his first album was another genre piece, the backbeat shuffle of *This Note's for You* (1988). The title track harshly attacked rockers who'd used their songs to hawk wares on TV commercials. A hilarious Julien Temple-directed video was refused by MTV, because it depicted Michael Jackson, Eric Clapton and other stars making fools of themselves. (In an odd twist, MTV eventually chose the send-up "Best Video of the Year.")

With Young's bluesy guitar riffs playing call-and-response with a large, sassy horn section, the album sounded more Memphis R&B than California rock. The ensemble playing couldn't obscure such typical Young fare as "Coupe de Ville" and "Twilight," however—which was more than could be said for the compositions that turned up on *American Dream,* the CSNY album finally released at the end of 1988. Rather than revitalizing the group, Young seemed to succumb to its blandness. As Anthony DeCurtis pointed out in ROLLING STONE, "The record's main failing is its banality."

Young's flub with CSNY was easily forgotten in the context of his many triumphs in 1989, however. In the credibility department, Young was "roasted" with a tribute album, *The Bridge,* on which his songs were covered by underground rock's hippest outfits—Sonic Youth, Dinosaur Jr, Nick Cave, the Pixies and Nikki Sudden, among others. Then, Young blasted through a hair-raising "Rockin' in the Free World," on *Saturday Night Live.* With this taste of his upcoming album, *Freedom,* Young demonstrated to an overwhelmed audience there was plenty of juice left in his forty-four-year-old body.

Freedom lived up to the promise of that television appearance. Consisting of his most inspired set of songs since *Rust,* the album mixed acoustic and electric material, some of which was originally intended for an album called *Times Square.* A bone-crushing set recorded in New York, five of the songs were issued on the EP, *Eldorado,* released only in Japan, New Zealand and Australia. A reworked version of the title track and a screeching cover of "On Broadway" were two of the songs from the EP ultimately added to *Freedom.* Young explained to ROLLING STONE's Sheila Rogers about the album, "I just kept juggling it around until I got something that I thought was more of an album than an assault. It's the first time I've felt like doing an album like this in years. On those other albums I was more into style. But I was losing track of what I wanted to do." ROLLING STONE critics certainly felt that Young was back on track: They chose *Freedom* "Album of the Year" as well as one of the Top 100 LPs of all time.

Young was on a roll: His next release, *Ragged Glory,* actually beat *Freedom* in terms of sheer energy and power. Young was wonderfully, chaotically flanked by Crazy Horse, who this time were clearly chomping at the bit, then letting loose with all the muscular fury they could muster. In 1990 the quartet was rocking as if it were 1969. Though Young contributed some compelling songcraft, particularly "Mansion on the Hill," the album's emphasis was on its glorious guitar workouts. Refusing to take themselves too seriously, the foursome raged through the Sixties garage-punk classic "Farmer John" and its Nineties counterpart "Fuckin' Up."

Quickly following on the album's heels was the Neil Young-Crazy Horse *Ragged Glory* tour. Young chose two longtime proponents of avant-noise-rock, Social Distortion and Sonic Youth, to open the shows. He told ROLLING STONE's Alan Light that he found it very "soothing" to hear the sound of feedback blasting through his dressing room's concrete walls before he went on. Adding to the already-high-powered set was its backdrop: the Persian Gulf War.

NONE OF THE TOUR'S shows could have been as surreal as the one I saw at West Point Academy, in Upstate New York. Surrounded by teenaged male and female cadets, buttoned down in their uniforms, I overheard one say to another, "I hear he rocks pretty good for such an old geezer." Young and Crazy Horse hit the stage to a vast roar. We'd already been subjected to a traditional "Star-Spangled Banner," piped through the house speakers; the military powers-that-be had refused Young permission to play the Hendrix version of the national anthem, which he'd used to open other shows. Missing as well was the peace sign projected on the Crazy Horse backdrop (also against the rules). Young greeted the crowd with a little nostalgia: "The last time I was here was in '67 with the Buffalo Springfield." The performance went on to become a nonstop display of unrelenting musical energy.

Young captured the highlights of the tour for the live double-CD set, *Weld,* released in 1991. Said Don McLeese in ROLLING STONE, "For anyone who thought Young and the band drove feedback to its outer limits on . . . *Ragged Glory, Weld* opens new dimensions of sonic turbulence." An in-your-face concert video, again directed by Bernard Shakey, was also released. And, for those who couldn't get enough white noise, a limited-edition set, *Arc,* comprised of feedback and other grunged-up sound bites, was issued at the same time.

As Young blazed into the future, surrounding himself with noise and new blood, he still hadn't forgotten the past. This became evident as he previewed his next release by performing a series of concerts in which he was surrounded by acoustic guitars, a piano and a harmonium. The performance I saw at New York's Beacon Theater, in February 1992, was unfortunately marred by the loudmouthed antics of Young fans whose ears were apparently still ringing from the *Ragged Glory* tour. Young seemed somewhat tentative as he tested his new material—soft-edged songs, a few with rather corny lyrics. Soon he just became annoyed, as cries of "Plug in, Neil!" wouldn't let up.

These songs comprised *Harvest Moon,* a sequel to *Harvest,* his most commercially popular album, twenty years in coming. Countrified and homespun, the album also featured the Stray Gators, Ronstadt, Larson and Taylor. Young explained that he couldn't maintain for more than six months the volume and energy levels necessary for *Ragged Glory; Harvest Moon* was, indeed, its diametric opposite. Though some of the material was a bit over-the-top in terms of plainspoken sentimentality, it was a much more successful "journey through the past" than Young's earlier attempt with CSNY. The public gobbled up *Harvest Moon,* making it his biggest seller in thirteen years, even garnering several Grammy nominations.

Also in 1992, Young joined artists from three generations to celebrate the fiftieth birthday of one of his earliest influences, Bob Dylan. Between sets by Johnny Cash and Pearl Jam (taking the stage after Sinéad O'Connor's run-in with the booing hordes) Young came across as the leader of the pack in conviction and vigor. In addition to his powerful versions of "Just Like Tom Thumb's Blues" and "All Along the Watchtower," his distinctive Gibson Les Paul sound rang out explosively in the power jam on "My Back Pages," and held together the grand finale, "Knockin' on Heaven's Door."

It seemed Young wasn't going to let a year of the Nineties go by without activity. He began 1993 continuing his acoustic performances; one two-hour concert, where Young was also joined by Lofgren and the Stray Gators, was filmed, with various portions later shown on PBS, VH-1's *Center Stage,* and MTV's *Unplugged. Unplugged,* which featured everything from *Harvest Moon* cuts to an updated "Trans," became available on CD later in the summer.

Another Young collection also came out in 1993. A final peace treaty with Geffen, *Lucky Thirteen: Excursions into Alien Territory,* compiled by Young himself, collected material from his tumultuous years at that label. As a piece, the album actually holds up, combining tracks, alternate versions, and outtakes from *Trans, Everybody's Rockin', Landing on Water, Life* and *Old Ways.* In his ROLLING STONE review, James Hunter pointed out, "*Lucky Thirteen* resequences and rethinks the imperfect but important Eighties work of an artist who recently contended that 'deep inside' his acoustic pleasantries, his distorted raveups, his troubled techno, his symphonic flights, lies 'the same stuff.' "

WITH THE MILLENNIUM JUST over five years away, what can we expect to hear from Neil Young, as he approaches his own half-century mark? He spent the latter part of 1993 performing concerts backed by Stax soul vets, Booker T. and the MGs, and featuring Pearl Jam as the opening act. For encores, he was joined onstage by Vedder and company for a volatile "Rockin' in the Free World." To the soundtrack of the Jonathan Demme film *Philadelphia,* Young contributed the devastating title track, a song with an utterly mournful loveliness reminiscent of parts of *Gold Rush.* Since the late 1980s, he's been working on the follow-up to *Decade,* which has been rumored to total sixteen CDs, to be released over time in sets of four. Bernard Shakey-directed archival videos may be issued as well.

And in early 1994 Young headed back into the studio with Crazy Horse. An advance cassette of their upcoming album, *Sleeps With Angels,* just crossed my desk as this book goes to press. What's on the tape is astounding: a sonic potpourri with elements of Young's music from across the decades, sounding at various times like *Everybody Knows This Is Nowhere, After the Gold Rush, Rust Never Sleeps, Freedom, Ragged Glory* and *Harvest Moon.* After numerous feverish listenings, the album seems to me to be Young's best work since *Rust.* Unless he pulls a fast one, as Young has been wont to do, songs such as the moody "Change Your Mind" and the sadly gorgeous title track (a tribute to Kurt Cobain) will be the soundscape accompanying the publication of *Neil Young: The* ROLLING STONE *Files.*

As for my guess about Young's future, I learned a long time ago to sit back and wait for the Surprise. As Young himself told Cameron Crowe in 1975, "Every one of my records, to me, is like an ongoing autobiography. I can't write the same book every time."

Through all the ups and downs, highways and byways, Neil Young has let his music describe his personal journey—any way he wants to, regardless of anyone's expectations. Indeed, with Young, only one thing's for sure: He'll continue to keep the top down and the engine roaring, leaving all those prognosticators spinning on the roadside as he disappears in great clouds of thick, gray smoke—only to return again.

BUFFALO SPRINGFIELD AGAIN
ALBUM REVIEW

THE BUFFALO SPRINGFIELD have once again produced a musically and vocally interesting album. The songs on this album are not always as distinctive as those on their first effort, but they are done well. What *Buffalo Springfield Again,* though, obviously lacks is cohesiveness.

Diversity is an advantage but sometimes goes too far and becomes disunity. This album sounds as if every member of the group is satisfying his own musical needs. Each of them has produced songs in his own bag. Together there is no blend, only a rather obvious alienation among the compositions.

Richie Furay has produced some pretty compositions that are suitable for his voice, such as "Sad Memory," and for Dewey Martin, the drummer, which comes off as an affected attempt at the Tamla-Motown sound with a touch of Otis Redding.

Neil Young, a very capable and original guitarist, should be strongly commended for his composition, "Mr. Soul," a gutsy contemporary blues. The song hangs together well. His second composition, "Broken Arrow," is an attempt at the latest trend in contemporary songwriting—the Beatle-esque freak-out. The song is over six minutes long. It goes through changes of tone, rhythm, instrumentation and vocal quality. The song begins with the screams of fans and a rather raspy vocal of "Mr. Soul" and moves to a slower tempo and a different song. Although he incorporates some excellent string tracks and piano tracks, the song, nevertheless, is unsuccessful. It doesn't hold up; it becomes tiresome and loses impact.

Steve Stills' songs and arrangements dominate the album. "Bluebird" is an earthy, original bluesy number with great drive. At the end of the track Stills changes the style, turning it into a sort of folky banjo-picking tune. In "Rock & Roll Woman" the group is at its vocal best and the instrumental track is perfectly coordinated.

Buffalo Springfield Again is hardly a failure. Far from it. It is simply a very good, but not great, second effort by a highly talented group.

CLAPTON AND SPRINGFIELD MEMBERS BUSTED

ERIC CLAPTON OF the Cream and three members of the Buffalo Springfield were arrested in Los Angeles last week on misdemeanor charges involving marijuana.

Booked with Clapton were Neil Young, Richie Furay and Jim Messina, along with nearly a dozen others, including Furay's wife, Nancy.

All were charged with "being at a place where it is suspected marijuana was being used," a misdemeanor offense. Bail was set at $1,250 for each person arrested—standard for this charge—and all were released within twelve hours.

Arraignment for the Buffalo Springfield and Furay's wife was set for Tuesday, March 26. Clapton, now touring the U.S. with his trio, reportedly had his arraignment continued to a later date because of prior engagements.

They were arrested when Los Angeles County deputy sheriffs answered a "noisy party" complaint at a private home in the wooded Topanga Canyon section, part of Los Angeles County but north of the city. Those present contend it was not a party, but a rehearsal, although two other members of the Buffalo Springfield—Steve Stills and Dewey Martin—were not present at the time.

The arrests were made late Wednesday, March 20.

Buffalo Springfield had other dope arrest problems recently. Messina, the bass player for the group, replaced Bruce Palmer, who had been deported to his native Canada following three marijuana arrests. The bust also comes on the heels of Neil Young's announcement that he is leaving the group to try it as a single.

BUFFALO SPRINGFIELD GOES TO PASTURE

T HE BUFFALO SPRINGFIELD, one of the most outstanding Los Angeles rock groups, disbanded on May 5 because of a combination
of internal hassle, extreme fatigue coupled with absence of national
success and run-ins with the fuzz. The group, formed in Los Angeles,
consisted of Steve Stills and Neil Young, who shared lead vocal and guitar
spots; Bruce Palmer, the original bass player to join the group; Dewey
Martin, drummer; and Richie Furay, who sang lead and played rhythm
guitar.

Although the group's blend of the voicings and rhythms of rock and
country music was highly regarded, only their third single, "For What It's
Worth," a song about the youth-police conflict on Sunset Strip in late
1966, was successful nationwide. The group had its own conflict on March
20 when Young and Furay were busted with Jim Messina (Bruce Palmer
had been busted months before and deported to Canada) in the same raid
that captured Eric Clapton of Cream, on charges of possession of marijuana.

Plans for individual members of the group are indefinite, although
Steve Stills says he would like to join another group, possibly replacing Al
Kooper in Blood, Sweat and Tears. Neil Young will try it as a single, and
Richie Furay and Jim Messina want to operate as a writing and producing
team.

BARRY GIFFORD

LAST TIME AROUND
ALBUM REVIEW

A S A FINAL TESTAMENT to their multi-talent, the Buffalo Springfield
have released *Last Time Around,* the most beautiful record they've
ever made.

This is the second record album by a largely Canadian group (the first
was *Music From Big Pink* by the Band) of major importance to be released
this month. They both have their country roots showing. The great difference lies in their separate "heaviness distinction." The Band are overwhelming seriousness and pointed profundity, and the Buffalo Springfield
are happier sounding, more sweet-country flavored. They sound, as Jim
Messina croons, like a "carefree country day."

"Four Days Gone" is one of the best tracks the Springfield has ever
done. Stills' vocal is, as usual, uniquely trembly. It's a sad, C&W-flavored
song about a guy on the road running from the government, trying to get
to his chick ("I'm four days gone into runnin' "), who can't tell his name
because he's "got reason to live." The piano tinkles [Floyd] Cramer-rily in
the background as Stills tells the story. "Government madness," he com-
plains.

Stills has written five of the cuts on the album. "Special Care" and
"Uno Mundo" show his amazing versatility as a songwriter. Both are
entirely different from the C&W-ish "Four Days Gone." "Special Care"
is a rock number in the finest sense. After a keyboard intro in the style of
Dylan's "Black Crow Blues," it's led by a furious, screaming guitar and a
crashing, closely following organ. Stills trembles the paranoid lyrics: "Hey
there you on the corner / staring at me / Would you like to shoot me
down?" The guitar's buzzing vibrato lays down the melody as he raves on
in the background, yelling at the people. It sounds as if he's being dragged
away.

"Uno Mundo" is a Latin-based maracas-congos-trumpet Jamaican ska-
beat politi-calypso blast at the world: "Uno Mundo / Asia is screaming /
Africa seething / America bleating / just the same."

On "I Am a Child," Neil Young sounds more like Tim Hardin than
Tim Hardin. It's not very often that this happens, that two performers

sound almost identical. Oscar Peterson sounds so similar to Nat "King" Cole that for years, during Cole's career, Peterson did not sing. Then, when Cole died, Peterson put out a memorial album dedicated to him—he sang all of Cole's best loved songs—an almost perfect duplication of the original recordings. And the similarity was unintentional, as is the likeness between Young and Hardin. Moreover, "Child" is done exactly in Hardin's electri-fied country-folk vein. It's a nice tune, very pretty, with some strikingly poignant lines: "You can't conceive of the pleasure in my smile." It's very simple and light. Even the harmonica bit reminds one of Herb Shriner playing "Back Home in Indiana."

Furay is a beautiful singer, and his best efforts here are the ballads "It's So Hard to Wait" and "Kind Woman." "Hard to Wait" is a plaintive love song: "I'll never forget you / I hope you care"—it moves slowly, backed by clarinet, acoustic guitar, drums and bass, all of which are played down appropriately, highlighting Furay's lingering falsetto. "Kind Woman" is similar and is performed just as nicely.

But the best track on the album is "Carefree Country Day." Messina's crackly-voiced lead vocal ("I get up in the morning with a cock-a-doodle-doo / I get myself together if and when I choose") has the most relaxed country flavor this side of Jack Elliott. Some great backup harmony by Furay and Stills and a funky "wha-wha-wha" horn interlude complement Messina's vocal superbly. It even has a "dot-in-doo-wah-wap-en-doo-wat-en-dah" fade-out, which is the finest bit of country doodling since Elliott's "Guabi Guabi."

Too bad this isn't the *first* time around.

GARY VON TERSCH

NEIL YOUNG ALBUM REVIEW

THIS ALBUM BY NEIL YOUNG (formerly of the Buffalo Springfield) and various friends is a flowing tributary from the overall Springfield river of twangs, breathless vocals and slim yet stout instrumentation. Especially vivid is Young's sense of melancholy and the ingenious clusters of images he employs in his lyrics (printed in full). In particular, one could very easily view this disc as an extension of Young's work on the *Buffalo Springfield Again* album, especially his compositions "Expecting to Fly" and the gaping "Broken Arrow," which closes the album.

This solo disc opens with "The Emperor of Wyoming," an instrumental that sets the tone musically for the side in a high-flying yet whining sort of way. It has that definite Springfieldian touch to it like wind between rocks or the people you see in dreams.

"The Loner" is a contemporary lament that features a nice blending of Young's guitar with strings in nonobtrusive fashion, allowing Young's balanced ice-pick vocal to chip effectively at the listener. The stance and imagery are much the same as in the earlier "Expecting to Fly."

The next two selections are pieces of the same puzzle. "If I Could Have Her Tonight" is a slow, crystal-like effort. It features a heavy drum line, Byrds-like guitar and mellow lyrics, which all together add up to that unique sense of melancholy yet joy in melancholy the Springfield captured so well—and which Young just continues doing. Like standing in all four corners of the night, "I've Been Waiting for You" is an extension of the theme, with a tinkly piano and organ.

The side ends with a longish song entitled "The Old Laughing Lady" that is so close to, yet so far apart from, Young's earlier song "Broken Arrow." A quivering piano and a halting string section move around and around the melody line, here peeking between his words, there showing sky between his phrasings. The two pieces also have a series of mood/tone changes between verses—the strings, for instance, get increasingly lusher and fuller in "Laughing Lady." The fadeout piano chord here is similar to the heartbeat fadeout on the earlier piece. The main difference between the two can be tersely put: The latter piece is tighter, more mature and has more of the quiet explosion to it that Young obviously intends.

The second side opens with a diminutive Jack Nitzsche piece entitled

"String Quartet From Whiskey Boot Hill." It is a slow, deliberate ethereal introduction to Young's vocal on "Here We Are in the Years." Musically the piece is string-dominated and very lush and full with Young's voice incising between—the scraping fadeout says it all.

"The Last Trip to Tulsa" closes the album. It is nine minutes long and is the most stylistic, anti-Springfield piece on the album. Here we have only Young's chameleon voice and guitar—no strings, drums or piano. It proceeds to build from verse to verse—the vocal gets wilder, the guitar more abandoned, more wanton. An innovative close to, in many ways, a delightful reprise of that Springfield sound done a new way.

CROSBY, STILLS AND NASH ADD YOUNG

NEIL YOUNG HAS JOINED Crosby, Stills and Nash, making it Crosby, Stills, Nash and Young, an alliance that already is being described as "the best-sounding law firm in pop."

The "super group" has also added Bruce Palmer on bass, and recording sessions have already begun.

Young had been working and recording as a solo the past year, since the Buffalo Springfield collapsed in May 1968. His joining the triumvirate of David Crosby, Stephen Stills and Graham Nash adds another "heavy" to the group and reunites him with Stills, who is also a former Springfield member.

The announcement that Young had joined the group followed several weeks of rumors that such a move would take place, although it was also considered a possibility that Stills would leave the combine and with Young and Palmer reform the Springfield. Palmer was that group's first bassist.

Oddly enough, this does not mean Young will abandon his solo career. He said he would continue to perform alone whenever he could—actually with a band called Crazy Horse backing him—and continue to make solo LPs for Reprise. In fact, Young made his comments about joining Crosby, Stills and Nash while remixing his first of two solo LPs, saying he didn't like the original pressing and indicating that so long as he was staying a single at least part-time he wanted his solo efforts to be as good as possible.

Crosby, Stills and Nash have released one album thus far, on Atlantic, and this is where the new alliance will remain. It is possible for Young to record for the two companies simultaneously because both are part of Warner Bros.-Seven Arts.

Young said the six-man band (Dallas Taylor continues on drums) has recorded four songs so far, three of which probably will be included in the first Crosby, Stills, Nash and Young LP.

The guitarist said that the group hoped to have an album complete by the time the band performs its first engagement, July 25 at the Fillmore East.

"When we do the Fillmore East, there won't be anyone else on the bill," he said. "We'll be doing a two-hour show, with an intermission.

"It's not a rock & roll group, y'know. Crosby, Stills and Nash will come out and play three or four songs from the first LP. Then I'll come out and join them for a couple more. Then we'll play a couple of new songs. And so far it's all acoustic—and no bass or drums for most of the first half.

"Then we have an intermission, and not until the second half will we start playing electric. If the people aren't quiet, they won't be able to hear us."

Young said he would be sharing the organ playing as well as lead guitar with Stills. He seemed well aware that this same combination of talent (some say ego) contributed to the death of the Springfield.

Young said he would not be contributing many vocals—although in remixing his own solo LP the major thing he was doing was bringing out the voice he had buried in the mix a year ago.

"When I was with the Springfield, I held back," he said. "I was paranoid about my voice. So on my own first LP I buried my voice intentionally. The second LP I brought it up more. I had more confidence. That's what working with Crazy Horse has done. It's given me confidence. That's why I want to continue as a single. But I won't be singing that much with the new group. Mostly just playing a lot."

Bassist Bruce Palmer's return to the U.S. pop scene came as a surprise in that as a member of the Springfield he was arrested three times on assorted charges (mostly dope) and twice deported to his native Canada. All problems with Immigration have been resolved, however, and Palmer has been quietly living in Los Angeles for about two months.

BRUCE MIROFF

EVERYBODY KNOWS THIS IS NOWHERE ALBUM REVIEW

NEIL YOUNG DOES NOT have the kind of "good" voice that would bring praise from a high school music teacher. But you only have to listen to Judy Collins mangle "Just Like Tom Thumb's Blues" to realize that rock & roll does not flourish because of "good" voices. The best rock vocals (for example, those of Mick Jagger or the Band's Richard Manuel) are usually gritty or even harsh. Negating a formula prettiness, they push forward the unique temperament of the singer ("It's the singer, not the song"—Mick Jagger). Such vocals can never function as background music; they demand that you listen to them and feel them. Their essence is their intensity—and in light of that intensity the products of "good" voices usually sound pallid and dead.

While Neil Young is a fine songwriter and an excellent guitarist, his greatest strength is in his voice. Its arid tone is perpetually mournful, without being maudlin or pathetic. It hints at a world in which sorrow underlies everything; even a line like "you can't conceive of the pleasure in my smile" (from "I Am a Child") ultimately becomes painful to hear. And because that world is recognizable to most of us, Young's singing is often strangely moving. In a natural and moving way, Neil Young is the Johnnie Ray of rock & roll.

Everybody Knows This Is Nowhere is Young's second album since the demise of the Buffalo Springfield. In several respects it falls short of his previous effort. Young's new material is a little disappointing; nothing on this album touches the aching beauty of "If I Could Have Her Tonight" and "I've Loved Her So Long" or the quiet terror of "The Old Laughing Lady." His guitar work also suffers by comparison; the lyricism of the first album can only be found in faint traces here. But despite its shortcomings, *Everybody Knows This Is Nowhere* offers ample rewards. Young's music partially makes up for its lack of grace by its energy and its assurance. And his singing is still superb. Listen, for example, to the conviction which he gives to the title cut, a song about the need for and the impossibility of escape from Los Angeles.

The most interesting tracks on the album are "Running Dry" and

"Cowgirl in the Sand." Building on a traditional folk melody, "Running Dry" interweaves electric guitar and violin into a disquieting blend. Its aura of strangeness is somewhat reminiscent of Young's magnificent "Out of My Mind." The lyrics are a bit overdramatic, but the music and vocal manage to transcend them, creating the feeling of a dimly understood tragedy.

On "Cowgirl in the Sand" everything works. The lyrics are quietly accusative, while the lead guitar, alternately soaring, piercing and driving, keeps the song surging forward. But it is Young's singing that is the real key to the success of this track. "Cowgirl in the Sand" demonstrates quite clearly the peculiar depths of Young's voice. It indicates how rock manages, again and again, to triumph over high school music teachers and their legions.

CROSBY, STILLS, ETC., A SELLOUT, ETC.

CROSBY, STILLS, NASH AND YOUNG made an auspicious hometown debut last month, selling out all seven nights at Los Angeles' fashionable Greek Theater.

Capacity of the outdoor theater is approximately 4,400, which means the musical alliance drew more than 30,000 during the week-long engagement. They also earned a tidy $70,000 for the gig.

What makes this noteworthy is that when CSNY were booked to appear in the Griffith Park amphitheater, they'd not yet appeared anywhere publicly, and the Crosby, Stills and Nash album for Atlantic hadn't even been recorded yet.

And, although Tom Jones and the Fifth Dimension—both proven acts, remember—both preceded CSNY at the Greek, the theater generally is known for presenting the likes of Johnny Mathis, Henry Mancini and Don Ho, also scheduled during the current season.

"It was a gamble," a spokesman for promoter Jimmy Doolittle said midway through the engagement. "At first we thought we'd made a mistake," she continued. "The act was very weak in advance sales, and we were afraid many of those who had season tickets weren't all that interested in an act like this. . . . Let's put it this way: The people who usually come to the Greek Theater aren't used to seeing quite that much hair on men."

But, she said, "Opening night ended our worries. The kids may not have had season tickets and they may not have been much in the advance sale department, but at the box office it was incredible. They came out of the hills in trucks. Now we've sold out every show, and opening night we had to turn hundreds away."

As for the show itself, it, too, was exceptional. David Crosby, Stephen Stills, Graham Nash and Neil Young—sharing the bill with Joni Mitchell— earned standing ovations and encores nearly every night.

The first part of the group's performance, each played two or three songs alone, limiting the accompaniment to acoustic guitar. The drums of Dallas Taylor and bass of Greg Reeves, the latter recently added to the band, were not even in view. With Joni Mitchell preceding them, it was for more than two hours essentially a folk concert.

Songs played during the initial half of the CSNY set included the song

Stills wrote to Judy Collins, "Suite: Judy Blue Eyes" and Nash's "Lady of the Island," both from the album recorded when it was Crosby, Stills and Nash; "4 + 20," a new song by Stills; and Young's "I've Loved Her So Long."

Following this gracious, uncluttered opening, a curtain behind the quartet of singer/songwriters opened, revealing banks of huge amplifiers, electric guitars, organ, drums and bass. It was time for some rock & roll.

Joined by Taylor and Reeves now, CSNY played, among others, Young's composition "Sea of Madness" and "Wooden Ships" (by Crosby and Stills) and "Marrakesh Express" (by Nash), the latter two from the Crosby, Stills and Nash LP and the last of the songs the band's hit.

This was the group's third public appearance and came only nine weeks after Crosby, Stills, Nash and Young first got together. They had previously performed at the Woodstock Music and Art Fair (at 5 A.M. on Monday) and at the Chicago Auditorium. Several earlier dates had been canceled because of nodes on Nash's vocal cords.

Following the Greek Theater engagement, they were to videotape appearances on three television shows, *Tom Jones, The Music Scene* and *Hollywood Palace*.

After that they were scheduled to perform at Fillmore East in New York September 19 and 20 and at the Fillmore West in San Francisco October 1, 2 and 3.

■ **RANDOM NOTES** (November 29, 1969)

Neil Young's first album for Reprise has been re-mastered to bring Young's voice out and is to be released in November as *Neil Young's First Album Again*.

■ **RANDOM NOTES** (December 13, 1969)

Quickies from Crosby, Stills, Nash and Young: Crosby is having "Wooden Ships," which he wrote with Stills and Jefferson Airplane's Paul Kantner, turned into a movie by sci-fi writer Theodore Sturgeon. It'll probably feature the entire band. . . . The next LP is complete, with mixing being finished at Studio 3 in L.A. It will probably be called—what else?—*Crosby, Stills, Nash and Young*, and should be out by mid-December. . . . Young, meantime, is definitely his own man—he and his other band, Crazy Horse, are working on their third LP for Reprise (it'll include a Neil Young rendition of Don Gibson's "Oh, Lonesome Me"); he is building a sixteen-track studio at his Topanga house with help from Wally Heider, and his Crazy Horse will do a tour beginning in February.

BEN FONG-TORRES

CROSBY, STILLS, NASH, YOUNG, TAYLOR AND REEVES

BEHIND THEM, A CREW IS setting up the curtains that'll hide their electric gear until their acoustic "wooden music" is finished. The curtains are black; there'll be no light show behind Crosby, Stills, Nash and Young. It's Thursday, 5 P.M., rehearsal time at the Winterland Auditorium in San Francisco. Four hours before showtime, a guard is already stationed at the old Ice Capades auditorium's doors, brusquely challenging all visitors. Outside, in brisk autumn weather, a line has already begun, a sidewalk full of hair and rimless glasses and leather and boutique colors. These people know Crosby, Stills, Nash and Young won't go on until 11:30, maybe midnight. No matter. They'll grab good places, on the hardwood floor at the foot of the stage. And they'll wait.

Dallas Taylor, the drummer, is moving along the foot of the stage now, out of view from Stephen Stills, who's on the stage testing out the piano. Taylor is edging toward Stills, a mischievous smile splitting his wide face. Suddenly Taylor springs, with a shout, up behind Stills, his right hand now a pistol, and kills him. Stills stiffens, falls off his seat, and plunges straight into David Crosby and his guitar, causing a crashing cacophony.

Across the floor, in the first row, Graham Nash is stirred alert by the noise. He's trying to put together the order of tunes they'll do that night. He calls out to Taylor, who's scampered off to stage center by now: "Hey, man—not around *axes,* man! Not when you're near an *ax!*" Taylor nods, but he knows that any minute now, Stills will have to come back and kill him.

More puttering around the stage, and suddenly it happens. Stills pantomimes the biting of the ring off a hand grenade, waits three seconds, and stuffs it into Taylor's mouth. Taylor dies beautifully, jumping out of his skin at the "explosion," then falling six feet down off the stage, tumbling, landing on his back.

Nash looks up again. No guitars in the way this time. He smiles, shakes his head, and goes back to work.

CROSBY, STILLS AND NASH coasted up the charts effortlessly this summer behind Blind Faith, Creedence Clearwater Revival and Blood,

Sweat and Tears. Then their single, "Marrakesh Express," hit the Top Twenty, then "Suite: Judy Blue Eyes," then *Crosby Stills and Nash* surged up again, past Blind Faith and the others.

And here's Nash, sitting atop a softly vibrating bed in Stills' motel room in San Francisco. "We didn't have a *band* with just the three of us," he is saying.

Crosby, Stills and Nash was Crosby and Nash and Stills, and Stills on organ, and Stills on bass, and Stills on lead guitar and overdubs of additional guitar tracks.

"We could sing the LP," Nash said, "but we couldn't play it." For their concerts, he said, "we knew we'd have to represent the sound we had on the album."

Dallas Taylor, with the trio from the beginning—which was a year ago—has been joined by Greg Reeves, a quiet, nineteen-year-old bassist right out of Motown's studios. And in the foreground—for most intents and purposes—is Neil Young.

Young, composer, guitarist, singer with Buffalo Springfield, has written a couple of tunes for the next album—"Country Girl" and "Helpless," the latter including a chorus featuring the high, soaring harmonic blend of Crosby, Stills and Nash—the blend that is perhaps the prime attraction of the group.

But mostly Young is a luxury, a utility man as well as yet another creative force. In the studios, where Stills reigns but shares the reins with opinionated co-producers Nash and Crosby, Young is a solid fourth corner. "We may shape the album," Stills says, "but Neil'll come along and give us that extra thing."

Nash elaborates: "He gives us that bit of direction we may need to resolve a question. He's good at making records."

Young was brought in, says Stills, because "we wanted another life force. I always wanted another rhythm section. But instead of a keyboard man, we thought, why not a guy who could do other things—write songs, play guitar, be a brother and stuff."

HERE COME THE LIFE forces into their dressing room at Winterland. It's 1:30 A.M. Sunday now, and they've finished their third of four nights. Dimly lit in red, the room is small, attic-like, but serves as an adequate shelter. Crosby, Stills, Nash and Young—and Taylor and Reeves—want some quiet. David's voice is out, and he's slumped into an old couch, his doctor standing over him.

David had had a sore throat since midweek and that day—Saturday— had wrecked it at the Vietnam Moratorium rally in Golden Gate Park. "He got carried away a bit," Nash had explained that evening backstage. "After the first thing he yelled he realized he'd gotten carried away." By the time he'd reached the stage at the Winterland, with each of the 5,000 onlookers able to shout louder than he, he knew he'd paid the price. He could talk best by nodding, smiling and crinkling his 'stache up and down. At the mike, Nash explained Crosby's ailment, and the crowd cheered at their disabled compatriot.

Stills, seated with an acoustic guitar on his lap, and facing Crosby, went into "Suite," and the audience, just itching for the group to justify the adulation they'd already poured onto them, whooped it up. Slowly, surely they galloped through the number, until the verse beginning, "Chestnut brown canary, ruby-throated sparrow." And when David reached the high note (. . . "thrill me to the MARrow"), he couldn't make it, and the crowd applauded, anyway, while he grinned sheepishly and held his throat.

From that point on—what, five minutes into the set—Crosby was pretty much out of it, and the program had to be overhauled. Crosby's usual solo, "Guinnevere," was dropped, along with a couple of duets with Nash. Young stepped in to sing a medley of Buffalo Springfield tunes, on acoustic guitar, with Stills. Later, during the electric half of the set, Crosby came back to spend the remains of his voice on a hoarse facsimile of "Wooden Ships," and Stills substituted for him on "Long Time Gone," a song clearly Crosby's.

The audience, like the ones in New York and Los Angeles and Big Sur, cheered everything they did, of course, but Crosby, Stills, Nash and Young knew better. The night before, they had done their now-standard encore number—a brief, softly sung untitled Stills composition about freedom, once submitted to *Easy Rider*—and gone offstage and around the rim of the old ice capades rink and settled into their dressing room and lit up a snack, and those 5,000 freaks on the other side of the curtains were still stomping on the floor, in their seats high in the distant balconies, screaming for MORE! MORE!

Now, tonight, it was pretty quiet by the time they'd reached the room, and Stills is looking up. "Hey, you should have been here last night," he says, clear eyes dancing. "Tonight was okay, but it was nothing. You know, we were *bored* out there."

And you know he's being straight. "Down by the River," the Young composition used as the set-closer, seemed interminable, with Stills and Young trading lead guitar runs and strums as laconically as two men lobbing a medicine ball back and forth. Nash, he of the high, silken voice, sang out a trade-off riff of his own and knocked Young out for a second, but that was a second out of thirty minutes. Still, the audience went crazy.

Crosby, Stills, Nash and Young can do no wrong.

IT COULD BE THE flawless harmony—tight as the Everly Brothers, soft as Simon and Garfunkel, melodic as the best of the Springfield. It could be reports, words-of-mouth about the mini-Woodstocks they'd created wherever they performed, sending out those effortless good vibes and coming off like "gentle free spirits." It could well be a mass appreciation of their aversion to the kind of hype that flooded Blind Faith, making them an instantly high-priced, out-of-reach act.

Young speaks: "See, the thing is, everybody—especially David—is a controversial character. Everybody has an opinion. Like, I like to watch David just to see what he'll do next." Crosby, of course—the Byrd who was canned because he wanted to speak and live as well as sing his political piece. He was deeply hurt when Roger McGuinn fired him, and over the months since his departure, Byrds interviews seemed to build a picture of Crosby as a huffy, moody, intolerable sort of man.

"This is the best music I've made with other people," Crosby beams. Away from the microphones, he spends most of his time behind and to the side of the control board, hand-cleaning future refreshments or bouncing up and down, his jacket fringes dancing to the music of his band.

LAMENT OVER LOST LOVE provided the theme—if anyone ever listened to the words—of the first CSN LP. But where "Suite: Judy Blue Eyes" opened and paced that album, a song called "Carry On," written by Stills, will set the tone for the second:

Rejoice,
Rejoice!
There is no choice!

Stills, for what it's worth, is apolitical. In that song, written when the war was still largely confined to Sunset Strip, he wrote of pickets proclaiming nothing stronger than "Hooray for our side." In the song he wrote for *Easy Rider,* he encapsulated the movie:

Find the cost of freedom
Buried in the ground
Mother earth will swallow you
Lay your body down.

—But it was a synopsis, rather than any analysis.

And at the Vietnam Moratorium rally at Golden Gate Park, he pounced on the piano to pound out a searing, machine-gun-paced version of "For What It's Worth"—but only after shouting to the 125,000 marchers: "Politics is bullshit! Richard Nixon is bullshit! Spiro Agnew is bullshit! Our music *isn't* bullshit!"

As Young put it: "Steve's trip comes to its head when he sings."

Stills is the one most intensely involved in the group's music. Onstage he bounces from acoustic guitar to piano to organ to electric lead. In the studio he directs most of the sixteen-track traffic, writing and singing the most songs, overdubbing the most tracks, staying the longest time. On several occasions, working on the second LP, he put in sixteen-hour days at Wally Heider's studios, located on the fringe of San Francisco's greasy Tenderloin district. He stayed at a motel a few blocks away. It was like he was on call to the burgeoning music, constantly in labor, in his head.

"We—Dallas and Bill [Halverson, their engineer] and I—spent last night till six doing *this,*" he said one evening at Heider's, holding up a stack of one-inch tapes. "Drunk out of my head playing the piano," a backing track for one of the tunes on the new album. "That's what you can do when you've had a gold record." Beaming like a newsboy who's just won a trip to Disneyland and gets a day off school.

IN THE STUDIOS, STILLS is a man of restrained excitement, of quiet pride, of nonstop devotion to the task of making records. "Steve's whole thing right now is the group," Young says. "It'd be impossible to have everybody into it as much as him. It'd be complete bedlam."

In the studios, Young, who so often clashed with Stills in the illuminating but frustrating Springfield days, generally stands back with his scowling demeanor, big-eyed, glowering stares shining out between messy black curtains of hair. He seems content in the shadows, thrashing his guitar mercilessly, like a country bluesman possessed. Young is a satisfied man—secure with his own band, Crazy Horse, on Reprise Records, as well as this insane, perfect gig with this superb, if not "super," group.

While Young and Reeves work out their backing for Young's "Country Girl," Stills hovers over engineer Halverson, and, with Nash, act as unofficial conductors. Nash picks out the slightest flaws in tuning, pacing, whatever—and relays his thoughts to Stills. It's a stop-go-stop-go process, of course, but somehow a song flows, maintaining its vitality and spontaneity, through the constant self-interruptions.

Young, the fourth corner, is wandering off from the control room following a playback on the track he and Reeves have just done. "What we've got to do is listen with an eye to simplicity," he says. "Think how we can make it bigger by simplifying it."

Stills was the leader of Buffalo Springfield, but Young stood out the most—tallest, darkest, fringiest, flashiest writer of some of their best songs ("Nowadays Clancy Can't Even Sing," "Expecting to Fly," "Flying on the Ground is Wrong"). And he was the most mercurial, quitting the band twice before they folded, saying he never wanted to be in a group anyway, just like you wouldn't have Dick Nixon to kick around anymore.

But this is different. Young is in two groups, right, but, as he explains, "Before I joined Crosby, Stills and Nash, I made it clear to both sides that I belong to myself."

First, there was Crazy Horse, who'd backed him up on his excellent second LP, *Everybody Knows This Is Nowhere,* and who're working with him now on his third album. They're also setting up a concert tour beginning in February.

"I didn't want Crazy Horse to die just as we were getting it together," he says. Crazy Horse is important to Young as a counterbalance to the tight, structured kind of music Crosby, Stills, Nash and Young put out. "Crazy Horse is funkier, simpler, more down to the roots." Young has production control with Crazy Horse. "I dig a lot of bass and drums, man. To my mind, the bass drum should hit you in the stomach. Listen to *Nowhere* at the same volume as *Crosby, Stills and Nash* and you'll know what I mean."

Young will do Don Gibson's country classic, "Oh, Lonesome Me" on the LP with Crazy Horse. He couldn't hope to do that kind of thing with CSNY. "But then, see, I have another side to me, and it's technically too far advanced for Crazy Horse—so the other band plays that. They complement each other inside me."

Young is contracted to Reprise and has a "temporary contract" with Atlantic, the remains of his five-year pact as a Buffalo Springfield. Hassles are few since both companies are under the Warner Bros. umbrella. Neil works out his tour schedules so that both bands know when they can have him.

With Crosby, Stills and Nash, Young sings lead on his numbers—with the three others building waves of smooth harmony behind his high, hard-edged voice. He does very little harmony singing himself. "I don't consider myself to be a background singer."

AWAY FROM EITHER BAND, Young is getting into the movies—writing a song for *Strawberry Statement* and doing the score—with Crazy Horse—for *Landlord,* "a racial comedy about a white guy who buys a tenement house in Brooklyn and kicks out the floor to build a New York City-type townhouse out of it and gets into all kinds of shit . . . voodoo fights and things—with the neighbors."

Young is also getting into filmmaking, beginning with a brand-new Super 8. He and Susan (who he met last year at a Topanga Canyon cafe she ran) are planning to move slowly toward "the big time," when they'll blow their scored films up to 16mm and have showings at the Topanga Community House, where the local women's club usually meets.

Young, married for a year now, plans to stay at his redwood, hillside Topanga Canyon house, their home since August 1968. He's even building a sixteen-track recording studio under the house.

Crosby has settled into a ranch in Novato, in north Marin County, and Stills is looking for a house in Marin County. Reeves lives about ninety miles north of San Francisco, in Guerneville. If Young moves, he says, it'll be to either Big Sur, on the Pacific Coast, or back to Canada.

Whatever the specific moves, there is a migration, of spirit, at least, to San Francisco. Stills and Crosby are close friends of Jefferson Airplane and the Grateful Dead family. Stills joined the Dead at the Winterland at one of Bill Graham's San Francisco Band nights and he and Garcia got it off for four or five numbers. And Garcia, in return, is now an unofficial member of CSNY. Garcia dropped by a session at Heider's one night and ended up playing steel pedal guitar on Nash's light "Teach Your Children."

"We just sat down and fiddled awhile," Stills said, "and we got an incredible take. The opening lick will just curl your whiskers."

Jerry Garcia and Neil Young, and young mojo man Greg Reeves, cool half-black/half-Indian bassist, and Clear Light Dallas Taylor, all in addition to Crosby, Stills and Nash. If the first LP was a milestone, this new one should be an event.

On that first LP the lovingly intertwined harmonies and impeccable instrumentation overshadowed the lyrics. Back when the first LP was being recorded, Stills, the construction engineer, had said, with tongue only slightly in cheek, that all he wanted to do was produce "the best album of the year." Nash says, "Our main complaint on that LP was that it sounded so constructed. This will change with Dallas and Greg, and with Neil and me branching out more."

Next time around, Nash says, it'll be the same as before: "Our main thing is to set some kind of a mood; our only rule when it comes to choosing our music is to pick something that gets us off."

At this point, Crosby, Stills, Nash and Young are coasting. Their next album is pre-sold gold, judging by their success across all fields of music— Top Forty, "underground" and "middle of the road" (their LP even reached Number Thirty-five on *Billboard*'s Soul chart). Their concerts, stage-managed by Chip Monck Industries, are near-perfect, the group relaxed in subdued light, making love with their soft, bluesy, acoustic music, slapping palms, soul style, after a particularly well-executed number, then charging on with a full load of amps and speakers, then collapsing in a circular embrace at the end of it all.

And their heads are straight. Stills, aglow with recognition as some sort of musical genius after those two years with Buffalo Springfield ("a sheer case of frustration," he calls them), won't play huge arenas where sound is sacrificed for a bigger gate. "And we won't have any ball-busting one-night tours. So you make your million dollars in thirty days instead of fifteen, right?

"The good thing," Stills says, "is to do a concert and instead of giving them one big flash, leaving them with flash after flash, and people come up and say—softly—'Thank you . . . thank you, man.' "

■ RANDOM NOTES (February 21, 1970)

Crosby, Stills, Nash and Young were a smash at Albert Hall, according to reports. But the daily London press failed to be amazed. Reviewing the concert, the *Evening Standard* moaned: "It was so extravagantly boring. On and on they went, from acoustic to electric, from close harmony to counter melody, from whimsical folk tunes to heavy hard rock and from dullness to dire drabness." The *Observer*, after putting down a Nash composition he misquoted as "Our bodies were perfected in afterglow," dismissed the group's onstage raps as "an exercise in low camp" and their show as "a crashing, witless bore."

Both reviewers admitted, however, that the audience loved—"raved," that is—CSNY. And that counts a little, too, we suppose.

■ RANDOM NOTES (March 7, 1970)

Crosby, Stills, Nash and Young's new album, *Déjà Vu,* should be out by this week. Generally expected by early January (although there has been no official release date), the record was delayed by the printer doing the cover, which will be a heavy grade of paper made to look and feel like leather, with gold-leaf embossing. From what we've seen, it'll look more like a book than an album. . . .

JOHN MORTHLAND

"OH, LONESOME ME"
SINGLES REVIEW

THIS IS PERHAPS THE greatest non-single yet. Neil Young has taken the old Don Gibson soliloquy and stretched it out to an agonizing 3:55. Whoever plays harmonica sounds like he's going to swallow it any second, and then Young's own shaky voice enters: "Everybody's going out and having fun / I'm a fool for staying home and having none / I can't get over how she set me free / Oh, lonesome me." Crazy Horse moves the song along, Young's guitar finally breaking in right when it begins to fade. Brilliant, but hardly Top-Forty material, since it sucks you in slowly rather than grabbing you with the first chords and then shaking you for three verses.

Prove me wrong. Buy "Oh, Lonesome Me," and let Neil Young and Crazy Horse haunt you for four minutes.

RANDOM NOTES (April 30, 1970)
Talk about gold: Crosby, Stills, Nash, Young and Company's *Déjà Vu* had orders totaling $2 million before it was in the stores. "Woodstock," meantime, is pushing up the singles charts steadily. . . .

ELLIOT BLINDER

NEIL YOUNG Q & A

NEIL YOUNG STRUTTED OUT of the swanky Americanese coffee shop at the Fenway Commonwealth Motor Hotel, on Commonwealth Avenue near Fenway Park, where the Boston Red Sox play ball. He had just finished eating lunch instead of breakfast after waking up late from a midnight concert at the Boston Tea Party, which is opposite Fenway Park.

The Tea Party had spent the week before broadcasting and advertising the one-night, one-show performance, and conservative estimates said that 200 people were turned away and another 2,000 or so were sardined in, elbow to elbow and elbow to head.

Young came on after several hours of intermissions and other groups, laboriously tuned three guitars, walked offstage, came back on and played and rapped an acoustic set of old Buffalo Springfield songs, warming everybody up for a beautifully long set with Crazy Horse. Standing ovation, hoots and howls.

Next morning I couldn't conceive of the pleasure in his smile when we sat down on your average American motel room twin-double and got into the kind of stoning session I might have expected to get into had we been longtime friends living on opposite coasts.

HOW LONG HAVE YOU *been playing guitar?*
About nine years.
How old are you now?
Twenty-four. I'm gettin' tired of this too. Really it's groovy, but I don't know how much longer I can do it.
Why is that?
I just want to do something else.
Other than music or other than touring?
After this next album I don't know how much longer it'll be before I put out another one, of any kind, with anyone. I think I'll just stop for a while.
Do you lead the kind of life where you're busy every day with more than one thing?
Yeah, it's like living two different lives. People who see me and come

over and want to talk to me because of Crosby, Stills and Nash are weird compared to the people I know through Crazy Horse; and then there's the people I know who don't have anything to do with either one of them, who are a whole other trip, and by the time the day's over I'm just completely screwed up. I start off real well depending on which one I see first.

Is that a reflection of what was in "Broken Arrow," of being a rock & roll star?

Yeah, that was when I was living in Hollywood, though, that's a whole other number I was into then. I was a Hollywood Indian.

You were?

I guess so, everybody thought I was an Indian. That was when it was cool to be an Indian. I was wearin' fringe jackets and everything. I really loved these fringe jackets I used to have with the Springfield. I dug wearing them.

What happened to them?

They died with the Springfield. A lot of changes went down in everybody's heads when the group broke up. When we got together we thought we were gonna be together about fifteen years. We really thought it was gonna last a long time because we knew how good it was. Nobody else did, though.

You must get this question a lot, but it's a question a lot of people want to know the answer to, so that's probably why you get it a lot, but how do you feel now about the Springfield and ever playing with those four people again?

I sometimes think about that and I would like to do another couple of concerts with the original Buffalo Springfield, the original. I think if we could get everybody together, I'd like to do that. It'd be fun.

Has anybody tried to get it together?

No.

Do you think it's on Jim Messina's mind, and . . .

Well, I know it's on Dewey Martin's mind, and, uh, it's on Messina's mind probably. Although I don't know who Stephen [Stills] and I would want to use if we could get Bruce [Palmer]. But you see that brings up a touchy subject of who we could get, or if we could get Jim Fielder too, from Blood, Sweat and Tears. . . .

You could use them all, if you could . . .

Yeah, but we tried, uh, just a minute. . . . [*Young begins searching for something.*]

What are you looking for?

I was just looking for another number.

We were just talking about bass players. . . .

Yeah, well, I don't know what bass player we'd use.

*A*LL THE WHILE WE *talked over in one end of the room, Susan Young milled around—as much as one can mill in a motel room—gathering things, and getting ready to go out and see what she could see in the ninety minutes that was left over from touring a nation. Young had spoken earlier to people from Right-a-Wrong (RAW), who were sounding him out on what he might be willing to do to help RAW's campaign to legalize marijuana. Young said he thought they were doing good things, but it was obvious that he was too far into his four guitars and two bands and one wife and home in Topanga Canyon. One of the RAW people came up to the room and a brief rap on politics and ecology ensued.*

*F*IVE YEARS THEY'LL COME around, five years. This is just starting. The hassle about pollution isn't gonna go away. The people aren't gonna get less uptight about it. So naturally the rate at which people respond is gonna get faster. I think five years is when things are really gonna start being done about it.

RAW: It might be a lot sooner, man.

I don't think so. You won't get these big plants to shut down and change things so . . .

RAW: Within four or five years there might be a very violent revolution, man, that will stop every wheel turning!

I can dig it. I hope not though, 'cause if it is I'll be in Big Sur (laugh). I'll be in Big Sur with my guns.

With his guns . . .

Yeah, I'll get a big cannon if they're gonna have a revolution. I'll sit up on top of my studio there, with my material gains after the game, and, uh, contemplate my future. . . .

You were talking before about not making any more records for a while . . .

Well, I'm not sure really what I want to do because I think ahead: I'm finishing this tour, then I go home and make a Crazy Horse album, then I go out on the road for thirty or forty days with CSN. It's getting to be a lot of work. It's getting to be no privacy at all.

Couldn't you just say, "No, we're not playing this week, or next week?"

No, I couldn't do that. Crosby, Stills and Nash have been resting for two or three months, right; they're ready to go back on the road, so it's hard for me to say, "Let's not go on the road now, let's wait, because I've been on the road playing with Crazy Horse." That just doesn't seem like a very good reason to them.

Well, couldn't they tour as Crosby, Stills and Nash and as Crosby, Stills, Nash and Young?

The reason that they asked me to join in the first place is 'cause they couldn't tour just as Crosby, Stills and Nash, 'cause they haven't gotten anybody to play the instruments.

What about Dallas Taylor and Greg Reeves?

Well, yeah, bass and drums. So what have you got? Bass and drums, rhythm guitar and Stephen. It's not enough for that big sound. They want more. Few guitars, organ at the same time as piano, they wanted a big group, I guess.

How do you feel now about what has gone down with Crosby, Stills, Nash and Young?

I think, uh, the tours we've done have been pretty successful. I don't know, it's blowing my mind—a lot of the applause, a lot of the reaction and everything. I don't know how it got so big—I knew it was gonna be big and everything because when I joined them they had a lot of hype out and everything. They had a good album out, you know, and they had a rapport there . . . so I mean I knew they were gonna be pretty big, but I didn't think it was gonna be as big as this. It's big. Makes a lot of money, and it's hard to relate to after what I was doin' before.

I meant musically, though. . . . I've not seen the four of you play together, but from what I've picked up in the media, you seem to take a backstage role in the group.

Yeah, I don't really . . . well the main thing with that group is their singing, the three of them singing, you know, and they sing those three-part harmony things and occasionally I sing a fourth part, but not often. It's the same sort of general role I played in Buffalo Springfield: I play lead guitar and occasionally I'll sing a song, and I'm quite happy to do that as long as I can do my own thing, because my songs actually require a different kind of thing than that anyway, so I'm quite happy to do them with Crazy Horse. We do most of them, they're just different. I couldn't do *Everybody Knows This Is Nowhere* with Crosby, Stills and Nash.

Did they ask you to join the group . . . how was the contact made?

Yeah, Steve came over to the house one day and asked me to join. First they didn't want to be called Crosby, Stills, Nash and Young. They just wanted it to be Crosby, Stills and Nash. They said, "Everybody'll know who you are, man, don't worry about that."

They wanted you to do a George Harrison. Crosby, Stills, Nash and Friends.

No, just Crosby, Stills and Nash . . . but anyway we got that all straightened out because, you know, the music is good, the music is exciting to me, it's more pop than Crazy Horse. Crazy Horse is liable to have a bad night, you know, and I think Crosby, Stills and Nash just isn't liable to have a bad night because the personalities are there. If the music isn't happening that night, just the fact that those three guys are there makes it cool. You know if you see Clapton having a bad night, you're still seeing

Clapton . . . and that's the way the kids feel, there's still that other trip happening. . . .

People come to see and to hear.

Yeah, but with Crazy Horse, nobody knows who they are really, nobody's familiar with them, except for maybe Jack (Nitzsche), and now when we go out to play . . . we're used to playing at home, playing in the studio.

We have a studio underneath the house, a P.A. system and wood walls and everything, and it's really groovy, and we play in there and that's where we get sound . . . and like we don't play together very much, 'cause there's no time. Now we've been playin' together for almost a month, and before that it was six months off, and together for three months before then, and that's all we've played together, so we're like about as loose as you can get.

Why did it take you so long to tune up last night?

Listen, I'll tell you . . . last night didn't take me nearly as long as the two days before that.

Really, people had waited for hours and hours for you to come on, and waited through bands that were doing a completely different type of thing than what they were waiting for, and then you came on . . .

Oh, you mean when we came out front and tuned up. . . . We were tryin' to be careful so it didn't happen during the show. It did happen during the show anyway, but something's been happening to my guitars during this trip where they just aren't staying in tune at all. We were just being ultra-careful, rather than have Crazy Horse come out in the middle of the thing, after I'd done six acoustic songs, and then tune right in the middle of things, it wouldn't make it, you know what I mean. . . .

Right, but I think it was really interesting 'cause what happened was that you had not wanted to come out and tune in the middle of a show, but that little thing that you did with tuning those four guitars became a show in itself, and everybody really got into it, and then you walked off, everybody sat there in a kind of limbo . . . like we were talking about people coming to see you as well as to hear . . . well, we'd just seen you tuning up for fifteen minutes and then you disappeared.

If there had been a curtain there . . . it happens every time we play a place without a curtain, but I just won't go out and get everything together right in the middle. . . . I guess it was kind of weird, though, 'cause I did tune three guitars.

That white one you really had trouble with, people wanted to come up and help you. . . . About Crosby, Stills, Nash and Young, when I asked you before about what had gone down, I meant musically, because Graham Nash particularly does a really different style of music than you do. . . .

Yeah, I know what you mean . . . well, on the new album, I play on about five songs and sing on three. . . .

Three different from the five or three out of the five?

No, three of the five . . . and the ones that I play on we mostly recorded live. Like my two songs, "Helpless" and "Country Girl," I did the lead vocal while I was playing, all at the same time, so the drums and bass, guitar and piano were all going at once, and I was singing the lead, so my things sound different, from overdubbing, you know. I mean, I probably could have played on all of them, 'cause you know, I can make up lines and put 'em down. . . .

Was there any particular reason they were taken live?

Yeah, that's the way I like to do it, and David likes to do it that way too, 'cause he likes to get off, he really likes to get off. So one of David's songs, "Almost Cut My Hair"—yeah, that's the name of the song—there's gonna be a lot of reaction to that song. It's really Crosby at what I think is his best. It's like all live, three guitars, bass, organ and drums, and it's all live and there are no overdubs, one vocal and the vocal was sung live—we did it in San Francisco at Wally Heider's—and then there's the other way of recording, which is the way they recorded their first album. And on this second album there are about five songs that sound sort of like the first album. . . .

To tell you the truth, I didn't like the first album. I like individual parts of it, but as an album it sounds too much like studio music. It's the kind of thing that gets into music through the back door; it's this computer sound that comes out.

Yeah, yeah, I know what you mean. The sound doesn't really come out of the studio, it comes out of the musicians, it's true. That's what I figure is the fault of the first album—as is the fault of my first album. It was overdubbed instead of played. People like to hear these people play together, I think. Playing live is very exciting, especially the guitars really get me off, and everybody playing at once is really groovy; but some bands prefer to do it that way.

Some bands have got to. . . .

The Beatles do it that way and that accounts for the difference between the Beatles and the Stones. The Stones almost always have at least four or five guys playin' at once . . . and that's where that funny feel comes from, 'cause if you ever tried to overdub that you can't have it, 'cause you'd get everything right. . . . When somebody makes a mistake, and some other guy does another thing because a guy made a mistake, to make the mistake feel good, and somebody else comes back in, and that is all happening every beat with the Rolling Stones . . . it's human and you're hearing it. . . .

It's great; that's what was happening last night . . . but when you first were talking about live, were you talking about playing before an audience?

No, I'm talking about live in the studio, you know, everybody doing it. . . .

Rather than one guy playing it and later having another guy see where it fits.

Yeah, or not even knowing what it is when he played the first one.

And CSN's first album was done that way. . . .

Yeah, it was all overdubbed, because Steve Stills played the organ and the guitar and the bass and the other guitar and the other organ and the keyboard . . . because they didn't have anybody else who could play, I mean there wasn't anybody in the group who could play any other instruments.

Well, why couldn't they put down the basics and then add to it. . . .

They did in some cases, but a basic putdown is like bass and drums, and Dallas plays drums and Steve plays bass and sometimes they'd do it that way. It's just a different way of making records, that's the way they do it. I don't know how to really explain it, 'cause it isn't my way. I did one album that way and, although in a lot of cases I was happy with what happened, especially in the new pressing of that first album, it just doesn't get off, doesn't get off.

Except for one song, which is great: "I've Been Waiting For You."

Yeah, yeah, that's the only one that sounds like it got off, but you know all those things were played at different days, every instrument. On that cut, isn't it incredible . . . you see that's how it can work, every once in a while. Because when I put on the lead guitar I was really into it that day, you know, and all the moods I was in at all the times that I put those things on. See, what I do is . . . in the beginning, we put down acoustic guitar and bass and drums, that's the smallest track that I ever did, one guitar, bass and drums . . . and then the acoustic guitar had a bad sound and the bass wasn't playin' the right notes and was a little out of tune, so we did both of these over again; so then we have only one original thing on it, which was the drums . . . but I played along with the things that I'd done before and Jimmy Messina, who played the bass on it, played the bass part over, and then he made up a different bass part so we took off the first one completely and played a whole new one . . . and then we dropped the acoustic guitar, 'cause it didn't fit with the other things that I put on . . . so then there was nothing left except for the drums. The pipe organ was put on. . . . Part of these things were done in different cities. . . .

What about the vocal? The vocal seems to be the thing that really holds it together.

The vocal was done at a different studio. . . . It does stick together though. It's very rare. It'd take you a long time to get a whole album of records like that, it's just not easy to do.

Were you not satisfied with the album as a whole, when it came out?

The first album? I was satisfied with what I'd done, as much as I could be. But then when the mastering job came out on it, it blew my mind, because I couldn't hear what I'd done . . . but now it's been remastered and you can almost hear it. It was badly mixed.

They're putting out new ones now, of the first album?

Yeah, the new ones are much better, much clearer. There's much more life on it.

Man, an announcement should have been made of it.

I know an announcement should have been made, but they just can't seem to get it together.

Y*OUNG GOT UP TO GET a glass of water, as our throats were apparently parched. I got up and noticed a pile of variously sized, colored and assorted pills. My vitamins, said Young.*

"What do you eat?"

When I'm on the road I eat anything. I eat meat, anything. The guys, Crazy Horse, they don't eat meat, most of them. . . . They're really down, I don't know if you can tell by lookin' at 'em, but they're not your usual bunch of rock & roll guys . . . they're just not that way. They're very funky, I think they're great. I don't know if you have to live with them to know how great they are or what. I don't know if the people are really hearing what I hear, you know.

How did you meet Crazy Horse?

I met all of them during the first six months that I was in L.A., when the Buffalo Springfield was just getting together, and they didn't know how to play at that time, not very well . . . they were just hangin' out, and I was starting to work with the Springfield, and I met Jack Nitzsche shortly after that and then he joined. . . . They were called the Rockets.

When is your new album coming out?

Which one, with Crazy Horse? It'll be out in about two months. It's really gonna be funky, it's really gonna be a dirty album. We're gonna do some things on it, some really old things, but we're gonna do them right. Like I think I might do this one country song that I learned in high school, when I was goin' through church dancing, junior high, I guess. I just remember the song; I don't remember who wrote it or anything.

There was this one record they played, sounds like an old Hank Williams song, we might do that one. And then there are some other songs, some songs that I wrote that are gonna be sort of . . . I don't know how to explain it. I'm trying to make records of the quality of the records that were made in the late Fifties and the Sixties, like Everly Brothers records and Roy Orbison records and things like that. They were all done with a sort of quality to them. They were done at once. They were done in Nashville. . . .

It doesn't matter where you do it. Nashville, it happened to be done there. Could be done anywhere. It's just a quality about them, the singer is into the song and the musicians were playing with the singer and it was an entity, you know. It was something special that used to hit me all the time, that all these people were thinking the same thing, and they're all playing at the same time.

Like the early Beatles.

Yeah, yeah, right. That's what I'm tryin' to get. That's what I want to get, on this next album. I started approaching getting it on the last album, on *Everybody Knows This Is Nowhere*. It happens on a few cuts, you can hear it. It's there all the time. . . .

Which cuts would you say?

Uh, I think "Cinnamon Girl," uh, "Everybody Knows This Is Nowhere," and, uh, "Round and Round" has that feeling of togetherness, although it was just Danny [Whitten] and me and Robin Lane.

I thought that one was really a little bit too long.

Well, it depends on where you're at, you know. A lot of people like that better than anything else on the album. I do things like that.

Like "The Last Trip to Tulsa," in my opinion, after I did it, I didn't like it and I didn't want it. After the album came out that's the one I really didn't like, you know, and I still don't, but a lot of people really dug that better than anything else on that whole album. See, it's strange. Just because it doesn't happen to be my favorite part, and I know a lot of people really didn't like it, you know, and I can dig why. Because it sounds overdone. It just sounds like it's a mistake to me, and luckily it's cool. It's the same thing with "Round and Round" on the second album. The acoustic live thing bores a lot of people.

Is that what that was, "Round and Round"?

Yeah, it was all done at once. Did you ever listen to it with earphones on?

Always.

Yeah, because the sound of that record, if you get into the sound of it and you know what's happening, thinking of the fact that there were three people sitting like you and me, and then another, and six microphone booms coming down, absolutely stoned out of our minds in the studio, singing a song with the guitars, three guitars goin' at once. If you listen to it, "Round and Round" is one of my favorites on the second album, because of some of the things—I guess you sort of have to listen to them, 'cause I didn't bring them out very much—but the echo from the acoustic guitar on the right echoes back on the left, and the echo from the guitar on the left comes back on the right and it makes the guitars go like this . . . one line starts goin' like da-da-daow . . . and then you can hear like one voice comes in and out, and that's 'cause Danny was rockin' back and forth. . . . Those things are not featured, they're just in it, you know, and that's what I'm trying to get at. I think they last longer that way. Doing it live and singing and playing all at once just makes it sound more real.

Do you remember "Cinnamon Girl" last night, you did it second to last, or so?

Oh, yeah, I remember that.

I thought that was a really great version, better than the album version.

Yeah, it probably was. The album versions weren't that hot. We'd only been together for eight weeks when we cut that album. Really literally, we'd only been together for six or seven days when "Down by the River" was cut.

Was there any reason that you did it that soon, instead of waiting?

I just wanted to go ahead and do it, I just wanted to catch it . . . because there is something on those records that was recorded . . . like it was when we were really feeling each other out, you know, and we didn't know each other, but we were turned on to what was happening. So I wanted to record that, because that never gets recorded. And that's what that album is, it's just the bare beginnings. And the change between that album and the next album is really gonna blow a lot of minds.

JOHN MORTHLAND

A STATEMENT OF A SINGLE MAN

EVERYTHING ABOUT NEIL YOUNG'S approach to music has become so highly personalized that when he performs, he seems at first to be oblivious of his audience. That impression is a superficial one, though, for his music demands rapt attention, and he quickly establishes such an intimate relationship to the audience that even a college gym seems like a cozy little club.

That's what he did here, at the Contra Costa Junior College gym, across the Bay Bridge from San Francisco. And the word from other cities along this, their first tour together, is that wherever he and Crazy Horse went, they won over the crowds in no time. Young is finally getting the recognition he has deserved ever since those frustrating days with Buffalo Springfield.

Like a Crosby, Stills, Nash and Young concert, a Neil Young concert begins with an acoustic set. Young plays acoustic in a hard, percussive manner, while still keeping intact his captivating melodies, like the tender "I Am a Child." He also does "Broken Arrow," the electronic collage from *Buffalo Springfield Again,* as a solo number now. And he closed out the acoustic set with "The Loner," on which he stretched out the lyrics in a Dylanesque manner: "Knohohoh when you see hiiiiimmm / Nuuuthiiiing can freeeee hiiiiimmm / Step aside / Open wide / It's the Lohohohohnerrrrr." It was as powerful a statement as a single man can make.

Crazy Horse—guitarist Dan Whitten, bassist Billy Talbot, drummer Ralph Molina, and electric pianist Jack Nitzsche—joined for the rest of the set. Crazy Horse is a strong band that gives Young all the support he needs. They opened with "Everybody Knows This Is Nowhere," did a new one, and then went into "Down by the River."

This was the one the crowd had been waiting for, the one they knew best. With Crazy Horse rolling along steadily behind him, Young displayed amazing virtuosity. Pacing the stage in his patched blue jeans, his head jerking up and down with the music, he picked guitar lines seemingly out of nowhere, piling them up one staccato note on top of another, never once letting you forget those lyrics. "I shot my baby!"

Between songs he charmed the audience with stories about near-accidents and observations on grass, his voice taking on the inflections of the fall guy in a comedy team. They responded by applauding each song with the first few chords, even the new ones that they didn't recognize.

The set calmed down slightly with another new song, "Wondering," and Whitten's "Come On Baby, Let's Go Downtown." (A whole album of songs written by Crazy Horse members is in the works.) Then it started building again with "Cinnamon Girl," which won a standing ovation even though it wasn't the last song. "Cowgirl in the Sand," Young's most romantic and most fully realized performance thus far, was the finale, and it gave Young another vehicle for long screaming improvisations.

Part of Young's power rests in his imagery, which, while sometimes strange, is almost always rich and evocative. Another asset is his high quivering voice, which is also unique. He seems most at ease with Crazy Horse, and they in turn fit his style better than any of the other bands he's worked with. On this night they could do no wrong anyhow, and, on leaving the gym, I noticed that most everyone was going home happy. It's easy to see why.

LANGDON WINNER

DÉJÀ VU ALBUM REVIEW

A LONG WITH MANY OTHER people, I had hoped that the addition of Neil Young to Crosby, Stills and Nash would give their music the guts and substance the first album lacked. Live performances of the group suggested that this had happened. Young's voice, guitar, compositions and stage presence added elements of darkness and mystery to songs that had previously dripped a kind of saccharine sweetness. Unfortunately, little of this influence carried over into the recording sessions for *Déjà Vu*. Despite Young's formidable job on many of the cuts, the basic sound hasn't changed a whit. It's still too sweet, too soothing, too perfect and too good to be true.

Take for example all of side two. Here we have a splendid showcase of all the Crosby, Stills, Nash and Young strong points—precision playing, glittering harmonies, a relaxed but forceful rhythm and impeccable twelve-string guitars. But are there any truly first-rate songs here? If there are, I don't hear them. David Crosby's "Déjà Vu" has little or no tune and fails totally to capture the eerie feeling that accompanies a real *déjà vu* experience. "Our House," by Graham Nash, is a flyweight ditty with nothing to say and makes this clear through its simpering melody. Steve Stills' "4 + 20" conjures up some quiet enigmas, but with such tepid questions at stake, who really cares? Neil Young's "Country Girl" continues his tradition of massive production numbers, which includes the masterful "Broken Arrow" and "Down by the River." But compared to his earlier work, the piece is sadly undistinguished. In both this song and the next one, "Everybody I Love You," Young's voice is absorbed in the major key barbershop harmonizing of the other singers. CSNY could probably do the best version of "Sweet Adeline" in recorded history.

One's disappointment with the album is heightened by the absurdity of its pretensions. The heralded leather cover turns out to be nothing more than crimpled cardboard. What a milestone—fake leatherette! The grainy portrait of the "Old West" characters on the cover looks less like Billy the Kid, the James Gang and Buffalo Bill than the waiting room for unemployed extras for Frontier Atmosphere Inc. "Now then, which of you desperados is next?" And, of course, the pretty gold-leaf lettering turns out to be yellow Reynolds Wrap. *Déjà Vu* would like to convince you that it has roots deep in the American soil. But a closer inspection reveals that its taproot is firmly implanted in the urban commercial asphalt.

There is much on this album of real merit. "Helpless," "Carry On" and "Teach Your Children" are excellent songs, well performed. But for me Crosby, Stills and Nash—plus or minus Neil Young—will probably remain the band that asks the question, "What can we do that would be really heavy?" And then answers, "How about something by Joni Mitchell?"

■ **RANDOM NOTES** (May 14, 1970)

Talking to KSAN-FM for a three-hour special on Warner Bros./Reprise Records, Neil Young casually dropped a bomb: "I'm not working with Crazy Horse anymore; I've got a new group behind me." Later in the conversation, pressed for more details, Young told how "One morning I just got up and decided to do something new. . . . You know, I go through different bags." So he let Crazy Horse go and has gotten a three-man band behind him. "The only clue I'll give is that none of them is known—except that on bass it'll be Greg Reeves." The upheaval means no Neil Young/Crazy Horse LP, leaving only a single, "Oh, Lonesome Me," for fleeting memories of a dynamite combination.

THEY JUST DON'T WANT RIP-OFFS

CROSBY, STILLS, NASH, YOUNG and company are the indirect targets of a boycott move in St. Paul, Minnesota, aimed at knocking down high concert prices.

Their concert, scheduled for May 24 at the Metropolitan Sports Center in St. Paul, is priced at $5, $6, $7 and $10, according to John Kane and Barry Knight, boycott leaders.

"We're saying the $10 price is too high and the $5 tickets are still too high for mediocre seats," said Knight.

Kane, a student at Macalester College in St. Paul, has been working with friends to organize boycotts through head shops and record stores. They also hope to stage a "free or minimum cost" show the day of the concert, to call attention to their crusade.

The fight, Kane said, is against the promoter of the concert, Mike Belkin, more than the band. "Still, they're asking for $25,000 or 60 percent of the gate," he said, "and that's pushing the price up, too."

In Los Angeles, Elliot Roberts, manager of the band, said he hadn't known about the price scale. While defending the group's price by pointing out massive traveling and equipment expenses, he agreed that the $10 top was "outrageous." The highest-priced seats are located in what is known as the "plush circle" of the auditorium and are generally available for music industry bigwigs to buy for media people and friends.

Roberts told ROLLING STONE that he would try and get whatever remaining $10 tickets chopped down, and announced 300 of the $5 seats changed to $2.

David Crosby also called the $10 price "outrageous," but said he couldn't be aware of all technical and business details of each stop along the upcoming eighteen-city tour.

"We're not against Crosby, Stills, Nash and Young," the boycotters said. "We just don't want promoter rip-offs in this area."

The Sports Center holds some 14,000; the nearest alternate site would be a college hall with a capacity of some 2,000.

The band, meanwhile, is finishing up rehearsals for the twenty-seven-day tour. Steve Stills' fractured wrist has healed, and now, at his second home in Laurel Canyon (number one now is the house he just purchased in Surrey, Ringo's old $100,000 mansion), he's directing rehearsals, trying out "Helplessly Hoping" on piano, working out three-part harmony for Tom Rush's "Urge for Going," and adding Buffalo Springfield riffs atop "Suite: Judy Blue Eyes."

And, in other CSNY news, the band has involuntarily joined the ranks of the bootlegged. The LP, now on sale around Los Angeles, on the Canyon label, features the fanciest bootleg cover yet, with a high-quality photo of the band (similar in tone to the *Déjà Vu* cover photo) beneath the title, *Wooden Nickel*. Tunes on the acoustic side, which both Nash and Crosby admit to be "good quality sound," are "Guinevere," "Birds," "4 + 20," "You Don't Have to Cry," and "Suite: Judy Blue Eyes." The flip is the electric side, and it's awful, in terms of audio reproduction. "It's just shit," Crosby said, "probably taped right off the P.A." Songs are "Listen Once Again to My Bluebird," "Sea of Madness" and "Down by the River."

Even the timings of the cuts are given, with "Down by the River" running nearly fourteen minutes and "Suite" taking 7:44.

According to Bill Halverson, who engineered both *Déjà Vu* and *Crosby, Stills and Nash,* the record sounds like a taping of a recent Pauley Pavilion concert in Los Angeles.

"It's a burn on everybody," Crosby said. Band manager Roberts says he's taking legal action against record shops that handle the record. "And not just cease and desist orders," he said. "If they sell 'em, we'll press them right up through the courts."

■ **RANDOM NOTES** (June 11, 1970)

About those rumors about Crosby, Stills, Nash and Young breaking up: They were true—for a day and a half. The band split up last Thursday (May 14) in Chicago, just before a concert there. But by Friday night they were back together again in Los Angeles, except without Taylor and Reeves, who were fired.

Chronologically, here's what happened: Steve Stills, left wrist still tender from an auto crash/fracture, went out to a ranch in Newhall, California, to ride a horse two days before the first concert in Denver. He was thrown off the horse and tore a knee ligament. Then Greg Reeves was fired the night before that concert, requiring a pickup man to learn the CSNY electric repertoire on twenty-four hours' notice. Crosby and Nash were suffering from throat infections from rehearsals. In Denver, Stills reportedly upset the group with his dramatics—climbing on stage on crutches, then acting like a formal tutor/orchestra leader through the set—while the bass player fell apart. Then Dallas Taylor, drummer with CSNY from the very beginning, was fired. "Everyone felt the music was suffering on the rhythm section," explained manager Elliot Roberts.

So it was a combination of medical and morale reasons that forced the cancellation of eight dates taking the band up through May 24. But, even while talking about the breakup Friday morning, David Crosby had said: "I'm sure we'll be back together again in some form very soon." And at least for now, they are, after a therapy session in L.A. The band resumes touring May 29 in Boston and will either make up the lost dates or play free concerts in various cities, according to Roberts. And, he added, they'll begin another album sometime in September.

TIN SOLDIERS AND NIXON'S COMING

OUT OF THE CROSBY, Stills, Nash, Young, Taylor and Reeves "breakup" last month comes one of the biggest spurts of productivity in the band's short history: Neil Young has come out with a tune called "Ohio," and the band has resumed its tour with a new bassist and drummer.

The new men are Johnny Barbata, thin but powerful drummer formerly with the Turtles, and Calvin "Fuzz" Samuels, bassist. Samuels joined the band on a day's notice last month when Greg Reeves was fired just before the band's concert tour began. He played the one CSNY show—in Denver—before the group began canceling dates.

The band is now back on tour.

As for "Ohio": Neil Young had gone off to the redwoods of Pescadero with Crosby and the band's road manager and light man, in the aftermath of the band's unofficial disbanding. When he got back to town, on Wednesday, May 20, he had a new tune to sing to Crosby, Stills and Nash.

The next day, the band was in the studios. By that night, two songs had been recorded and mixed: "Ohio" and "Freedom" (the short exercise in harmonic grief that the band used as the encore number on its previous concert tour), and the master tape was sent to Atlantic Records in New York. By Monday, word had gotten back that "Ohio" was being pressed and would be released within a week. And KMET-FM in Los Angeles already had a tape of "Ohio" on the air.

If AM stations put "Ohio" on playlists, it will mean two CSNY singles on the charts at once. "Teach Your Children" had been released just two weeks ago, one week before Young's Pescadero retreat.

But whether or not AM radio in general will program "Ohio" is doubtful. "I don't think they'll touch it," Crosby said. "This one names names."

"Neil surprised everybody," Crosby said. "It wasn't like he set out as a project to write a protest song. It's just what came out of having Huntley-Brinkley for breakfast. I mean we've all stopped even watching the TV news, but you read headlines on the papers going by on the streets."

Young's own comment, said Crosby, was: "I don't know; never wrote anything like this before . . . but there it is."

■ RANDOM NOTES (July 9, 1970)

If any radio station explains that they're not playing "Ohio" by Crosby, Stills, Nash and Young because it's been banned by the FCC, that's bullshit. The song, which names "tin soldiers and Nixon" as the villains in the death of six Kent State students (two more have died since the first major burst of reports), has so far been heard only on FM. But the FCC, despite Chairman Dean Burch's repressive noises last year and Commissioner Robert Lee's current campaign against smutty lyrics, has never outlawed a song from the public airwaves. So if your local rocker cops out, take it to the station's general manager.

■ RANDOM NOTES (September 3, 1970)

Neil Young's album, *After the Gold Rush,* should be out now (release date was August 22, at the latest). The album includes tracks with Crazy Horse, which Young has reassembled for a tour beginning in November. A Crosby, Stills, Nash and Young live two-album set was going to be culled from six sets taped at the Fillmore East. But as the Fourth of July concert in Chicago approached, Nash, Stills, and Crosby had individual flashes and, without telling the others, asked that the show be recorded by engineer Bill Halverson (who'd *also* suggested recording the concert). The result: an expectedly excellent evening and a possible all-Chicago album, due out around November.

Also upcoming: a film of the entire tour, including, according to manager Elliot Roberts, "all the shit that came down with the individual cats." CSNY aren't expected to tour again until next May. Between now and then, Nash and Crosby will be doing recording work in San Francisco, and Stills, if all goes well, will take off with a ten-piece band, including Booker T., a horn section, and some female singers.

TOP 100 SINGLES OF THE LAST 25 YEARS

OR A TRIBUTE TO the rock & roll 45, ROLLING STONE writers and editors chose the top 100 singles of the twenty-five years spanning 1963 to 1988. Crosby, Stills, Nash and Young came in at Number Seventy-six, with "Ohio," which entered the *Billboard* charts on June 27, 1970.

#76 "Ohio," Crosby, Stills, Nash and Young

"I had the *Time* magazine there, with that girl looking up from a dead student lying on the ground with the blood and the whole deal," Neil Young says of his inspiration for "Ohio." "I just wrote it. It just came out right there on the porch."

Rock and politics met head-on in "Ohio," Crosby, Stills, Nash and Young's raging response to the killing of four students by National Guard troops at Kent State University on May 4, 1970. In its evocation of the senseless violence at Kent, it sent a chilling message to the counterculture: "Tin soldiers and Nixon's coming / We're finally on our own / This summer I hear the drumming / Four dead in Ohio."

Young composed "Ohio" while on a redwood-country retreat from CSNY following a temperamental (and temporary) breakup. David Crosby, who was with Young at the time, said in a 1970 interview with ROLLING STONE, "It wasn't like he set out as a project to write a protest song. . . . It's just what came out of having Huntley-Brinkley for breakfast."

"Ohio" was cut live in the studio, with Crosby's unrehearsed cries of "Why?" and "How many more?" audible on the fade. It possessed a craggy opening guitar figure and a fiery six-string interplay from Young and Stephen Stills. "Ohio" and its flip side, Stills' hymnlike "Find the Cost of Freedom," were recorded and mixed the same evening and rush-released as a single. Despite concern that AM radio might find it too controversial—and regardless of the fact that the band had another single, "Teach Your Children," out at the time—"Ohio" rose to Number Fourteen. "It was really like the folk process at work," Young says. "You know, that was really like music as news."

SONGWRITER: Neil Young. **PRODUCERS:** Crosby, Stills, Nash and Young. **HIGHEST CHART POSITION:** Number Fourteen. **RELEASED:** June 1970. **ALBUM:** *So Far*. Atlantic Records.

ED WARD

"SUGAR MOUNTAIN" SINGLES REVIEW

THIS IS A RATHER OBSCURE Neil Young cut, recorded live at Ann Arbor's Canterbury House. Five and a half minutes of Young and his guitar weeping away acoustically. Part of his next album may be like this, and here's a chance for a preview. On the B side is "Cinnamon Girl."

LANGDON WINNER

AFTER THE GOLD RUSH ALBUM REVIEW

NEIL YOUNG DEVOTEES WILL probably spend the next few weeks trying desperately to convince themselves that *After the Gold Rush* is good music. But they'll be kidding themselves. For despite the fact that the album contains some potentially first-rate material, none of the songs here rises above the uniformly dull surface. In my listening, the problem appears to be that most of this music was simply not ready to be recorded at the time of the sessions. It needed time to mature. On the album the band never really gets behind the songs and Young himself has trouble singing many of them. Set before the buying public before it was done, this pie is only half-baked.

"Southern Man" is a good example. As a composition, it is possibly one of the best things Neil Young has ever written. In recent appearances with Crosby, Stills and Nash, the piece has had an overwhelmingly powerful impact on audiences. But the recording of "Southern Man" on *After the Gold Rush* fulfills very little of this promise. By today's standards, the ensemble playing is sloppy and disconnected. The piano, bass and drums search for each other like lovers lost in the sand dunes, but although they see each other's footprints now and then, they never really come together. Young tries to recover the dynamics of the piece with his voice alone, but can't quite make it: On this and the other really interesting tunes on the album—"Don't Let It Bring You Down" and "I Believe in You"—the listener hears only a faint whisper of what the song will become.

Another disturbing characteristic of the record, oddly enough, is Young's voice. In his best work Young's singing contains genuine elements of pathos, darkness and mystery. If Kafka's story "The Hunger Artist" could be made into an opera, I would want Neil Young to sing the title role. But on this album his intonation often sounds like pre-adolescent whining. The song "After the Gold Rush," for instance, reminds one of nothing so much as Mrs. Miller moaning and wheezing her way through "I'm a Lonely Little Petunia in an Onion Patch." Apparently no one bothered to tell Neil Young that he was singing a half octave above his highest acceptable range. At that point his pathos becomes an irritating bathos. I can't listen to it at all.

There are thousands of persons in this country who will buy and enjoy this record. More power to them, I suppose. But for me the test of an album is whether or not its quality is such that it allows you to grow into it a little more with each subsequent listening. And I find none of that quality here. To the seventy or eighty people who wrote to ROLLING STONE in total rage that I could be anything but 100 percent delighted with *Déjà Vu*, I will simply say: this record picks up where *Déjà Vu* leaves off.

THE TOP 100
THE BEST ALBUMS OF THE
LAST 20 YEARS
AFTER THE GOLD RUSH

IN 1987, ROLLING STONE asked seventeen rock writers to submit nominations for the 100 greatest albums of the last twenty years—albums initially released between 1967 and 1987. Neil Young's *After the Gold Rush* came in at Number Seventy-one.

#71 *After the Gold Rush,* Neil Young

Along with Crosby, Stills, Nash and Young's album *Déjà Vu,* the brooding, apocalyptic *After the Gold Rush* is the record that brought Neil Young his curious brand of superstardom. The album's back cover has a note that reads, "Most of these songs were inspired by the Dean Stockwell-Herb Berman screenplay *After the Goldrush.*" In effect, the album was a soundtrack to a movie that was never made. "The film fell through, and there I was with a record," Young told ROLLING STONE in 1979. "So I put it out. Would have made a great movie."

Such offhand ironies somehow seem appropriate to Young, who has followed strangely contradictory career paths—at times actively courting mass success, at other points fleeing popularity as if it were a deathtrap. At the time of the album's release, Young's eccentricity was apparently just beginning to annoy some observers. In his ROLLING STONE review of *After the Gold Rush,* critic Langdon Winner compared the mournful title track to "Mrs. Miller moaning and wheezing her way through 'I'm a Lonely Little Petunia in an Onion Patch,'" and declared, "I can't listen to it at all."

However, it has since become clear that *After the Gold Rush* holds up as one of Young's most moving, satisfying and wide-ranging albums. The title track is a stirring, romantic meditation on the passing of the Sixties; its key line—"Look at Mother Nature on the run in the 1970s"—proved all too prophetic. "When You Dance I Can Really Love" features guitar playing that raises dissonance to the heights of lyrical beauty and falsetto singing that seems the very definition of longing. The churning "Southern Man" took on the issue of racism and generated a response from Lynyrd Skynyrd in the song "Sweet Home Alabama," which asserted, "I hope Neil Young will remember/Southern Man don't need him around anyhow." With characteristic perversity, Young later said, "I'd rather play 'Sweet Home Alabama' than 'Southern Man' any time. I first heard it and really liked the way they played their guitars. Then I heard my own name in it and thought, 'Now *this* is pretty great.' "

On this album, Young explores various facets of his psyche without stopping long enough to establish a firm identity. But if his persona was elusive, the sound he established on *After the Gold Rush* was unmistakable, a combination of dense, muscular rock and world-weary innocence that has made Neil Young one of the most important rock artists of his generation.

RECORDED AT: Neil Young's house, Topanga Canyon, California, late 1969 and early 1970. PRODUCERS: Neil Young and David Briggs with Kendall Pacios. ENGINEERS: Ray Thompson and Henry Zazouski. RELEASED: July 1970. HIGHEST CHART POSITION: Number Eight. TOP FORTY SINGLE: "Only Love Can Break Your Heart" (Number Thirty-three). TOTAL U.S. SALES [as of 1987]: 700,000. Reprise Records.

PLENTY OF C AND S AND N AND Y

CROSBY, STILLS, NASH AND YOUNG are still very much intact, but there won't be any public, live evidence of that fact until probably next June.

Between now and then, however, there'll be plenty of each of them—through individual albums and on tours featuring Neil Young as a soloist, Steve Stills as head of a big band, and David Crosby and Graham Nash as a folky duet.

The most definite project concerning CSNY as a group is the live album, comprised of tapes from the band's performances at Fillmore East and in Chicago. The album, according to manager Elliot Roberts, is being mixed by Stills and Young.

Stills, whose arraignment for his coke bust in La Jolla, California, in August is still upcoming (it's been postponed a couple of times) is in England, putting together a band with a Memphis horn section. The band will tour and do an album. Stills already has a "solo" album (featuring any number of horn and gospel wailers behind him) ready. It should be out by October 26.

Stills' album is expected first, then the live album, then a solo effort by Crosby, which is being finished up at Wally Heider's in San Francisco and Los Angeles. Crosby has two or three tracks to go, and it could be out by December.

Crosby and Nash are also in England—with manager Roberts—to do a BBC-TV special spotlighting Nash as a composer. Crosby is a guest star, as he was for the show featuring Joni Mitchell. Nash, who's been helping out on albums for both Crosby and the Jefferson Airplane's Paul Kantner, is also more than half-finished with his own album. His solo effort is backed up by, among others, Neil Young on piano and the L.A. Symphony.

A Crosby-Nash tour, Roberts said, is a possibility, but not as much a certainty as the Neil Young tour, mapped out for three weeks beginning next January. Before the tour, Young does a Carnegie Hall number—on December 4. The tour, Roberts said, "will have Neil by himself, just acoustic. He's always wanted to do a small acoustic tour." Dates will include clubs (the Cellar Door in Washington, D.C., is booked) as well as concert halls (Berkeley Community Theater) and will probably include "a few Canadian dates," the manager said.

Young's irregularly regular backup, Crazy Horse, will continue on by its lonesome, with veteran composer/pianist/arranger/producer Jack Nitzsche part of the band. A Crazy Horse album is nearly complete, and—well, of course—"Neil sings on a track or two."

Finally, Crosby, Stills, Nash and Young—together—will do a tour in June, 1971, Roberts said. But that's only a guess. By that time, they may be working on another CSNY studio album . . . or Neil Young might be doing his fourth LP. . . .

RANDOM NOTES (February 18, 1971)

Neil Young's finished with his tour and punctuated it with a taping session for *Johnny Cash on Campus*, along with Linda Ronstadt, James Taylor, Tony Joe White, and Albert Brooks. The show was taped at Vanderbilt University in Nashville and will be aired February 17 on ABC-TV.

RANDOM NOTES (March 4, 1971)

Neil Young, in Nashville with James Taylor, Linda Ronstadt, and others to tape a Johnny Cash TV show, dropped by Elliot Mazer's Quadraphonic Sound Studios to do a bit of work, and ended up with three complete tunes for his next album, original tunes called "Bad Fog of Loneliness," "Old Man" and "Heart of Gold." Young's backed by Kenny Buttrey on drums, Tim Drummond (from Mother Earth) on bass, Ben Keith (also Mother Earth) on steel, James Taylor and Linda Ronstadt on backing vocals, and Tony Joe White on lead guitar on one of the songs. Taylor also takes a turn or two on lead guitar with Young. Mazer, who part-owns the new studios, engineered the sessions, which lasted two long weekend evenings. Young, he said, will be back to do more.

CSNY'S PRE-ROAD UPS AND DOWNS

THE NEWS ABOUT Crosby, Stills, Nash and Young is news about Stephen Stills getting off easy on his San Diego drug bust, Stills going off on tour beginning in July, and the whole group thinking about a cross-country tour early next year.

The four got together at Crosby's place in Los Angeles last week and pretty much agreed to do another tour in February, according to their manager, Elliot Roberts. They even sang a few numbers during the harmonic evening, he reported.

Stills was on the coast last week not only to reunite with his superbuddies and help plan his tour and the release of his next album, but also to go to San Diego to get his wrist slapped with a $1,000 fine (plus probation) for his not-often-celebrated coke bust in a La Jolla motel last August. The charges—originally for possession of "dangerous drugs" (cocaine and barbiturates) got cut down to a misdemeanor. Roberts wouldn't elaborate on the penalty. "It's over now, so we don't talk about it."

Stills is also doing final mixes on his next album, working at Atlantic's Criterion Studios in Miami toward a June deadline.

As for his tour, it'll be a big one, with Stills backed by a five-piece rhythm section including CSNY bassist Calvin "Fuzzy" Samuels. Though not all booked up yet, the tour—with Crazy Horse as the supporting act—will hit twenty-five stops over seven weeks and will begin July 2 in Portland and conclude with concerts at the Coliseum in Oakland and the Forum in Los Angeles.

Neil Young, finished with his tour (he was welcomed back by *Young Man's Fancy,* a double-album bootleg job from his Los Angeles concert in February), is finishing up his next album, recorded in Nashville. At the moment, he's moving—painfully—back and forth between traction in a friend's house and the doctor's office. His back, hurt once this year when he slipped a disc during his tour, suffered another slip on a recent trip to Nashville.

Graham Nash has a solo album due out within the week called *Songs for Beginners.* And David Crosby is at work with comedy writer-actor Carl Gottlieb on their film for United Artists, *Family.*

GEORGE KIMBALL

4 WAY STREET ALBUM REVIEW

BETWEEN TWO MISERABLE bootleg albums—*Wooden Nickel* and *Live at the Forum,* atrocious not so much due to the production imperfections common to bootleg recording but largely because of the wretched workmanship of the group themselves—and six cuts on the two *Woodstock* albums, which collectively constituted a monumental disaster in the history of live recording, it seemed to me that, however one might view their two studio albums, Crosby, Stills, Nash and Young had about as much business recording live concerts as did the Monkees.

But *4 Way Street* is a surprisingly good album. To begin with, CSNY all sing and play in the same key on almost every single cut. One of the principal failures of their previous live work was that they attempted to duplicate those tight, three-part harmonies that required numerous takes and overdubs in the studio, but this double album is for the most part a showcase of solo material by each of the four. The exceptions—"Long Time Gone," "Pre-Road Downs" and "Carry On"—are still pretty ragged live, but in the latter case this is mitigated somewhat by the fact that "Carry On" serves as the vehicle for some long, exciting Stills-Young electric exchanges.

Young and Stills also really get it on together on the other extended number (thirteen plus minutes), Neil's "Southern Man," trading off some steaming riffs that compare favorably with the Danny Whitten-Young guitar work on the original *(After the Gold Rush)* version. Neil Young's "Cowgirl in the Sand" (done by himself with acoustic guitar) is a strangely different song from the recording with Crazy Horse, but it is utterly exquisite all the same. Young also does lovely acoustic solos of "Don't Let It Bring You Down" (from *Gold Rush*) and an old Buffalo Springfield tune, "On the Way Home." Even "Ohio" is no worse (though no better) than the single—but then the message is the medium anyway, I guess.

About a year ago (in a review of *Déjà Vu*) someone remarked that CSNY's principal weaknesses were Crosby's singing and Nash's songwriting. I tend to disagree, and I think this album goes a long way in refuting both points. As for the first argument, well, his solo album aside, Crosby does two excellent songs here. One of them, "Triad," is particularly notable, for the song was one of the major bones of contention leading to

Crosby's departure from the Byrds. The haunting "The Lee Shore" is a treasure, and while "Long Time Gone" is pretty well botched here, it is not so much the fault of Crosby's vocal inadequacy as the fact that the song—like, among others, "Suite: Judy Blue Eyes"—is one of those in CSNY's repertoire which is difficult enough to be beyond the group's ability to competently perform it live.

And while Nash's songs are, to be sure, pretty lightweight, they rarely pretend to be anything else. The worst thing you can say about them is that they're harmless, and most of them are actually damned nice. They *have* suffered from some incredibly saccharine, overly slick renditions on the first two albums—sometimes so disgustingly sweet they make you want, as Dorothy Parker once put it, "to fwow up." Nash's "Right Between the Eyes," though, is one of the high spots of *4 Way Street,* and "Teach Your Children" is one of the few cuts on the record where the whole group sings together without blowing it. (While there's no Jerry Garcia steel guitar on this version of "Children," somebody picks a fine mandolin.)

In point of fact, if criticism of somebody's *writing* is to be levied in connection with CSNY, one might well point to a couple of the Stills numbers. Stills jumps from "49 Bye-Byes" into a latter-day version of his Springfield-era "For What It's Worth" called "America's Children." It is a patronizing, gratuitous piece of drivel (the liner notes describe it as a "poem"), which is presumably supposed to heighten the political consciousness of all us "children." Stills' "Love the One You're With" has been roundly criticized as being offensive to women. It is not merely offensive to women; it is insulting to human beings. About the only good thing that can be said about the song is that, in the absence of that background chorus and hokey arrangement, it *sounds* better here than on his solo album.

CSNY's latest backup duo, Johnny Barbata on drums and Calvin Samuels on bass, perform creditably if unspectacularly. The album does clearly point up their limitations as a group, but Crosby, Stills, Nash and Young are all performers of unquestionable talent, and—mostly because they stay out of each others' way—*4 Way Street* must surely be their best album to date.

RANDOM NOTES (August 5, 1971)

Neil Young is off the boards for a spell, backaches and all, and he's working on a documentary movie about himself and the last CSNY tour. Young is reportedly financing the film and doing a soundtrack for it. Christmastime release, he hopes.

RANDOM NOTES (October 28, 1971)

Screams Outside the Limousine Dept.: Stephen Stills and Neil Young have been joining Crosby and Nash on recent concert dates in upstate New York and will probably continue to do so for the remainder of the Crosby-Nash tour. There's a good chance the four will tour together formally in the spring.

TIM CAHILL

CROSBY, NASH—STILLS? YOUNG?

RAHAM NASH SAID IT not so many months ago: Crosby, Stills, Nash and Young "were never a group in the accepted sense of the word. We're just four lads who get together from time to time to make records or do stage shows." A loose arrangement, certainly, and one that allows for four separate solo acts as well as various duets and trios. So when Crosby/Nash announced a fall tour together, there were none of those press conferences to talk about "our sound," none of that amputee's courage, appearing onstage not quite whole. Crosby and Nash like their duet sound well enough to have a new Atlantic LP in the works.

On the last Thursday in September, Stills joined the Crosby/Nash tour for a set at Carnegie Hall. That weekend, Neil Young did a few songs with the other three in Boston. The audience treated it like some monumental rapprochement. Never mind that there had never been any breakup, announced or implicit. Never mind that these surprise jams have been a bonus feature on the four-way street for some time. Never mind that every interview with these guys indicates that they love to play together. People get uneasy about CSNY.

First of all there was that three-day breakup in Denver a little over a year ago. And then there's the fact that all four split from successful groups—Crosby from the Byrds, Nash from the Hollies, Stills and Young from Buffalo Springfield—before coalescing into one of the few genuine supergroups around. So whenever all four appear onstage together for no other reason than the joy of playing together, it becomes an *event*.

The next concert date was Sunday in New York and rumor had it that they would be together again. Atlantic Records was noncommittal but they acknowledged that, yes, all four were in town; and, if they wanted to, if the vibes were good, if they *felt like it,* there was a possibility that they might all appear together.

Sunday the usual street people were doing their spare-ticket routine on people two blocks from the hall in any direction. The concert was sold out and a huge crowd at the door hassled and bargained for admission. Inside everyone knew, or had heard it from an unimpeachable source: Young was there but Stills wasn't, neither Young nor Stills was there, both Young and Stills were there and they had brought Bob Dylan with them.

Crosby and Nash came out and sang "We Have All Been Here Before," for which the crowd cheered wildly. They tuned for a while and were cheered for that. Crosby, who usually mentions somewhere along the way that he has laryngitis or a sore throat, was in such excellent voice that he opted for Lebanese flu. In point of fact, he did have a cold, as did most everyone else on the tour; but it was Nash who was the most ill. He had an accumulation of air under one lung that made it difficult for him to take deep breaths.

About 10:30 Stephen Stills stepped onstage, and Carnegie Hall echoed with a long standing ovation that ended in a raggedy-ass rush to the stage. Stills, a man who once dedicated a song to Jose Cuervo Tequila, stumbled a little picking up his guitar; but when he sang, he sounded fine. The songs were new and they pleased Crosby and Nash as much as anyone. The three exchanged palm slaps, soul style, just like CSNY of old. Except, of course, for . . .

At 10:45 Neil Young came out of the wings and there was a longer, stronger ovation. An ovation partly for Young and partly for the fact that here they were, *the four of them,* together.

"We thought we'd all come out and sing for you," Nash said.

"It's gonna be pretty loose though," Crosby warned. And it was. There were a couple of false starts and a dropped verse at one point, but no one really cared because it all felt so good. They sang "Helpless," "Triad," "Chicago" and "Ohio," while the crowd stomped and whistled between songs, yelling out their favorite titles sometimes even before the last number was finished. Crosby finally asked them to knock it off.

Stills and Young both left projects of their own to appear at Carnegie Hall. Young had come up from the south where he was filming a movie, tentatively titled *Journey Through the Past,* reportedly a *cinéma vérité* type documentary. He had also just finished cutting a solo album, *Harvest,* soon to be released on Reprise. Stills, too, had come up from the south— Miami—where he was working on his solo album, *Stephen Stills 3,* on Atlantic. Crosby/Nash taped performances in Boston, New York and Berkeley for *their* new album.

Berkeley was on the last leg of the tour, and a lot of CSNY fans were expecting another Boston or New York. The night of the concert, University Avenue was jammed with cars from Castro Valley and Salinas and Redwood City. People were stopping at gas stations to get directions to the Berkeley Community Theater, and telling one another that they had it from a very reliable source out there in the Livermore Valley that all four of them would be in town tonight.

Crosby and Nash were greeted with a long hand followed by a brief buzz of whispered conversation. They broke into some gentle, moody tone songs, losing the words behind intricate harmonies. Crosby did a few songs onstage by himself, notably "Triad," one of the high points of the night. Nash sang his new songs, "South Bound Train Going Down" and "Immigration Man," at the piano. His voice sounded a little raw and he had to stop once in mid-verse to catch his breath; but the new songs were good enough to carry him. Late in the set Young walked out to a tremendous hand that he cut short by launching right into "Helpless."

Toward the end of the concert, Young sang a new song, "Alabama." Nash and Crosby put down their guitars to sing gentle harmony behind Young's distinctive lonely voice. Like most Young songs, it needed hearing more than once; but some people evidently had other things in mind. Just as the last chord of "Alabama" vibrated into silence, some pimple in the second row took advantage of the quiet to stand up and shout at the top of her voice.

"Where's Steve?" she demanded.

Stills was 3,000 miles away, back in Miami, and those who want to be assured of seeing CSNY together will have to wait until June and July when a tour is scheduled. There's a CSNY album in the works, too. It will probably be finished this spring, though Crosby says he isn't holding his breath on it. It really depends on how they all *feel,* you see.

■ **RANDOM NOTES** (December 9, 1971)

Neil Young's *Harvest* won't be in the stores for a while now, Young wants final okay on the cover art. The tapes are complete and he'll give them to Reprise when they show him the art.

■ **RANDOM NOTES** (February 17, 1972)

Neil Young's *Harvest* definite now, perhaps, for February 15. On Young's side, it's a matter of approving the test pressings, three each from three different plants; Warner/Reprise says they're holding everything a few extra days so the album will be fully protected by the new federal copyright law, which is effective February 15. Which doesn't exactly clash with Young's feelings about bootleggers. One scene in the film he's making shows him in a record store spotting, and seizing, a clutch of pirated tapes, and he answers the clerk's protests: "You have no right to sell these; I made them and they're mine!"

■ **RANDOM NOTES** (March 2, 1972)

Just a shot away: Expecting, happily, are Neil Young and Carrie Snodgress, about six months from now.

JOHN MENDELSSOHN

HARVEST ALBUM REVIEW

A T THE END OF THIS, five'll getcha ten, most of you are going to be exclaiming lividly, "O what vile geeks are rock critics! How quick are they to heap disapproval on one whose praises they once sang stridently at the first sign of us Common Folk taking him to heart *en masse*! How they revel in detesting that which we adore!" However often I might second with a hearty "right on!" such a perception of the critic/audience chasm, though, I will swear under oath before the highest court in the land that such an exclamation is far from apt in the case of a displeased review of Neil Young's *Harvest*.

Different folks, it must be seen, respond to overwhelming mass acceptance with different strokes. While some respond to commercial prosperity as a means to realizing all those brainstorms that a lack of loot formerly made impossible, to expanding and growing as an artist through the exploitation of heretofore unattainable resources, others either wilt artistically in the face of a mass audience's expectations—resorting to conscious imitations of what was once instinctive and spontaneous—or greatly relax the standards by which they once judged themselves, having concluded (usually quite correctly) that once one attains superstar status the audience will eagerly gobble up whatever half-assed baloney he pleases to record.

On the basis of the vast inferiority relative to his altogether spectacular *Everybody Knows This Is Nowhere* of the two albums he's made since teaming up with Crosby, etc. (and thus insuring that he'd never again want for an audience), it can only be concluded that Neil Young is not one of those folks whom superstardom becomes artistically.

Harvest, a painfully long year-plus in the making (or, seemingly more aptly, assembling), finds Young invoking most of the L.A. variety of superstardom's weariest clichés in an attempt to obscure his inability to do a good imitation of his earlier self.

Witness, for example, the discomfortingly unmistakable resemblance of nearly every song on this album to an earlier Young composition—it's as if he just added a steel guitar and new words to *After the Gold Rush*. Witness his use of said steel guitar to create a Western ambience worlds less distinctive than that conjured in earlier days by his own vibrato-drenched lead guitar.

Witness, in fact, that he's all but abdicated his position as an authoritative rock & roller for the stereotypical laid-back country-comforted troubadour role, seldom playing electric guitar at all anymore, and then with none of the spellbinding economy and spine-tingling emotiveness that characterized his playing with Crazy Horse. Indeed, his only extended solo on the album, in "Words," is fumbling and clumsy, even embarrassing.

Young's Nashville backing band, the Stray Gators, pale miserably in comparison to the memory of Crazy Horse, of whose style they do a flaccid imitation on such tracks as "Out on the Weekend," "Harvest" and "Heart of Gold." Where the Crazies kept their accompaniment hypnotically simple with a specific effect in mind (to render most dramatic rhythmic accents during choruses and instrumental breaks), the Gators come across as only timid, restrained for restraint's sake, and ultimately monotonous.

With that going on behind him, Young's lyrics dominate the listener's attention far more than befit them. Young's verbal resources have always been limited, but before now he's nearly always managed to come up with enough strong, evocative lines both to keep the listener's attention away from the banality of those by which they're surrounded and to supply the listener with a vivid enough impression of what a song is about to prevent his becoming frustrated by its seemingly deliberate obscurity and skeletal incompleteness. In his best work, as in *Everybody Knows,* wherein Crazy Horse's heavy, sinister accompaniment made unmistakable the message (of desperation begetting brutal vindictiveness), which the almost impenetrably subjective words hinted at only broadly, the basic *sound* of a song further vivified what lyric fragments suggested.

Here, with the music making little impression, the words stand or fall on their own, ultimately falling as a result of their extremely low incidence of inspiration and high incidence of rhyme-scheme forced silliness. A couple are even slightly offensive—"The Needle and the Damage Done" is glib, even cute, and displays little real commitment to its subject, while "There's a World" is simply flatulent and portentous nonsense. Only "A Man Needs a Maid," in which Neil treats his favorite theme—his inability to find and keep a lover—in a novel and arrestingly brazen (in terms of our society's accelerating consciousness of women's rights) manner, is particularly interesting. Nearly everything else is limitlessly ponderable, but in a scant, oblique way that offers few rewards to the ponderer.

It might be noted (with remorse) that neither of the symphony-orchestrated tunes of *Harvest* even approaches "Expecting to Fly," from 1967, in terms of production or overall emotional power. Would that the two unreleased movements of that earlier masterpiece, originally conceived as a trilogy, been given the grooves used for "Maid" and "There's a World."

(Apologies if "The Emperor of Wyoming" or "String Quartet from Whiskey Boot Hill," from *Neil Young,* or "Broken Arrow" are in fact the missing two-thirds.)

"Alabama" aspires to the identical effect of "Southern Man" but contains nothing nearly so powerful as that *Gold Rush* song's "I heard screamin' and bullwhips crackin'," followed by a vicious slash of Danny Whitten's rhythm guitar and a stinging lead line from Young. The first line of "Old Man" promises a lot more than the song ever delivers in terms of compassionate perception. The basic conceit of "Heart of Gold" would be laughed off the airwaves coming from another solo troubadour. "Are You Ready For the Country," like "Cripple Creek Ferry," seems an in-joke throwaway intended for the amusement of certain of Young's superstar pals. The title tune is lyrically cluttered and oblique, and "Out on the Weekend" is puerile, precious and self-indulgent, not to mention musically insipid.

Truth be told, I listened to the entirety of *Harvest* no less than a dozen times before touching typewriter to paper, ultimately managing to come up with only one happy thing to say about it: Neil Young still sings awful pretty, and often even touchingly. For the most part, though, he's seemingly lost sight of what once made his music uniquely compelling and evocative and become just another pretty-singing solo superstar.

Which can't help but bring me down.

■ RANDOM NOTES (June 22, 1972)

Neil Young will wait till winter—November 15, to be very exact—to do his next big tour, fifty shows in ten weeks in the U.S. then to Europe—with backup from the Stray Gators.

■ RANDOM NOTES (July 6, 1972)

Neil Young rush-released a single, "War Song," in time for radio exposure before the California primary. The song, which he wrote and recorded with Graham Nash, will benefit George McGovern's campaign fund. Young even made the rounds of San Francisco radio stations to urge a few spins.

■ RANDOM NOTES (November 9, 1972)

Carrie Snodgress gave birth September 8 to Zeke Snodgress Young, the father being Neil. Zeke joined the jam at Young's ranch near San Francisco.

■ RANDOM NOTES (March 1, 1973)

Neil Young interrupted his New York concert January 23 to read a note just handed him. "Peace has come," he read, throwing the audience into a ten-minute fit of hugging and kissing and whooping and crying. The Stray Gators then joined Young in "Southern Man."

JON LANDAU

NEIL YOUNG PERFORMANCE REVIEW

Carnegie Hall, New York

January 23, 1973

NEIL YOUNG ALMOST DID it all in New York. He showed up with the Stray Gators—the near-perfect backup band from *Harvest*—and a bunch of fine new songs. More important, he left behind the case of nerves that marred several concerts during his last tour. This time out his attitude was relaxed and engaging, one that allowed him to ignore both the indifference of the mostly trade audience that filled the orchestra and the belligerently fruitcake fans that stood standing and screaming in all of the balconies.

Young was least effective in his opening solo spot, where the occasional shrillness and flatness of his voice grated against the excessively simple acoustic guitar background. The balance between voice and background found its natural meeting ground only with the addition of the band, and as he sat playing acoustic guitar, with Kenny Buttrey playing only the sketchiest of drum parts for "Out on the Weekend," Young began to sound better and better. After "Heart of Gold," he switched to his Lonnie Mack-style electric and revved up the volume.

For the rest of the concert we were alternately treated and subjected to some beautifully intense singing, dazzling new songs and interminably mediocre jamming. Halfway through the performance it struck me that Young's talents are, in descending order, as a vocalist, arranger, melodist, lyricist, rhythm guitarist and lead guitarist. His often sentimental words are an almost always sufficient vehicle for his musical ideas. That combination of simple lyrics and intense delivery was especially evident on his best new song, "Don't Be Denied," an autobiographical piece that left him screaming about the paranoia that comes from ". . . seeing the world through a businessman's eyes."

Another told of the joy of watching a woman expecting their child. Both, however, were marred by those seemingly unnecessary guitar solos, which often clashed with Ben Keith's high-pitched pedal guitar noodlings and meanderings.

Young hit his peak with the most familiar songs, including an explosive rendition of "Cinnamon Girl," an improved "Everybody Knows This Is Nowhere" and a solid "Southern Man." For me, everything was overshadowed by one song—"Alabama." I think it has the best chorus he has written, and in performance, it builds with a majestic sway characteristic of the Rolling Stones at their best.

Young was not especially well received, all things considered. The performance was too short and he barely won an encore. Just the same, the morning after, I found myself admiring him as much as a person as a musician. In "Don't Be Denied," he offers one of the few attacks on the star system that a rock musician has made creditable. And he makes it so because his performance and style seem free of any taint of cynicism. He knows everything the pop world has to offer and intends to enjoy himself in spite of it.

As for the people who at one time or another think they are using him—whether in his professional or personal life—he doesn't even seem to mind, because he knows that while he isn't going to change them, they haven't changed him either.

JIM MILLER

JOURNEY THROUGH THE PAST
ALBUM REVIEW

NEIL YOUNG HAS BEEN INVOLVED in a lot of memorable rock music over the last seven years. He was one of the most interesting songwriters in Buffalo Springfield, and his own solo work with Crazy Horse still sounds fresh today. At his best, Young transformed his thin voice into a distinctive vehicle for a haunting, frail style, while his lead guitar bristled with a concise energy. His most satisfying work, especially the superb *Everybody Knows This Is Nowhere,* captured an intimate *presence* that was both unassuming and engaging.

The title of Young's newest record, *Journey Through the Past,* suggests a selection of tracks from the various phases of Young's career. Unfortunately, the album instead palms itself off as a film soundtrack, although whether the existence of any film could justify the existence of this record is questionable. To be sure, there *are* selections by the Buffalo Springfield and Crosby, Stills, Nash and Young here. But, oddly, nothing with Crazy Horse is included, and Neil's evocative "Sugar Mountain," which has never been on an album, is also absent. If old concert tapes of "Rock & Roll Woman" are being dredged up, why not include the full-length "Bluebird"?

It's sad but true that the best stuff on *Journey* is by the Buffalo Springfield. The album opens with a hilarious introduction of the group on television that segues into a truncated version of "For What It's Worth," followed by "Mr. Soul," apparently from the same television show; Young's driving vocal and guitar work on "Mr. Soul" possess a vitality almost completely absent from *Journey*'s other cuts. From "Rock & Roll Woman" on, the record quickly degenerates into a depressing combination of sloppy music and verbal filler for a two-record set that lasts barely over an hour. The first side ends with CSNY doing "Find the Cost of Freedom" and "Ohio" in concert. Both songs are available on *4 Way Street* in similarly unmemorable live versions; if Young wanted these songs re-released, he would have done better to use the superior single takes.

"Southern Man," which was originally one of *After the Gold Rush*'s highpoints, is also resurrected for the third time, in a ragged concert version that again seems to feature CSNY singing off tune (the album's fancy packaging somehow manages to omit a listing of who performs what on which tracks). It is tediously crammed together on side two with a new take of "Alabama," an unblushing rehash of "Southern Man" first issued on *Harvest; Journey*'s new version is only distinguished by the pointless addition of some studio small talk. Young's *Harvest* band, the Stray Gators, is a stone bore on the two other tracks culled from the *Harvest* sessions. If the outtake of "Are You Ready for the Country" is merely annoying, *Journey*'s version of "Words" is downright offensive. Occupying all of side three, it winds on for fifteen tortuous minutes, with nary an interesting thematic development in sight; Young's hapless attempts at a guitar solo are so inept as to be embarrassing. All three of the *Harvest* songs actually sounded better in their original incarnations.

The one new song on *Journey*, "Soldier," is performed by Young alone on the piano. It's a lousy recording, and the song is hardly up to Young's normal standards; perhaps it serves some function in the film. Apart from "Soldier," the fourth side is given over to sheer dreck: a bit of Handel's *Messiah*, the theme from *King of Kings* (?), and, just as strange, Brian Wilson's moody instrumental "Let's Go Away for a While," pulled off the Beach Boys' *Pet Sounds*. There's really little excuse for issuing these tracks on a Neil Young album—but then, there's not much more excuse for issuing inferior new versions of old Neil Young material.

In fact, some six minutes of Buffalo Springfield songs and the approximately three minutes of "Soldier" are all that might conceivably edify the purchaser of *Journey Through the Past*. It is outrageous that this album was ever released. It is frankly exploitive of a faithful audience that deserves better from one of its favored performers. There have been many moments in his career when Young has produced some fine rock. *Journey Through the Past* contains virtually none of those moments. It is the nadir of Neil Young's recording activity.

■ RANDOM NOTES (April 12, 1973)

More reunion news: For some time now, and especially since the original Byrds got back together, there've been questions about a possible reunion of Buffalo Springfield. We asked Poco's Richie Furay, who replied: "It's all up to Neil right now," which indicates that the wheel is in motion.

The originals would be Neil Young, Stephen Stills, Furay, Bruce Palmer and Dewey Martin. "I'm sure Stephen wants to do it," said Furay. "In fact he's mentioned it to me several times. I'd do it, and everybody else could use it for some reason or another. But Neil doesn't need it. Whether he wants to spend the time to do it is up to him. Probably it's not gonna come down until someone with higher authority starts bringing the idea down upon everybody."

■ RANDOM NOTES (April 26, 1973)

His heart is still of gold: *Disc,* a rock magazine in England, reported Neil Young canceling his European tour because of a "serious heart infection" requiring an operation. Not true. Young just has hardened lymph nodes in his throat.

JANELLE ELLIS

NEIL YOUNG'S FIRST FILM SHOWN
A docu-autobio-musico-*Journey*

Journey Through the Past *comes off as sort of a cinematic contemplation of the navel. The film will probably disappoint those fans seeking the music of Young and be of value primarily to those searching souls looking for a view of the outside world from inside the hectic, confused, and confusing world of rock music.*

—Bob Porter, *Dallas Times-Herald*

NEIL YOUNG'S FIRST FILM, *Journey Through the Past,* premiered at the U.S. Film Festival in Dallas, Texas, on April 8. Only a third of the 3,500-seat Memorial Auditorium in the Dallas Convention Center was filled for the Sunday afternoon screening; at Young's request, none of the papers had mentioned anything about Neil Young himself showing up. Still, *Journey*'s two showings that day drew the largest crowds of the week, including the festival's handful of celebrities: Vincent Minnelli, Jack Nicholson, Lou Adler and Carrie Snodgress. Minnelli was being honored during the week with a retrospective of his films; Nicholson, who directed *Drive He Said,* was on a panel discussion; Adler, whose record label is heading toward video (he'll be filming parts of the Carole King tour for a movie or TV special), had a weekend to spare, and Snodgress was there to be with Young and their six-month-old son, Zeke.

As the title implies, and as Young himself explained later, "Basically, the film is about me. It's a collection of thoughts. Every scene meant something to me—although with some of them I can't say what."

Or, as producer Fred Underhill (whose previous credits include work on *Marjoe* and *Woodstock*) put it, "It's a conscious attempt to not do a music film, a performance film. He ventured into fantasy, and did fictional sequences. But it also had his music and some historical context for it, from TV films of Buffalo Springfield through today. But I keep asking Neil what it's about, too."

Young's thoughts are expressed through a character known as the Graduate, played by Richard Lee Patterson, who appears throughout the film. In one Fellini–like sequence, the man, in cap and gown, gets beaten senseless; he's dropped off in the middle of a desert, and from there begins to wander; the church, the military and Big Business are portrayed as the main threats to his Constitutional rights. There is a morbidly drawn-out scene of a junkie fixing up (Young later indicated that he had witnessed such scenes backstage); shots of Jesus Freaks on Hollywood Boulevard putting the word on Young, and a re-creation of a recurring dream of his: twelve black-hooded men on black horses sweeping down a beach toward a man and his pickup truck. Although Young said he couldn't explain its significance, the scene serves as the illustration for the soundtrack album.

Another scene has Young in a junkyard under a busy freeway. He sits in a '57 Buick, opens his lunchbox and talks ecology: "Like, man, you know, rebuilding old cars instead of manufacturing new ones."

Bob Porter of the *Times-Herald,* the only critic who covered the film, called its philosophy "simplistic—unless there is a gigantic put-on taking place. . . . It seems at odds that someone so organized and craftsmanlike in his music would approach another media so unstructured. Young expressed the determination to do other films. He is artist enough that he may grow with that. With *Journey* he stands as a filmmaker somewhat like he would as a beginning musician."

NEIL YOUNG BEGAN TALKING about making movies about four years ago, when he was still with his ex-wife, Susan, in Topanga Canyon. At that time, his 8mm camera was a new toy, and his dream was to blow up some of the best of his home movies to 16mm for "the big time"—to show to neighbors at the Topanga Community House. Young had recently joined Crosby, Stills and Nash, and they soon began plotting out a movie of themselves—a documentary of their live concerts and of their lives. David Myers began shooting them on the road, with L.A. Johnson doing sound and Underhill as a production assistant.

"After we'd shot a lot of stuff, they looked at it and did nothing," Young said. But whoever might want the footage, it was agreed, could have it. Young then began plans for *Journey Through the Past,* through his own production company, Shakey Pictures, in conjunction with Myers, Johnson and Underhill, whose own company is called Taut and Gripping, Inc., from a Judith Crist film review.

In the credits, *Journey* is identified as "A film by Neil Young." Young is also credited as editor—"that's what he's most proud of," said Underhill—although he also directed scenes and conceived of most of the fantasy bits. He also went to TV networks in New York to look through stock footage, coming up with, among others, ABC-TV's coverage of Billy Graham and Richard Nixon at a youth rally in the South, singing "God Bless America" together.

By last January, the movie, eighty minutes long, was finished, and Warner Bros., the distributor, released its soundtrack album. But legal problems developed: Clearances had to be obtained for everything from Jesus Freaks to the man who composed "God Bless America," Irving Berlin. Now, the film is scheduled to be released in June, pending a few more clearances, with openings in New York and Los Angeles.

In Dallas, when the film began and Young's name appeared on the screen, the audience burst into spontaneous, spirited applause. At the end, the applause was more . . . polite, and scattered. Young had watched the film from inside the projectionist's booth and listened to the response. He judged himself safe and bounded down the aisle, completely surprising the audience. Joined by Underhill, Myers and festival director L.M. "Kit" Carson (who'd worked with Myers on *Marjoe* and invited Young's participation in this year's festival), he sat on the edge of the stage, legs dangling over the front row.

"Not used to this," Young began. "We don't have question-and-answer periods after our concerts." The audience immediately warmed up and shot questions at him for half an hour—the usual inane ones ("Were you drinking gasoline from that jug?" "No, that was apple juice." Young smiled at Snodgress and winked), the technical ones (Underhill said the film cost about $350,000), and some musical ones (Young brushed aside most of the questions, about a Buffalo Springfield reunion, about how often Stills seemed to appear in the film, about Crosby, Stills and Nash). Young appeared hyperexcited through the session, like a high school kid who'd just won in the Science Fair, but still nervous over his first film.

The consensus, from his friends, on the film: a decent first try, even if not exactly Academy. "It was a nice film," said Lou Adler (himself a star of such rock movies as *Monterey Pop, Brewster McCloud* and *A Model Shop*). "Neil's touch is great, as it is in his music." But, Adler added, he'd actually be more enthusiastic to see Young's second and third tries. "Anyone coming out of one industry and going into another has to still be learning the mechanics of the new one," he said. "And now he'll have something to bounce off of."

Young's co-manager, Elliot Roberts, agreed. "This film is not as proficient as his next endeavor," he said. "But it was made with a lot of care and love."

■ RANDOM NOTES (July 5, 1973)

Crosby, Stills, Nash and Young have decided to postpone their tour, says a Stills aide, because Young "wants to spend time with Carrie and Zeke." The tour may get going in October. Meantime, the group is rehearsing in San Francisco. "The music is incredible," says one observer, surprising no one, and the LP may be finished before the tour.

■ RANDOM NOTES (August 30, 1973)

From a source close to the group, we understand that Crosby, Stills, Nash and Young are closer than ever to an actual album. The latest step began with Crosby taking off on one of his occasional trips to Maui. Young, needing a rest after his recent tour, decided to go over, too, and joined him. The two were sitting around in Lahaina when Stills called up to find out what was going on. Nothing was, he was told, so he flew over to the island. Finally, Nash split from his Haight-Ashbury digs and joined into what became a round of serious rehearsals. Last we heard, they booked time in a San Francisco area studio for an album. If that gets done, a fall tour is still possible.

JUDITH SIMS

NEIL YOUNG OPENS THE ROXY THEATER

THE ROXY THEATER, the long-awaited rock club rival to the Troubadour and the Whisky, finally opened September 20 with Neil
Young headlining two shows a night for four sold-out nights.

A crowd lined up on Sunset Strip outside the building—formerly a strip
joint called the Largo—to look at celebrities, while inside, the customers
shrieked and leaped as the famous entered, Elton John, Carole King, Helen
Reddy, Jackson Browne and Herb Alpert among them. (Later in the week,
customers included Bob Dylan, Alice Cooper and various members of the
Allman Brothers Band.)

Originally scheduled to open sometime last spring, the Roxy and its
owners have been plagued by demons and heavy changes. Peter Asher
(manager of James Taylor) and Elmer Valentine (owner of the neighboring
Whisky) dropped out as partners recently. (Asher left, he said, because "I'm
not in a position to have that kind of money sitting around waiting for
something to happen"; Valentine was not available for comment.) The
splits left the Roxy to Chuck Landis, owner of the building; Ode Records'
president Lou Adler; Elektra-Asylum head David Geffen, and Bill Graham,
who will do the booking for the club.

Seating capacity is 500 (compared to the Troubadour's 350); admission
will be around $5 (plus a two-drink minimum, drinks averaging $1.25).

On opening night Grin was scheduled to open, but Graham announced
that Nils Lofgren had a sore throat; instead we got Cheech and Chong, who
continue to wallow in sexist, dopist tastelessness: "How about that Billie
Jean King beating Bobby Riggs? Well, it wasn't the first time a man got
licked by a girl." Their set was mercifully brief, as was Graham Nash's.
Willie looked and sounded awful, enthralling the crowd with new songs,
one of which whined about the disparity of marijuana laws between states.

After Nash the house lights went up, a hot R&B record hit the turnta-
ble, and a crew of dancers from *Soul Train* burned up the aisles, encircling
the delighted audience. Absolutely the best part of the evening.

Young finally emerged, wearing dark glasses, and an ill-fitting white
sport coat over untucked T-shirt. Still, his presence is powerful. Young the
man is always interesting; unfortunately, Young the songwriter is often
banal. He performed only new tunes (except for the encore), in two of

which he used the same line, "Think I'll roll a number." The best of the bunch was "Tonight's the Night," about former CSNY roadie Bruce Berry, who died recently of a heroin overdose.

Young was backed by Nils Lofgren on guitar and off-key harmonies; Ben Keith on pedal steel; Ralph Molina on drums and Billy Talbot on bass, the latter two of Crazy Horse. The stage was set with a tall spindly tree, a wooden Indian, a glittery platform shoe, and lots of boots hanging from the grand piano. "Welcome to Miami Beach," Young said.

■ **RANDOM NOTES** (November 22, 1973)

Neil Young, getting bombed in the press for his latest album, his first film and his live shows, won't be daunted: He's got another album ready for January release called *Tonight's the Night*, from his smack-saga song of the same name. This one's not live, but Young went for the live sound by cutting it at an L.A. rehearsal hall with Crazy Horse, using a remote unit parked outside . . . Correction: In our review of Young at the Roxy, the dancers were not from *Soul Train,* as announced by Bill Graham. They were the local Lockers and will be on *In Concert* November 23. . . . Later on in Young's week at the Roxy, we hear, he offered a silver boot to any woman who would walk on stage topless. As if on cue, one did: his own Carrie Snodgress.

BUD SCOPPA

TIME FADES AWAY ALBUM REVIEW
Neil Young's Unorthodox Live Album

THIS ALBUM MAY DO FOR Neil Young's declining image what *Pat Garrett & Billy the Kid* did for Dylan's. But like Dylan's much-maligned movie soundtrack LP, *Time Fades Away* has its virtues when taken on its own terms and not as the latest major work of a major artist. Here, Young seems to have consciously avoided the sober sense of importance that accompanied *After the Gold Rush* and *Harvest* by recording his new material live and rough. Mistakes and fluffs dot these performances, and Young has made no attempt to correct them. For whatever reason, he's made a startlingly unorthodox album.

If *Time Fades Away* isn't the standard big statement we've come to expect from such performers, neither is it the standard live album of the successful artist. There are no hits, no familiar tunes; for that matter, there's hardly any audience response—it's quickly faded out at each song's end. More than any of his earlier works, this record shows Young's reticence about being a public figure.

Young's privateness has always been at the heart of his writing and performing, right alongside his staunch moral sense. These two elements have been both his prime virtues and his main flaws. Both elements are evident in this new material, with uneven but sometimes positive results.

There is an overbearing sense of self-righteousness in the title song, with its images of nervous junkies strung out on the street. But it's saved by a sharply ironic chorus, in which the junkie's weak parent whines: "Son, don't be home too late / Try to get back by eight / Son, don't wait till the break of day / 'Cause you know how time fades away. . . ." The lyric is energized by hard, jerking instrumental work from the Stray Gators and by Young's jagged, piercing vocal: He's still the best whiner in rock & roll. And he expresses anguish like no one else.

Young's is a pain-dominated, rather Old Testament sensibility, and nowhere is all this more obvious than in "L.A." Young's self-righteousness becomes absolute, and he depicts himself as some neo-Israelite prophet warning the unhearing masses of the inevitable apocalypse. Young's blanket condemnations, "Southern Man" and "Alabama" included, are as simplistic as they are venomous, but their fire makes them compelling nonetheless. That "L.A." is reflectively sung while the two earlier songs sounded impetuous makes this one's content and tone that much more ugly.

It's hard to believe that the same person who conceived "L.A." could write and sing the delicate "Journey Through the Past," "The Bridge" and "Love in Mind." These are small-scope, understated songs, and they're performed convincingly by Young, with only his own simple piano.

The best song on the album is "Don't Be Denied," which continues the tone but expands the scope of his quiet, personal songs. It is a complete autobiography in four verses, and the most effective part deals with his childhood. In this section, Young cuts rapidly through scenes that depict the private trials of a rather delicate kid in a rugged land. This song seems an explicit re-expression of the emotional content of Young's moving but impenetrably private "Broken Arrow." The latter part of "Denied," in which Young deals with the problems of being a celebrity, forgoes universality for the writer's personal complaints but is no less credible for it. A lack of honesty in his work has never been one of Young's problems; if anything, he's gone too far in the other direction, saying what would have been better left unsaid and looking bigoted or just plain foolish in the process.

He comes off rather silly in "Last Dance," a long, ponderous song that sounds like Young's parody of his own *After the Gold Rush* hard-rock style. And he's out of control on "Yonder Stands the Sinner," which is self-deprecating in what seems to be a more intentional way. His voice breaks when he squeal-shouts the word, "sinner!" as if he were disclaiming the moralistic fury of "L.A."

If Young appears foolish and arrogant at various points on the album, he seems to be allowing us a glimpse of these flaws, rather than letting them slip through and spoil his big moments without his consent, as happened on *Harvest. Time Fades Away* is an idiosyncrasy from one of rock's most idiosyncratic artists. If it isn't a resounding success, the album is still a revealing self-portrait by an always fascinating man.

■ RANDOM NOTES (April 11, 1974)

Crosby, Stills, Nash and Young to play several summer rock festivals (although Crosby told us, at Dylan's post-tour party at the Forum, that the latest attempted reunion had been "sacrificed at the altar of ego").

■ RANDOM NOTES (June 20, 1974)

Neil Young showed up unexpectedly at the Bottom Line in New York City on May 16, where he played a full set after Ry Cooder and Leon Redbone had finished theirs. Young stayed onstage for an hour of mostly new material, soon to be heard, to be sure, on his new album, now entitled *On the Beach*.

BEN FONG-TORRES

CSNY'S REUNION
A Show of Strength

MINUTES AFTER CROSBY, Stills and Nash and then Young, hit the stage in Seattle for the first concert of their reunion tour, it was clear that no other group ever had a chance of replacing them while they were apart—not America, not Bread, not Poco, not the Eagles, not Seals and Crofts or Loggins and Messina or Souther, Hillman and Furay. Not even Manassas or the reunion of the original Byrds.

It's been four years since the last tour, and each of the principals has gone through weighty changes. But onstage, you can hardly tell. The 1969 Woodstock language is still there; Crosby is still the group mouth; Nash the gentle presence; Stills and Young the fabled guitar stars. And although a couple of the voices have measurably changed, the meat of the group is still the high vocal harmonies.

But if any one action proved that the group hadn't changed since the old and golden days, it was their utter lack of foresight and discipline in planning, then executing, the first show. As Crosby, his voice wrecked, would say the next evening, just before the Vancouver concert, the group had mapped out forty-four songs for what they figured would be a three or three-and-a-half-hour stand. And when they found themselves with fully nine more numbers on their list at 12:35 A.M., three-and-a-half-hours after they had opened with "Love the One You're With," they decided to plunge ahead, what the hell, first show and all.

And it ruined them and their Vancouver show. Not that the audience noticed; in both Seattle and Vancouver, packed houses of 15,000 and 17,000 gave their heroes heroes' receptions and continuing waves of ovations. But the group, of course, knew, and they scuttled and shuffled songs around to accommodate Crosby's sinking voice.

Backstage in Vancouver, after the opening electric set, Nash, standing with producer Bill Graham, was shaking his head, wondering out loud if the group could survive a tour of thirty shows in two months. Later, during the solo sets, Neil Young would enter the dressing room in a foul mood, saying the show, now trimmed by ten minutes, was *still* too long, that the concert—organized to begin electrically, break, and then build from acoustic (with the whole group, then solo sets) back to electric—should revert to the old CSNY formula—acoustic, electric, finish. Nash himself would report: "David is really bummed out."

After the concert, at a Denny's coffee shop, some fans gathered to complain about Crosby. "He's singing this song, 'For Free,' and he's trying to tell everybody to shut up so he could sing," said one young woman. "How can you tell 17,000 people to quiet down? Then he got pissed off because it wasn't quiet enough for him and stopped the song right in the middle."

Said Crosby: "I don't bum out on people onstage. There were too many people yelling, 'Sit down.' I asked them and asked them to be quiet. But it was very loud and I had great difficulty, and once I stopped, I didn't have enough emotional momentum to start that song over again, so I went right into 'Guinnevere'—and did a fucking good job on it!"

But Crosby was clearly unhappy. "During rehearsals [at Young's ranch in La Honda, south of San Francisco], we never had time to go all the way through the show, see how long forty-four songs would take," said Crosby. "It was an honest mistake. I gave too much and ended up cheating Vancouver. I felt bad. I'd let them down and I'd let the band down." But, as Nash and Stills and manager Elliot Roberts said, the group cannot contain itself, once onstage. Crosby agreed. "I get to a song like 'Ohio' [which closed the opening electric set] and you know me. To hold back on that . . . Well, I don't believe in controlled mediocrity."

Crosby, Stills, Nash and Young are uniquely attractive, for some obvious musical reasons and, not insignificantly, for some more mysterious personal ones. The fact that the group broke up at the height of success in 1970 was puzzling enough. That Graham Nash would later attribute the split to "stupid, infantile ego problems" made it only more interesting. Then came the annual announcements of impending reunions, followed by almost ritual withdrawals of those announcements. The most recent was last winter, when the four got together in Hawaii, sang together and even worked up some new material. "We realized how good it could be," said Crosby. "But," and he slowed the next sentence down: "We—weren't—quite ready—to—do it. A couple of us weren't."

Elliot Roberts said, "It started to look like bullshit." Roberts, who manages Crosby, Nash and Young, finally went to each man, got summer cleared, and began mapping out the season's biggest rock & roll tour, some thirty dates, most of them much larger than the kickoffs in Seattle and Vancouver July 9 and 10. Two shows at the Oakland Coliseum July 13 and 14 drew a reported total 76,000; another outdoor shot—at the Ontario Motor Speedway in Southern California August 3—was expected to draw

somewhere near 200,000, and 40,000 and 50,000 were projected atten-
dance figures in Houston, Denver, St. Louis, Kansas City, Milwaukee and
several other spots. Unofficial total gross estimates ranged from $6 million
to $10 million, with between 800,000 and a million persons paying an
average ticket price of $8.50.

Were CSNY back together only for the money? "Well," said Roberts,
"it's not a benefit. But I'd have to say that money is not a factor." Crosby,
while admitting that he has spent most of his money over the years,
maintained that he does not need CSNY income in order to survive. The
reason for the reunion, he said, should be clear: "It's the best goddamned
music any of us has ever played—and we all know it."

In keeping with CSNY's nature, the schedule was not totally firm a
week into the tour; a date had not yet been fixed for the closing show at
Madison Square Garden, and whether a mid-September stop in London, at
Wembley Pool, might extend to other parts of Europe, was still to be
figured out. At the last minute, an invitation to Kenny Passarelli, who'd
worked with Stills, to be the group's bassist was canceled, and the backup
band consists of Tim Drummond, from Neil Young's tours and the *Harvest*
and *Time Fades Away* albums, on bass; Joe Lala, from Manassas, on percus-
sion, and Russ Kunkel, who backed Crosby and Nash on their tours and
duet album, on drums.

The first show was a show of strength and of health, Stills looking
bright-eyed and snappy in one of his collection of football and hockey
jerseys; Young with his hair drastically trimmed and smiling out from
reflective shades; and Nash and Crosby maintaining their respectively un-
derfed and overnourished appearances. The four soul-slapped, back-patted
and hand-shook their way through the first part of the show, shifting seats
and instruments with ease through "Love the One You're With,"
"Wooden Ships," "Immigration Man," "Cowgirl in the Sand," "Change
Partners," "Traces" (a new Young song), Nash's "Grave Concern," preceded by a group litany of Watergate gibberish ("I don't recall" . . . "I can't
seem to remember" . . . "To the best of my recollection . . ."), "Black
Queen," "Almost Cut My Hair" and "Ohio." Stills was giving Young
plenty of room to roam on lead guitar, a comment for those who remember
stories about Sunset Strip duels between the two major forces of Buffalo
Springfield; Stills would later shine for himself on his banjo number,
"Know You've Got to Run," and several Latin-beaten jams.

The hour-long electric set was followed by an acoustic session that first
aroused the crowd with "Suite: Judy Blue Eyes," which suffered from a
poor mix and a few offed keys, and "Helplessly Hoping." A beautiful
"Blackbird," a group favorite since the earliest days in Laurel Canyon, was

followed by a Young lament, "Human Highway," which he only recently discarded along with an entire album called *Tonight's the Night*, in favor of the just released *On the Beach*. The song showed off Young's new voice, the high end seemingly chopped off, the whine now more a moan. Nash sang "Prison Song" and a lovely new love song, reminiscent of "I Miss You" on *Wild Tales*, and Crosby began the solo spots with a new tune reflecting his own maturity—"Carry Me"—then a tribute to his "favorite song-writer" with "For Free" by Joni Mitchell, and "Guinnevere," which had Nash sneaking up to weave in a perfect laser beam of harmony. Here, the audience was stilled, many on the main floor assuming Fifties civil-defense huddle positions, heads sunken between knees. Nash followed with "Sleep Song" and "Our House," which earned an ovation, and he gave way to Stills for "4 + 20" and the banjo workout. Young then performed two more new compositions, both musically lighthearted: "Love Hard Blues" and "Long May You Run," which he wrote for his refurbished '48 Buick Roadmaster. When he finished "A Man Needs a Maid," it was 12:35, and people could be seen packing up and leaving. But the transition back to electric had just begun, with "Don't Be Denied," then several Stills numbers that extended into lengthy jams, along with "Déjà Vu" and "Pre-Road Downs." "Long Time Gone" and "Carry On" closed the show and ignited a full ten-minute encore call that got the group back on for "Chicago."

At 1:37 in the Pacific Northwest, with the monorail long out of commission and several hundred people suddenly needing rides, Crosby, Stills, Nash and Young wove together into a four-man hug. They had overdosed, and the next night would be a disaster. But they had proven that they were in it, more than anything else, for the music.

BEN FONG-TORRES

THE EGO MEETS THE DOVE
The Reunion of Crosby, Stills, Nash and Young

A S ELLIOT ROBERTS, their manager, so daintily put it, they were pissing in the wind, these boy wonders of his who could make a million at the snap of four sets of fingers.

And yet, year after year, this all-time favorite group from out of the Woodstock era, these symbols of harmony in music, would try to get back together and would fail. "We really did try, every year," Nash would say. "It just didn't fucking happen because it wasn't real."

From the beginning, in the spring of 1969, Crosby, Stills and Nash had been preparing the public for their breakup. I initially met them while they were cutting their first album and they were all saying, and this was the bottom line of my story, that they were not a group.

From the Byrds, the Buffalo Springfield and the Hollies, the three men had had enough, they said, of outsized egos. Now they would band and disband as they pleased, go solo or form various duos for tours and albums as they pleased.

They have been true to their founding principle. And it makes no sense.

After you've become the biggest in the biggest of all entertainment businesses, you're supposed to look the other way and slip right by those old principles, on the way to a four-way easy street. And if the public wants a reunion, a manager's supposed to make sure it damned well gets one. Even if his wonders have to stay in different hotels, travel in separate curtain-drawn limousines and sing from isolation booths.

But Elliot Roberts is a laid-back sort of guy. Anybody who's got a slice of several million dollars a year, who for four years sees the fortune's dissipation because, well, because "it wasn't real," and who doesn't commit horrendous acts of violence born of frustration—that person has got to be stone laid-back. Or he's happy with the fortune he's already made. Or he's a real friend. Roberts, it would be fair to say, is a bit of each.

"I have to give him a great deal of credit," says Graham Nash, "for his patience, to deal with the fucking mad people that we are." But Nash remembers the founding principle:

"I don't like that word, reunion," he says. "To be perfectly honest with you, I never felt that we were totally apart. I always felt that eventually we would grow up and realize what was happening. We've always been musically connected."

Musically, there is no question about CSNY. If you're into living-room rock, fireplace harmonies and just a taste of good old social consciousness, this is your group. At the concerts this time around, there were those who were there to remember. Instantly, they were thankful again for "Chicago" and "Ohio" as well as for "Suite: Judy Blue Eyes" and "Our House." Over the years, Crosby, Stills and Nash have shown up at a Young concert. Nash and Crosby have shown up at a Stills show. They've probably done a lot of visiting to each other's living rooms. There clearly is that musical connection.

So why couldn't they get along for long enough to work together? What tore them so far apart that even music couldn't reunite them for so long? They had, each of them, been unable to escape that mysterious thing called ego.

At the St. Paul, Minnesota, Civic Center, the lights are doused, 19,000 voices rise out of the darkness and all you see are the blue fluorescent lights playing onto the Indian rug; it looks like a snowdrift onstage as Crosby, Stills, Nash and bassist Tim Drummond face off to establish the rhythm. Neil Young, in a Buick service department jacket and patched cords, is behind the organ. The power builds—it's "Love the One You're With"—and a floorful of people are suddenly shake-hopping in place. On "Wooden Ships," springing up from central casting, there's your clenched fist, front center, just as the chorus begins.

In the middle of the acoustic set, Young introduces "For the Turnstiles" by saying: "Here's a song I wrote a long time ago. There's a couple of really good songwriters here tonight; I hope they don't listen too closely." Minutes later it's Stills, and he, too, pays tribute to a songwriter in the crowd:

"This one's for Bob," he says, "because I know I've been that mad before." Head bowed and hands flailing, he flies into "Word Game":

Would you knock a man down if you don't like the cut of his clothes
Could you put a man away if you don't want to hear what he knows
Well, it's happening right here . . .
("Word Game" by Stephen Stills © 1971 Rondor Music International,
Inc.)

Through most of this set, Bob Dylan, in cowboy shirt, jeans and shades, has been standing in the midst of a small group on the floor off to the side, behind backstage barriers. He stands, unnoticed by the audience, next to a woman in a DRUG HELP jacket.

Dylan is in his home state for a visit with family and friends. He's with Louie Kemp, his buddy from their childhood days in Hibbing, just north of here, and the word has spread quickly that he has taken an apartment in town, is moving back and buying some property just outside Minneapolis.

As the acoustic set makes its transition back into electric, Dylan wanders off by himself. He is willing to have a few words. Over Young's rock-star recall, "Don't Be Denied," Dylan shouts that he's in town to attend a funeral.

What about the talk that he's looking for some property here?

He flashes the half-smile: "I'm always looking."

I say I enjoyed hearing the album of the tour, that it sounds better than most of the nine shows I covered.

"Wait till you hear my next album!"

"How far along is it?"

"I haven't started yet!"

Dylan has been at the St. Paul Hilton that afternoon; Crosby broke away from an interview to have a visit with him. I ask Dylan how he's liked the CSNY show so far and he responds with questions about Frank Sinatra's problems in Australia and about the weather in San Francisco. A moment later, after he's absorbed some more music, he turns and shouts: "I like to play *small* rooms!"

"Your next record should be a comedy record," I yell.

"All my records are comedy records!"

Later that night—in fact, early the next morning—Dylan pops up again, into a fifteenth-floor suite of beautiful Midwestern women and weary rock & roll tourists. He talks briefly to Stills, eyes three guitars on the floor, picks one up and herds Stills into an adjacent room for a session of new Bob Dylan songs. The only other member of the audience, through the two-hour show, is bassist Tim Drummond.

"Aw, fuck!" Drummond laughs the next afternoon. He is staying behind while the tour moves immediately into Denver to allow Crosby, Stills and Nash to catch the Eric Clapton show.

"Dylan's got an album," says Drummond. "It's great and it's completely different from *Planet Waves*. It's gutsy, bluesy, so authentic. I heard eight or nine songs and it's the first time I've sat in a room and liked everything I've heard."

DRUMMOND, IT TURNS OUT, will provide most of the information I need about Neil Young. Young, the so-called reluctant star of the group, is the lone holdout—staying away by driving off after each show in a GMC camper van toward the next town and by staying busy before shows, meeting, joking and jamming with the others. Elliot Roberts will say: "Well, he just doesn't want to talk; he says he's got nothing to say." And later: "He never likes the way he comes out in print. He says it sounds like someone else." Young has his year-and-a-half-old son, Zeke, with him on this tour, along with their dog, Art (who swaggers around backstage wearing full photo-ID credentials), and he is determined to spend time with his kid and avoid hotels and airports. "He likes to be on the road," says Crosby. "He loves driving down the old highway." Graham Nash: "He doesn't trust a lot of people." Nash lifts a Coca-Cola and sings, "I don't know who to trust anymore. . . ."

So it is Tim Drummond who will trace Neil Young through the years, through the changes and up to the reunion.

Drummond, thirty-four, played with Conway Twitty ten years ago, split and settled in Cincinnati, got discovered by James Brown and became "the only paleface in his band." Tired of the road, he moved to Nashville to do session work. One day, he was walking down the street when a photographer friend stopped him. "He said Neil Young was at Quadraphonic Studios [Young was in town to be on the Johnny Cash TV show] and was jamming and needed a bass player. So I showed up and the first song we cut was 'Heart of Gold.' Later we went out to Neil's ranch [in La Honda, California, just south of San Francisco] and recorded in this old barn, with bird shit all over and holes in the ceiling and a remote truck parked outside. 'Alabama' and 'Are You Ready' are from the barn."

Drummond accepted Young's invitation to tour with him in a band whose name would come from Drummond's times with Brown.

"We'd be riding in a bus with James and get drunk and we'd call it 'seeing gators.' One guy would call out, 'There goes a flock of 'em, strayin' behind.' "

Young and the Stray Gators hit sixty-five cities in three months, beginning January 5, 1973, playing all big halls with capacities between 15,000 and 20,000, and the tour hit Young hard. He looked disheveled throughout; he was criticized for doing too short a show (the average was an hour and a quarter) and he had just completed a film, *Journey Through the Past,* that would fail to secure a distribution deal and would account for his least successful album ever.

"There was so much pressure on him," says Drummond. "It was just him in front of the mike." On the last four dates, Crosby and Nash showed up to help.

From there talk began again about an attempted CSNY reunion. The four wound up in Lahaina, on the island of Maui in Hawaii, worked up some new songs, and the scene then shifted to Young's ranch, where it crumbled in the fall. Drummond: "I came out in July to do this. We recorded about six songs for a new album." Included were Nash's "Prison Song" and "And So It Goes," which wound up on his own *Wild Tales,* and Young's "Human Highway," which was to serve as the album's title. "Then," says Drummond, "we decided to go on the road and get tight. Then we decided against it. Something wasn't right." Nash: "The four of us didn't feel it was solid enough to go out there and represent it as our level of competence." And Crosby: "There was a lot of disagreement about how to go about it. Plus others had commitments they felt were too good to pass up. The record's still there, but we're so much more together now than we were then. We are now to the state where two or three times we went into Neil's studio in the evening after rehearsals, just to fuck around acoustically, and got masters right away—first or second take."

Between the ditching of the tour and the rehearsals two months ago at Young's, Crosby, Stills and Nash all did separate tours while Young put together, then dumped, an album called *Tonight's the Night.*

"It was a flash," says Drummond. "He wanted to use Crazy Horse, he did, and he had an album. It was done live in his studio and it sounded like an old funky club, three in the morning." Elliot Roberts: "It was a drunken rock & roll party album." Crosby: "He wasn't satisfied with it."

Came the spring of '74, manager Roberts sprang again. Young, by now a father, was finished with another album, *On the Beach,* and had a few dozen new songs left over; he agreed to the reunion and offered his ranch, nestled in the redwoods, as rehearsal quarters, six days a week through the month of June.

"Neil played host in the most incredible fashion," says Crosby. "He built this full-size, forty-foot stage in the middle of a grove of redwoods and right across from his studios so we could record. He put half of us up and fed us all, had two chicks working. And the place, because it's so private and beautiful, was a natural to make us feel great and work hard."

Graham Nash: "At first I felt apprehensive, but as soon as I heard Stephen play, I knew it was all cool. Stephen's cooled out a lot. Just his sense of control, of space, of leaving room for Neil to play. He's become more aware of the 'us' rather than the 'I.' And Neil, because of his achievement on a personal level and because he's feeling comfortable with himself, is able to extend that hospitality to others. Before, he wasn't as open to doing that. He has gotten, from my own viewpoint, to gain a great deal of patience and consideration for other people."

And from his anchor position at bass and from working with Young since *Harvest* in Nashville, Drummond observes: "Neil's a changed man. He's really one of the boys now, a funky-ass musician. He's more open than he used to be. He's really into music—playing music—rather than being out front. I don't think he feels the pressure anymore. Just play, and fuck all that other shit."

EXCLUSIVE INTERVIEW WITH Neil Young, conducted July 22, Civic Center Coliseum, St. Paul, Minnesota:

"Neil, do you think you can find half an hour after the show to talk a bit?"

"Well, I'm taking off right after the show, and it's a twenty-two hour drive to Denver. You know, I'm not real good at giving interviews. But I'll tell you, I'm having a lot of fun and it's getting better every day."

We were talking about the space
Between us all
And the people who hide themselves
Behind a wall of illusion
("Within You Without You" by George Harrison © 1967, Northern
   Songs, Ltd.)

THREE YEARS AGO, one year after the "last" CSNY show in the summer of 1970, Stephen Stills had that song on his mind. "George Harrison wrote the summation," he said. But Stills had quoted only the first line, while in fact he was one of the people who hid behind illusion walls. He was sitting in the fourteen-room cottage in Surrey that he'd just bought from Ringo Starr for a quarter-million; he had adopted a stiff, squire-ish way of speech; he now owned two horses and insisted that the cover photo for his interview depict him atop either Major Change or Crazy Horse, without knowing that the magazine had not considered him for a cover in the first place. Stills copped from a novel to describe his inspiration for his songs. ("Well," he had said in his lazy, slightly pained way, "there are three things men can do with women: Love them, suffer for them or turn them into literature." Lawrence Durrell, writing *Justine* in 1957, had one of his characters say it first.) And on a mission to establish his own identity as a solo star, Stills would stumble through a tour he now calls "the drunken Memphis Horns tour," each show highlighted by a pounding, raging rendition of his Buffalo Springfield classic, "For What It's Worth," Stills attacking a piano and the audience with a political drift-rap he now admits was a "rant." He drank and ranted, he says, because of fear. "There were pressures on me to prove myself." From where? "The business."

What about the pressures of the old days and the ego fights?

"I know it's good copy," he says, "but I really don't think it's anybody's business. Because a lot of it had to do with all those things—musicianship, the ego that it takes to step out onstage and say, 'Look at me, mama,' which is Lenny Bruce's line which just hits it right on the head. You have to be one to know one. And I might say something about somebody in our little, in our . . . family . . . that they might be offended to see in print, so . . . I think we all went through a stage of growing as musicians. We went through one stage together and another separately and now we're going through another together.

"I missed 'em, you know. I missed Graham telling me when to stop and what was too much and I missed David's vocals and I missed Neil's collaboration on the sound of the records. I missed playing guitar with him, 'cause we really back each other up. Like the song we were doing this afternoon—I just love it, to sit there and listen to Neil tell the story, and a couple of times I had his phrase and just repeated it back to him. That kind of shit."

In March 1973 Stills married Veronique Sanson, the popular French singer, in London; they are now the parents of a boy named Christopher.

"So Neil and I, both of us, had babies, and that puts us in a place where we can really relate to each other. Some of the kid stuff we used to pull goes away. Just taking things the wrong way, not using your head about relationships with people."

Stephen Stills says he's grown up. Talking politics—he's a voracious reader and has Solzhenitsyn's *Gulag Archipelago* on the road with him—he concludes: "I could be totally full of shit, but at this point in my life, I don't care."

"Why do you say at this point in your life?"

"At this point in life? I really don't give a shit if ROLLING STONE thinks I'm stupid, jive, horrible."

"But why are you thinking that at this particular point of your life?"

"Because I've grown to the age where I can apply my own intellect to the situations I'm in and remain true to what occurs to me as a human being existing on this planet. Whereas at age twenty-three that was not true. There's a lot of creative thinking that goes on at that age, but you get surrounded by the kind of experience that I've had . . . I mean, man is the sum total of his experience. And you can only apologize for so much.

"I mean, hey, what did we all do, what the fuck were we all doing? David with the Byrds, and me and Neil with the Springfield, we were all trying to . . . I mean, Neil's got that beautiful song, 'Don't Be Denied.' It says, 'Pretty soon, matter of fact, played guitar. Used to sit on the back porch and think about being stars. . . .' And that's about as far as it goes."

We are in a Sportscoach camper van, on the way home to San Francisco after the first show at the Oakland Coliseum.

"People who play music or attack their art form in one way and then find themselves in a position of obtaining popularity and find that it means something entirely different to everyone else and trying to strike the balance . . . or in a lot of cases just totally reject what the fuck everybody else thinks . . . I mean, you could spend three months with me and maybe you'd get the idea of what it is. I mean, look how long—I don't mean to compare myself—but look how long it took everyone to understand Picasso. Look how long it takes people to understand artists, period . . . and I don't think there's a musician who has gotten popular support that hasn't been through the same thing. An artist cannot often be responsible for the effect his art has on his audience, be it a painter, sculptor, musician, actor, whatever. He just can't. If he gets hung up with that, he's going to lose it because he's gotta keep working at *his* shit. I mean there's that time when it's going down: It's now, not yesterday, not tomorrow. And what you play or how you sing right now is how you sing right now, and the only thing that lasts are the songs."

Stephen Stills will be thirty next January. Is that growth? From observation, he seems to be consciously reining in his take-charge ways of the past—the product, he says, of some military schooling in his background. The maturity—or simple awareness of what's needed to keep this show on the road—is obvious onstage. He is relaxed and lets the others have their ways; given his moments on electric guitar or acoustic or banjo, he sings and stings with his instruments, picking out some neat blues figures on the banjo. Vocally, he exercises two fine voices: the alcoholic scowl for his Texas-based blues and the frankly middle-of-the-road, sloping croon that gets me thinking, from a distance, how, in physical comparison with his coworkers, Stills comes across like a Bing Crosby in a hockey jersey—especially when he's got on pressed slacks and straw beach shoes to boot.

But I mean, if Dylan hadn't shown up at the hotel after the concert and spirited Stills away with a guitar, I might have spent three months with Stills all in one night. At three in the morning, we were heading into the second hour of this beery rap, Stills offering his thoughts on *Gulag* and Russian history, on the history of art and his own recent tries at painting; on how he wanted to find a publisher to do a Stephen Stills songbook in the fashion of an old hymn book.

The next afternoon—late the next afternoon—getting ready to leave for Denver, Stills tries to keep his eyes open long enough to look into mine, forms a smile, then laughs: "Bob sang all these great new songs and then he turned the guitar over to me and asked me to sing him a new one, and I was so wasted I couldn't remember the words!" Stills is genuinely amused. "Hey, all that stuff last night. I hope you disregard it."

EVEN FRIENDS DISMISS much of what Stills has to say when he's off the stage. He talks about moving back to California, to the Bay Area, in fact, where the rest of the group now have homes. Michael John Bowen, his manager and friend from high school days in Tampa, Florida, pshaws in his tart, jock-strapped voice: "That's *this* week." Stills had talked about the burden on Solzhenitsyn's shoulders and I relay what I recall of his thinking to Graham Nash, and Nash snaps back: "That's *this* book."

As he says, Stills doesn't have to apologize his entire past away; he can, in fact, be forever proud of much of it. Neither do audiences—the minority that have minded when Stills lost either his voice or his head—have to forgive. Still, today he does find it easier to admit or at least rationalize mistakes.

"When I did 'For What It's Worth' and did the rant and all that, you point out what an incredible bust it was for me. It was really dumb. But the last generation, that's what they wanted to hear and, of course, being an entertainer, I was behind it.

"And I'll blow records sometimes," he says, " 'cause I get so far into getting it recorded, and some of the mixes are so difficult, I'll get too hung up and blow the performance of the gig. But, you know, I'm learning."

In the studio, Stills used to be the seldom-disputed captain. He clearly and cleanly dominated the first album, producing, mixing, arranging and dubbing in most of the instrumentation (guitars, organ and bass) on the ten tracks.

Stills won't talk about the stories of battles over *Déjà Vu;* he thinks ahead to the next CSNY album, to be done after the tour. "That's going to be a whole different kind of thing to deal with," he says. "It'll be give and take and getting a consortium of opinion. The erroneous assumption is that we are gonna hassle about it, and nobody's into that anymore."

David Crosby has also talked about growth, about how "everybody's willing to give each other more room and respect."

Michael John Bowen breaks into a conversation Stills is having just before the show in Vancouver. "They're reworking the first set," his manager tells him. "Graham wants you. They want to put 'Cut My Hair' into it." Stills: "Okay, all right. We can do that instead of 'Black Queen.' " Bowen: "But Graham says 'Black Queen' follows 'Cowgirl' nicely." Stills finally excuses himself. The impression is that he'll go along with whatever anyone wants.

"Maturity," Crosby is saying, "has lessened the pressure between us.

I'm knocked out with how good partners we're being and how hard everyone's trying."

But doesn't stepping back and holding tongues approach a kind of dishonesty? Crosby says he's talking musically:

"You'll hear us playing along and we're playing to a place where we're storming and somebody, without even looking, will come to a peak"—Crosby, in his hotel room, mimes a lead guitarist creating a storm—"and everybody goes *fwhooop!* and drops *way* back, and one guitar will come out speaking right out of it, just clear. Now that's leaving room for people, and that happens when you're gettin' to be a band."

WHEN I FIRST ENTER his suite at the St. Paul Hilton, Crosby, dressed down to just shorts, is near to attacking his vanity mirror. He is five months into kung fu—that's maybe two months past the cut-off point for most faddists—and finds time to work out every day.

I tell him how much fun I had the night before and how Stills and Dylan stayed up to at least 5 A.M.

"I don't do that anymore," he says, like a kid who's had a pleasant bad habit forcibly changed. "It just doesn't pay off. It's mostly my throat. If I don't get enough sleep, I get a cold and blow it, and 18,000, 40,000, even 60,000 people don't get a righteous count. It sounds corny but it's true." He also wants to trim himself down (he's now a "bear-shaped" 155 pounds) before it gets too late. But most important: "When you're physically active, your mind feels better, you think more clearly and you're less likely to be irritable." Crosby says he's begun to control his temper, blamed for numerous Byrd flaps and untold problems within CSNY.

"There was a time," he says, "when I would stop that song last night ['Guinnevere'] and call that audience a bunch of inconsiderate, stupid assholes—the three- or four-hundred Quaalude freaks in front, I mean." [In Vancouver, Crosby had left Joni Mitchell's "For Free" unfinished after several attempts to quiet the crowd failed. The audience, festival-seated and jammed in like what Crosby called "vertical sardines," were being hooted by people in the back to sit down. It happens everywhere.] "Anyway," says Crosby, "at least I've escaped some of that. It does it naturally. Life knocks corners off of everybody, you just go along bouncing down the street, you know."

But Crosby, not long ago, worried about the apocalypse and wrote a song about escaping, by wooden ships, with a few friends, to some island where their common values would create an unimpeachable little utopia. For almost two years after CSNY, he was determined at least to locate and buy an island for himself. Instead, as he puts it, "I settled for a home in suburbia." He bought a house in Mill Valley a year ago. He is content to sail off once in a while in his boat, the *Mayan,* to Hawaii or to Tahiti. And he no longer has doomsday on his mind. "That lurks a bit further away than before," he allows.

"But you gotta admit," he says, "we all did feel apocalyptic at one point, didn't we?" Jackson Browne didn't, I say.

Crosby smiles and nods. "That's true. Jackson—well, there he is, 'Everyman.' He really said it. He made me sit down and think. He wrote it for me, I guess. [Crosby sang harmony on the track, in fact.] He stopped me cold in my tracks. He nailed a certain thing in me, that escapist thing, and he called on something in me that's very strong, that I really believe in—and that's human possibility. I have a basic faith in the transcendence of the human spirit over everything. The present condition is not encouraging, but I believe in the human potential to an astounding—almost religious— degree, and he called on me hard."

It is easy, of course, to take a man's words from four years ago and laughingly offer them back to him for lunch. It is also easy to look at someone's photograph from ten years ago and laugh. The sounds should be equally hollow. Return with me to those quotes of yesteryear and note that in 1970, while this loudmouthed, honey-dripping bear of a Hollywood hippie rock & roll star was saying things like "I want to blow this political system," he was also quite far along in having dug to the bottom of that system and found—not pigs, but robbers: the oil company barons. His onstage raving at the Monterey Pop Festival in 1967 about who killed Kennedy also seems a little less mad these days. As does his depiction back then of Lyndon Johnson and Richard Nixon as politicians "who've made their deal years ago, who sold out to the special interests and controlling powers in this country in order to gain power."

At any rate, Crosby's got fewer stress marks these days. "Watergate [which he and Stills follow avidly, the way some pop stars follow NBA finals] has made the people more aware of what government is, and that's enormously encouraging. I think things are pretty healthy now."

And, of course, there's an effect on Crosby, the writer of "Long Time Gone" and "Almost Cut My Hair."

"There's a lot less hollowness," he says, "a lot less loneliness. I've had an old lady for two, three years, and a wider circle of friends that includes a lot of people who have nothing to do with music—boat people. And it helps balance. Music itself is wonderful but the business needs a little balance from the outside world. It's a very good real world: They're a bunch of realistic people, and living on boats, sailing long distances, is very real. The ocean doesn't know who you are and doesn't care. I know it's helped me, given me a different perspective. When I was with the Byrds and living in L.A., I thought that was everything that was happening in the world. But there's stuff happening out there that has nothing to do with music, concerts, money and show biz."

Early this year, Graham Nash ascribed CSNY's inability to regroup to "stupid, infantile ego problems." In Denver, Nash is more specific: "It was between me and Stephen and it was over a lady. That's why we broke up that first time."

Crosby agrees with Nash's earlier description. "Ego being out of balance with intelligent cooperation makes you impossible to work with," he says, "and some of us were more guilty than others and it's nobody's business which ones they are." What about persistent stories about Stills and Young and their fights? "Oh, no," says Crosby. "It's not that simple. We're all four guilty as shit." Crosby laughs at the past. "The reasons . . . I could come back and forth with reasons all day, but it would sound like two high school kids arguing in homeroom about who did what to who first. I don't remember all that and I don't want to; that's like holding grudges. The basic thing is we all had to get to a point where we wanted to play with each other, where we felt like, 'Outtasight, I want to be in a band now, I want to play and sing harmony with *those* guys.' "

So Stills and Young didn't want to be with each other, or with Nash and Crosby, when they did their own tours?

"No," says Crosby. They were looking for "self-expression."

Crosby himself went out looking for his own audience—or, more accurately, "Elliot insisted I do it. He said it'd change how I felt about myself. It did. It gave me much more confidence."

First, he coupled up with Nash for a month-long acoustic tour in the fall of 1971, after the first attempted CSNY regrouping fell through. They toured again a year later, and, last fall, after another reunion dissolved, each took off for short tours through Eastern college towns, doing a half-dozen shows each.

"I flat loved it," says Crosby, "and I found all the weirdos who would come out just to see me. I found out that there is a group that likes my songs."

Earlier on the tour, Crosby has given the impression that he was an elitist about his music; that he considers some of the newer forces in rock—the noisier, splashier, bi-sexier acts—to be something less than valid. In St. Paul, Crosby seeks to clarify: "I've learned that it's different audiences out there. It is not the same people who go to a Uriah Heep concert as go to a Bob Dylan concert. I tell you what's been happening. There has been a change in the scene and it's mostly because we copped out, in a sense, in doing what we're supposed to do. Us and Dylan and, in a sense, Joni and James and other people who are word/music people. There was a hiatus there. The whole community of people who write word music, in that kind of changes and space and emotional context, the descendants of Dylan and the Beatles and folk music. We are not supposed to lead any segment of the population but I think we're supposed to reflect it and respond to it. But I think that segment hasn't been reflected musically in a long time and to that extent we just haven't been pulling our weight. Those people just didn't have concerts to go to until Dylan went out. That was the icebreaker. I bet him being out and us going out, you'll see a couple of other people try to get back out, too. Something's going on that I think is really good."

So Crosby won't dismiss even the crappiest music as crap. As he sees it: "We're back to 'Wooly Bully' and 'Tambourine Man' again. Two to one, 'Wooly Bully' outsold 'Tambourine Man,' and that's an *important fact.* Remember where that bell curve is. You got to know that the world's not like you."

"I have no quibble with that. I'm glad all those people have any music at all that they like; I'd rather have them listening to even music that I don't think is music than going out and street-fighting or laying around taking Quaaludes. If it's a party for them, good. I want everybody to have a party."

THE PIANO IS JUST being tickled to death; out comes "It Had to Be You." Over the central bar area, hanging off to the side of a display of circular ceiling lightbulbs, is the TV, tuned to the All-Star Game. Summertime in Denver, at the Hampshire House tavern, and Graham Nash is on his third Coke. He looks around. "Isn't this fuckin' bizarre," he says, soft and hoarsely. The observation is more in wonderment than in amusement.

Outside the hotel, he'd responded to a "how are you" with a "lousy." With the group's strategically relaxed schedule—roughly two days off for every concert—Nash is finding himself bored and depressed on this, the evening of his arrival.

We decide to have a drink. I ask him to paint a portrait of himself over the past few years since 1970. He proceeds to draw a surprisingly blue picture of the spoils of success and the elusiveness of inner harmony.

"When CSNY decided that emotionally it couldn't make it as a band, that we couldn't stand each other for more than the three hours it took to play together, I retreated. First I toured with David 'cause I still had that energy. Then I turned thirty and I took acid on my birthday at Vanessi's [an Italian restaurant in the San Francisco North Beach area that, along with North Beach, keeps late hours]. I went to mix my and David's album and I was trying to mix 'Where Will I Be,' which is musically very spacy and difficult to get on top of when you're—well, you just get side-tripped. 'What's on track two? Wow, what a *cowbell!*' But I decided that I finally really needed to find out who the fuck I was, what was important to me in terms of how much I could put up with to be able to live with myself. So I took a couple of years where I didn't do too much except finish my house [a Victorian in the Haight-Ashbury], write several songs and just stay away."

"What did you have to put up with in order to live with yourself?"

"There's a certain thing that goes on, you face a certain situation and you deal with it one way. But if that situation means that whoever you went through the scene with doesn't grow from that situation, you bullshit yourself. Like if someone pulls a trip and you let it go, you're not helping either yourself or the other person, and I decided I was going to try and be as honest as I could in my relationships. I changed dramatically as a person because I was always very easygoing and outward, and I'm not easygoing now. . . .

"And before, when I got depressed, I could always go to someone's room and yuk it up, just fake my way out of it. But I can't do that anymore. And girlfriends come up and hug me and I feel . . . I don't know, I don't feel *anything.* And I'm trying to figure out whether I've thought myself into a paralysis of feeling.

"There's something in me that automatically makes me do the positive thing in any given situation. It's because I've trained myself that way. The bad feeling is wondering whether I really mean it or whether I'm just on automatic pilot."

Once a thin man with a shaggy haircut and a neat goatee to dramatize a rectangular face, Graham Nash is now a thin man with a less-controlled look about the head and beard. He wears black high-top gym shoes, patched jeans and two shirts, one gray, one army tan, all four sleeves rolled up.

"All my aware life," he is saying, "from age sixteen, seventeen, eighteen, I've been an object. A fucking object. That's why I try very hard to be as unrecognizable as possible."

A reporter is by no means an analyst, although by the nature of the work, one learns to peel a head through questions. I offer a phrase I've heard from friends who've been in therapy—"self-love."

"Yeah," says Graham. "I've got to try and see the good things that I am. David is doing numbers on me every day, 'cause he sees me sinking and sinking. He was driving the car today—and he asked how I was. And I said, 'I don't know; I'm just glad that we're getting off onstage.' And he said, 'Feeling a bit shaky, hey?' And I said yeah. And he turned around—which for David is very unheard of—and he said, 'You should look at the good things that you are instead of the bullshit.' And he turned back and continued driving. But just the fact that he turned away—I mean, you know David and driving and Christine [Crosby's girlfriend, killed in an auto accident in 1969]. And I knew he sincerely meant it. David said, 'Look, you very rarely lie to others and you're as honest as you can be,' but that's not special or 'good' to me. I think consideration of others, general well-being and things like that are normal."

Earlier, Nash had depicted himself as a misanthrope. I venture, now, that he must find most "normal" people less than "good."

"I see mirrors," he says. "I see a reflection in everybody; I see somebody fuck up and I get mad and see me fucking up and it's so unlike me. I was always the other way, saying, 'No, come on, it's better than that.' I was always where David is now and David used to be where I am."

Nash looks up from his fourth Coke. "That's strange, I just realized that."

That evening David is at the wheel again, on the way with Stills and Nash to the Clapton concert. Stills is a friend of Clapton's from the days of Springfield and Cream. When Stills lived in London, the two had gotten together numerous times to talk, jam and record. Stills credits Clapton with teaching him "fluidity . . . in that style of real nicely constructed blues guitar." He is thinking of a jam tonight, but his head is still feeling the effects of his audience with Dylan.

"I don't know if I could play tonight, even if he asked me," he says in the car. "Usually it's the other way—I have to twist his arm to play with me." Crosby advises: "Well, there'll be other times." He doesn't turn his head.

At the concert Stills will stay on the sidelines, watching the show from a seat onstage. Nash, meantime, stays away from the action, standing early on by himself at the rear of the auditorium building.

Graham Nash's melancholy may be at least partly the product of rejection. All four members of the group have suffered declining album sales on their own (with Young the slowest to fall), but none ever failed to reach the charts—until this spring and Nash's *Wild Tales*.

"I *was* a little disappointed in the response," he says. It's an understatement. He continues: "It almost feels to me like no one heard it and that hurts for any artist trying to communicate. I haven't even asked about the sales." In contrast, he claims his first solo, *Songs for Beginners,* hit the Top Ten and the Nash/Crosby album reached Number Two. Atlantic Records, however, says that the two albums did not do as well as Nash recalls.

The first album, *Crosby, Stills and Nash,* has now reached 2.1 million units in sales; the first CSNY album has sold 2.5, and *4 Way Street,* the double live set, sold 900,000. Stills' two solo albums went 800,000 and 600,000, respectively; the first Manassas product, a double album, sold over 400,000 and *Down the Road,* with Manassas, is near 300,000.

Neil Young, whose pre-CSNY album, *Everybody Knows This Is Nowhere,* sold 1.3 million, hit two highs after joining the group: *After the Gold Rush* (1.8 million) and *Harvest* (two million). *Journey Through the Past,* the soundtrack to his largely unseen film, was a relative bomb at 300,000 and *Time Fades Away,* from the Stray Gators tour, is at 480,000. Crosby's one solo, according to Crosby himself, sold near 500,000.

In the last year, then, no single member—C, S, N or Y—approached the royalty riches of the old days. Still the group fends off the offensive notion that they might be doing this for the money.

"I think that assumption is very easy to come to," says Stills, who before the tour joked to one reporter: "The last time it was for the music, the art and the chicks; this time it's for the cash!"

Now, riding over the Bay Bridge, he's saying it doesn't matter what he says about the group's being back for the music. "Even if you write it down word for word, if somebody wants to believe it's bullshit, it's still bullshit. I think it has to do with everyone realizing that the service we can do each other was greater than how we were doing by ourselves. And without that, the other considerations never come into play. Of course the money's good. I mean, I can build the kind of studio I want to build and, you know, I ain't got no apologies to make. I don't think we're ripping anybody off. If people weren't interested they wouldn't come. That's the difference between business and art. And we are all four of us very, very dedicated to our art form." And that is word for word.

Nash reasons it out this way: "It can't be the money or we'd have been playing these last four years and making millions of dollars. When we left it, we were pretty hot. We could've continued for a couple years but we didn't because we couldn't stand each other."

And if that's not honest enough for you, Crosby weighs in. I had asked him not about money but about the future of CSNY.

"My guess," he says, "is that we won't stay together. We'll make an album and not stay together. I think the soonest you would see us come together again after we made the album would be the next summer. And even that might be too soon. Why? Because contrary to everybody else, who seem to want to just grind it out by the pound as fast as they humanly can—you know, 'make your hay while you can'—we like to do it when we feel like it, so that it doesn't come out sounding to you like it's been ground out by the pound. So we get together and play when it's exciting to do it—and it isn't exciting to do it all the time."

SOMEWHERE IN THE MIDDLE of "Suite: Judy Blue Eyes," on the line, "It's my heart that's a-sufferin', it's a-dyin'," Stephen Stills trills a stretched-out "heart," turns the word into a one-note blues number, and 19,000 people in St. Paul whoop it up. Moments later they rock the coliseum with an ovation that lasts, by my count, a full 170 seconds, during which matches get lit and lifted and firecrackers ignited. An attempt by Nash to speak—he gets out a "Jesus!"—is greeted by another wave of all the rabble a rock & roll crowd can crank up these days.

It is two more hours before the concert ends and the group files past the towel man, down the stairs and back into their dark dressing room. Outside the room in an adjoining, bright white bathroom, Crosby and Nash stop to talk. Crosby is wiping his forehead, keeping the dressing room door closed to outsiders and talking about the concert.

"Steve was outrageous," he says. "That was the best response we've ever had to that song." He turns to Nash. "Did we sing the suite or did we sing the suite?" Nash laughs and recalls the ovation. "That was ridiculous. I started laughing! I've never had to *stop* them before." He turns toward the dressing room and as Crosby pulls open the door, someone inside—it kinda sounds like that reluctant star—yells out: "A great show!"

STEPHEN HOLDEN

ON THE BEACH ALBUM REVIEW
Neil Young: The Sands of Time

SINCE HIS DAYS WITH Buffalo Springfield, the shifts in Neil Young's preoccupations have presented a barometer of a generation's attitudes toward itself, reflecting the dissolution of political idealism and, beyond that, the end of the romance of youth itself. Even in such early ballads as "Sugar Mountain" and "I Am a Child," Young gently warned against living with the illusion of perpetual youth, while his childlike vocals tantalized us with the possibility. The pain of facing adult reality at an age and in an era that encouraged prolonged adolescent fantasy comprised the underlying theme of Young's first three solo albums, a trilogy that culminated in *After the Gold Rush,* perhaps the quintessential turn-of-the-decade album by a folk-rock soloist.

Whereas Bob Dylan's music formed the aesthetic spearhead of generational rage and moral fervor in the mid-Sixties, Young's subsequently expressed, with equal credibility, the accompanying guilt, self-doubt and paranoia, especially in its obsession with time and age. Ironically, Young achieved superstar status with his most compromised album, *Harvest,* a sweetened rehash of ideas from *After the Gold Rush*. But Young resisted the temptation to venture further toward the MOR style that had cinched his audience; and his live album, *Time Fades Away,* released two years after *Harvest,* came as a rude about-face.

On the Beach is Neil Young's best album since *After the Gold Rush*. Though a studio album, its sound is raw and spare, as bracing as Dylan's *Planet Waves*. Mostly self-produced, *On the Beach* boasts fine instrumental support, notably by guitarist Ben Keith (who shares vocals with Young on two cuts), Rusty Kershaw (fiddle and slide guitar on two cuts), and Band members Rick Danko (bass) and Levon Helm (drums) on the album's most exciting track, "Revolution Blues."

The hard-edged sound of *On the Beach* is a contributing factor to its greatness, since the album poses aesthetic and political questions too serious to be treated prettily. Through various opposed personae, Young evokes primary social and psychic polarities that exemplify the deterioration of American culture. Though not named, the figures of Charles Manson and

Patricia Hearst appear as emblems of apocalyptic social dislocation in the album's two masterpieces, "Revolution Blues" and "Ambulance Blues." In each song, by empathizing with the emotions of both predators and victims, Young has dared what no other major white rock artist (except John Lennon) has—to embrace, expose and perhaps help purge the collective paranoia and guilt of an insane society, acting it out without apology or explanation.

"Walk On," a succinct rejection of Sixties fantasies, revolves around a bitter observation about growing up: "Sooner or later it all gets real / Walk on." "See the Sky About to Rain" and "For the Turnstiles," tremulous, fatalistic ballads, encompass images of violence, corruption and disintegration, their meanings contained in their cryptic titles, each a slogan, a mantra, a scrawl of graffiti. The driving, terrifying vision of "Revolution Blues" is counterpointed by the equally horrifying "Vampire Blues."

Two ballads, "Motion Pictures" and "Ambulance Blues," feature Young singing almost an octave lower than normal and sounding for the first time in his career morally arrogant. "On the Beach," the seven-minute title cut, is the album's most questionable inclusion, a lethargic, whining meditation on the reasons not to remain psychically isolated in Los Angeles. It shows Young immersed in self-pity—one of the taboos of rock that Young has long sought to redeem. Though Young's weariness of civilization also supplies the theme of "Motion Pictures," it is melodically fluent and the album's only direct message of love.

The nine-minute "Ambulance Blues," which closes the album, is the tour de force of Young's recording career. Doubling on acoustic guitar and harmonica and backed by Kershaw's eloquent fiddling, Young summarizes his entire musical/political past, beginning with the idealism of "the old folkie days," then impressionistically evoking specific social traumas, among them Watergate and the Hearst saga. He addresses us with a populist truism which he repeats in a voice that quietly spits in our faces: "You're all just pissin' in the wind." The last verse cites Nixon as both symptom and cause of a predicament that is frightening beyond comprehension:

> I never knew a man could tell so many lies
> He had a different story for every set of eyes
> How can he remember who he's talkin' to
> 'Cause I know it ain't me
> And I hope it isn't you.

In its appeal to a post-revolutionary, post-psychedelic generation of young Americans, "Ambulance Blues" stands as an epic lamentation, as irrefutable a piece of song–poetry as Paul Simon's "American Tune" and Jackson Browne's "For Everyman." I could not imagine anyone but Young singing it.

On the Beach is one of the most despairing albums of the decade, a bitter testament from one who has come through the fire and gone back into it.

■ **RANDOM NOTES** (February 27, 1975)

CSNY have been sneaking in and out of the studios since around New Year's with Lee Sklar, Russ Kunkel and Bill Kreutzmann assisting on bass and drums. Reports have them bickering intensely, chiefly Neil Young and Stephen Stills. Our source explains that Young is suffering lapses of concentration and complaining to Nash, Crosby and Stills that he "feels like he's somewhere else."

■ **RANDOM NOTES** (June 19, 1975)

Ex-Buffalo Springfield drummer Dewey Martin is suing Stephen Stills, Neil Young, fellow BS'ers Bruce Palmer and Richie Furay, ex-manager Richard Davis and Atlantic for $150,-000. Martin claims he was duped into signing away his interest in the group in 1968 and that the $150,000 represents royalties he would have earned since then.

CAMERON CROWE

SO HARD TO MAKE ARRANGEMENTS FOR YOURSELF

The ROLLING STONE Interview with Neil Young

NEARING THIRTY, NEIL YOUNG is the most enigmatic of all the super-stars to emerge from Buffalo Springfield and Crosby, Stills, Nash and Young. His often cryptic studies of lonely desperation and shaky-voiced antiheroics have led many to brand him a loner and a recluse. *Harvest* was the last time that he struck the delicate balance between critical and commercial acceptance, and his subsequent albums have grown increasingly inaccessible to a mass audience.

Young's first comprehensive interview comes at a seeming turning point in his life and career. After an amicable breakup with actress Carrie Snodgress, he's moved from his Northern California ranch to the relative hustle and bustle of Malibu. In the words of a close friend, he seems "frisky . . . in an incredible mood." Young has unwound to the point where he can approach a story about his career as potentially "a lot of fun."

The interview was held while cruising down Sunset Boulevard in a rented red Mercedes and on the back porch of his Malibu beach house. Cooperative throughout, Young only made a single request: "Just keep one thing in mind," he said as soon as the tape recorder had been turned off for the last time. "I may remember it all differently tomorrow."

Why is it that you've finally decided to talk now? For the past five years journalists requesting Neil Young interviews were told you had nothing to say.

There's a lot I have to say. I never did interviews because they always got me in trouble. Always. They never came out right. I just don't like them. As a matter of fact, the more I didn't do them the more they wanted them; the more I said by not saying anything. But things change, you know. I feel very free now. I don't have an old lady anymore. I relate it a lot to that. I'm back living in Southern California. I feel more open than I have in a long while. I'm coming out and speaking to a lot of people. I feel like something new is happening in my life.

I'm really turned on by the new music I'm making now, back with

Crazy Horse. Today, even as I'm talking, the songs are running through my head. I'm excited. I think everything I've done is valid or else I wouldn't have released it, but I do realize the last three albums have been a certain way. I know I've gotten a lot of bad publicity for them. Somehow I feel like I've surfaced out of some kind of murk. And the proof will be in my next album. *Tonight's the Night*, I would say, is the final chapter of a period I went through.

Why the murky period?

Oh, I don't know. Danny's death probably tripped it off. Danny Whitten [leader of Crazy Horse and Young's rhythm guitarist/second vocalist]. It happened right before the *Time Fades Away* tour. He was supposed to be in the group. We [Ben Keith, steel guitar; Jack Nitzsche, piano; Tim Drummond, bass; Kenny Buttrey, drums; and Young] were rehearsing with him and he just couldn't cut it. He couldn't remember anything. He was too out of it. Too far gone. I had to tell him to go back to L.A. "It's not happening, man. You're not together enough." He just said, "I've got nowhere else to go, man. How am I gonna tell my friends?" And he split. That *night* the coroner called me from L.A. and told me he'd OD'ed. That blew my mind. Fucking blew my mind. I loved Danny. I felt responsible. And from there, I had to go right out on this huge tour of huge arenas. I was very nervous and . . . insecure.

Why, then, did you release a live album?

I thought it was valid. *Time Fades Away* was a very nervous album. And that's exactly where I was at on the tour. If you ever sat down and listened to all my records, there'd be a place for it in there. Not that you'd go there every time you wanted to enjoy some music, but if you're on the trip it's important. Every one of my records, to me, is like an ongoing autobiography. I can't write the same book every time. There are artists that can. They put out three or four albums every year and everything fucking sounds the same. That's great. Somebody's trying to communicate to a lot of people and give them the kind of music that they know they want to hear. That isn't my trip. My trip is to express what's on my mind. I don't expect people to listen to my music all the time. Sometimes it's too intense. If you're gonna put a record on at eleven in the morning, don't put on *Tonight's the Night*. Put on the Doobie Brothers.

Time Fades Away, *as the follow-up to* Harvest, *could have been a huge album . . .*

If it had been commercial.

As it is, it's one of your least selling solo albums. Did you realize what you were sacrificing at the time?

I probably did. I imagine I could have come up with the perfect follow-up album. A real winner. But it would have been something that everybody was expecting. And when it got there they would have thought that they understood what I was all about and that would have been it for me. I would have painted myself in the corner. The fact is I'm not that lone, laid-back figure with a guitar. I'm just not that way anymore. I don't want to feel like people expect me to be a certain way. Nobody expected *Time Fades Away* and I'm not sorry I put it out. I didn't need the money, I didn't need the fame. You gotta keep changing. Shirts, old ladies, whatever. I'd rather keep changing and lose a lot of people along the way. If that's the price, I'll pay it. I don't give a shit if my audience is a hundred or a hundred million. It doesn't make any difference to me. I'm convinced that what sells and what I do are two completely different things. If they meet, it's coincidence. I just appreciate the freedom to put out an album like *Tonight's the Night* if I want to.

You sound pretty drunk on that album.

I would have to say that's the most liquid album I've ever made [*laughs*]. You almost need a life preserver to get through that one. We were all leaning on the ol' cactus . . . and, again, I think that it's something people should hear. They should hear what the artist sounds like under all circumstances if they want to get a complete portrait. Everybody gets fucked up, man. Everybody gets fucked up sooner or later. You're just pretending if you don't let your music get just as liquid as you are when you're really high.

Is that the point of the album?

No. No. That's the means to an end. *Tonight's the Night* is like an OD letter. The whole thing is about life, dope and death. When we [guitarist/pianist Nils Lofgren, bassist Billy Talbot, and drummer Ralph Molina Young] played that music we were all thinking of Danny Whitten and Bruce Berry, two close members of our unit lost to junk overdoses. The *Tonight's the Night* sessions were the first time what was left of Crazy Horse had gotten together since Danny died. It was up to us to get the strength together among us to fill the hole he left. The other OD, Bruce Berry, was CSNY's roadie for a long time. His brother Ken runs Studio Instrument Rentals, where we recorded the album. So we had a lot of vibes going for us. There was a lot of spirit in the music we made. It's funny, I remember the whole experience in black and white. We'd go down to S.I.R. about five in the afternoon and start getting high, drinking tequila and playing pool. About midnight, we'd start playing. And we played Bruce and Danny on their way all through the night. I'm not a junkie and I won't even try it out to check out what it's like . . . but we all got high enough, right out there on the edge where we felt wide open to the whole mood. It was spooky. I probably *feel* this album more than anything else I've ever done.

Why did you wait until now to release Tonight's the Night? *Isn't it almost two years old?*

I never finished it. I only had nine songs, so I set the whole thing aside and did *On the Beach* instead. It took Elliot [manager Elliot Roberts] to finish *Tonight's the Night*. You see, a while back there were some people who were gonna make a Broadway show out of the story of Bruce Berry and everything. They even had a script written. We were putting together a tape for them, and in the process of listening back on the old tracks, Elliot found three even older songs that related to the trip, "Lookout Joe," "Borrowed Tune" and "Come on Baby Let's Go Downtown," a live track from when I played the Fillmore East with Crazy Horse. Danny even sings lead on that one. Elliot added those songs to the original nine and sequenced them all into a cohesive story. But I still had no plans whatsoever to release it. I already had another new album called *Homegrown* in the can. The cover was finished and everything. [*laughs*] Ah, but they'll never hear that one.

Okay. Why not?

I'll tell you the whole story. I had a playback party for *Homegrown* for me and about ten friends. We were out of our minds. We all listened to the album and *Tonight's the Night* happened to be on the same reel. So we listened to that too, just for laughs. No comparison.

So you released Tonight's the Night. *Just like that?*

Not because *Homegrown* wasn't as good. A lot of people would probably say that it's better. I know the first time I listened back on *Tonight's the Night* it was the most out-of-tune thing I'd ever heard. Everyone's off-key. I couldn't hack it. But by listening to those two albums back to back at the party, I started to see the weaknesses in *Homegrown*. I took *Tonight's the Night* because of its overall strength in performance and feeling. The theme may be a little depressing, but the general feeling is much more elevating than *Homegrown*. Putting this album out is almost an experiment. I fully expect some of the most determinedly worst reviews I've ever had. I mean if anybody really wanted to let go, they could do it on this one. And undoubtedly a few people will. That's good for them, though. I like to see people make giant breakthroughs for themselves. It's good for their psyche to get it all off their chests. [*laughs*]. I've seen *Tonight's the Night* draw a line everywhere it's been played. People who thought they would never dislike anything I did fall on the other side of the line. Others who thought, "I can't listen to that cat. He's just too sad," or whatever. . . . "His voice is funny."

They listen another way now. I'm sure parts of *Homegrown* will surface on other albums of mine. There's some beautiful stuff that Emmylou Harris sings harmony on. I don't know. That record might be more what people would rather hear from me now, but it was just a very down album. It was the darker side to *Harvest*. A lot of the songs had to do with me breaking up with my old lady. It was a little too personal . . . it scared me. Plus, I had just released *On the Beach,* probably one of the most depressing records I've ever made. I don't want to get down to the point where I can't even get up. I mean there's something to going down there and looking around, but I don't know about sticking around.

You didn't come from a musical family. . . .

Well, my father played a little ukulele. [*laughs*] It just happened. I felt it. I couldn't stop thinking about it. All of a sudden I wanted a guitar and that was it. I started playing around the Winnipeg community clubs, high school dances. I played as much as I could.

With a band?

Oh yeah, always with a band. I never tried it solo until I was nineteen. Eighteen or nineteen.

Were you writing at the time?

I started off writing instrumentals. Words came much later. My idol at the time was Hank B. Marvin, Cliff Richard's guitar player in the Shadows. He was the hero of all the guitar players around Winnipeg at the time. Randy Bachman too; he was around then, playing the same circuit. He had a great sound. Used to use a tape repeat.

When did you start singing?

I remember singing Beatles tunes . . . the first song I ever sang in front of people was "It Won't Be Long" and then "Money (That's What I Want)." That was in the Calvin High School cafeteria. My big moment.

How much different from the States was growing up in Canada?

Everybody in Canada wants to get to the States. At least they did then. I couldn't wait to get out of there because I knew my only chance to be heard was in the States. But I couldn't get down there without a working permit, and I didn't have one. So eventually I just came down illegally and it took until 1970 for me to get a green card. I worked illegally during all of the Buffalo Springfield and some of Crosby, Stills, Nash and Young. I didn't have any papers. I couldn't get a card because I would be replacing an American musician in the union. You had to be real well known and irreplaceable and a separate entity by yourself. So I got the card after I got that kind of stature—which you can't get without fucking being here . . . the whole thing is ridiculous. The only way to get in is to be here. You can't be here unless it's all right for you to be here. So fuck it. It's like "throw the witch in the water and if it drowns it wasn't a witch. If it comes up, it is a witch and then you kill it." Same logic. But we finally got it together.

Did you know Joni Mitchell in those days?

I've known Joni since I was eighteen. I met her in one of the coffee-houses. She was beautiful. That was my first impression. She was real frail and wispy looking. And her cheekbones were so beautifully shaped. She'd always wear light satins and silks. I remember thinking that if you blew hard enough, you could probably knock her over. She could hold up a Martin D18 pretty well, though. What an incredible talent she is. She writes about her relationships so much more vividly than I do. I use . . . I guess I put more of a veil over what I'm talking about. I've written a few songs that were as stark as hers. Songs like "Pardon My Heart," "Home Fires," "Love Art Blues" . . . almost all of *Homegrown*. I've never released any of those. And I probably never will. I think I'd be too embarrassed to put them out. They're a little *too* real.

How do you look back on the whole Buffalo Springfield experience?

Great experience. Those were really good days. Great people. Every-body in that group was a fucking genius at what they did. That was a great group, man. There'll never be another Buffalo Springfield. Never. Every-body's gone such separate ways now, I don't know. If everybody showed up in one place at one time with all the amps and everything, I'd love it. But I'd sure as hell hate to have to get it together. I'd love to play with that band again, just to see if the buzz was still there.

There's a few stock Springfield myths I should ask you about. How about the old hearse story?

True. Bruce and I were tooling around L.A. in my hearse. I loved the hearse. Six people could be getting high in the front and back and nobody would be able to see in because of the curtains. The heater was great. And the tray . . . the tray was dynamite. You open the side door and the tray whips right out onto the sidewalk. What could be cooler than that? What a way to make your entrance. Pull up to a gig and just wheel out all your stuff on the tray. Anyway, Bruce and I were taking in California. The Promised Land. We were heading up to San Francisco. Stephen and Richie Furay, who were in town putting together a band, just happened to be driving around too. Stephen had met me before and remembered I had a hearse. As soon as he saw the Ontario plates, he knew it was me. So they stopped us. I was happy to see fucking *anybody* I knew. And it seemed very logical to us that we form a band. We picked up Dewey Martin for the drums, which was my idea, four or five days later. Stephen was really pulling for Billy Munday at the time. He'd say "Yeah, yeah, yeah. Dewey's good, but *Jesus* . . . he talks too fucking much." I was right though. Dewey was fucking good.

How much has the friction between you and Stills been beneficial over the years?

I think people really have that friction business out of hand. Stephen and I just play really good together. People can't comprehend that we both can play lead guitar in the band and not fight over it. We have total respect for musicianship and we both bring out the perfectionist in each other. We're both very intense, but that's part of our relationship. We both enjoy that. It's part of doing what we do. In that respect being at loggerheads has worked to our advantage. Stephen Stills and I have made some incredible music with each other. Especially in the Springfield. We were young. We had a lot of energy.

Why did you leave the band?

I just couldn't handle it toward the end. My nerves couldn't handle the trip. It wasn't me scheming on a solo career, it wasn't anything but my nerves. Everything started to go too fucking fast, I can tell that now. I was going crazy, you know, joining and quitting and joining again. I began to feel like I didn't have to answer or obey anyone. I needed more space. That was a big problem in my head. So I'd quit, then I'd come back 'cause it sounded so good. It was a constant problem. I just wasn't mature enough to deal with it. I was very young. We were getting the shaft from every angle and it seemed like we were trying to make it so bad and were getting nowhere. The following we had in the beginning, and those people know who they are, was a real special thing. It gave all of us, I think, the strength to do what we've done. With the *intensity* that we've been able to do it. Those few people who were there in the very beginning.

Last Springfield question. Are there, in fact, several albums of unreleased material?

I've got all of that. I've got those tapes.

Why have you sat on them for so long? What are you waiting for?

I'll wait until I hear from some of the other guys. See if anybody else has any tapes. I don't know if Richie or Dicky Davis [Springfield road manager] has anything. I've got good stuff. Great songs. "My Kind of Love," "My Angel," "Down to the Wire," "Baby Don't Scold Me." We'll see what happens.

What was your life like after the Springfield?

It was all right. I needed to get out to the sticks for a while and just relax. I headed for Topanga Canyon and got myself together. I bought a big house that overlooked the whole canyon. I eventually got out of that house because I couldn't handle all the people who kept coming up all the time. Sure was a comfortable fucking place . . . that was '69, about when I started living with my first wife, Susan. Beautiful woman.

Was your first solo album a love song for her?

No. Very few of my albums are love songs to anyone. Music is so big, man, it just takes up a lot of room. I've dedicated my life to my music so far. And every time I've let it slip and gotten somewhere else, it's showed. Music lasts . . . a lot longer than relationships do. My first album was very much a first album. I wanted to prove to myself that I could do it. And I did, thanks to the wonder of modern machinery. That first album was overdub city. It's still one of my favorites, though. *Everybody Knows This Is Nowhere* is probably my best. It's my favorite one. I've always loved Crazy Horse from the first time I heard the Rockets album on White Whale. The original band we had in '69 and '70—Molina, Talbot, Whitten and me. That was *wonderful.* And it's back that way again now. Everything I've ever done with Crazy Horse has been incredible. Just for the *feeling,* if nothing else.

Why did you join CSNY, then? You were already working steadily with Crazy Horse.

Stephen. I love playing with the other guys, but playing with Stephen is special. David is an excellent rhythm guitarist and Graham sings so great . . . shit, I don't have to tell anybody those guys are phenomenal. I knew it would be fun. I didn't have to be out front. I could lay back. It didn't have to be me all the time. They were a big group and it was easy for me. I could still work double time with Crazy Horse. With CSNY, I was basically just an instrumentalist that sang a couple of songs with them. It was easy. And the music was great. CSNY, I think, has always been a lot bigger thing to everybody else than it is to us. People always refer to me as Neil Young of CSNY, right? It's not my main trip. It's something that I do every once in a while. I've constantly been working on my own trip all along. And now that Crazy Horse is back in shape, I'm even more self-involved.

For sure CSNY put my name out there. They gave me a lot of publicity. But, in all modesty, *After the Gold Rush,* which was kind of the turning point, was a strong album. I really think it was. A lot of hard work went into it. Everything was there. The picture it painted was a strong one. *After the Gold Rush* was the spirit of Topanga Canyon. It seemed like I realized that I'd gotten somewhere. I joined CSNY and was still working a lot with Crazy Horse . . . I was playing all the time. And having a great time. Right after that album, I left the house. It was a good coda.

How did you cope with your first real blast of superstardom after that?

The first thing I did was a long tour of small halls. Just me and a guitar. I loved it. It was real personal. Very much a one-on-one thing with the crowd. It was later, after *Harvest,* that I hid myself away. I tried to stay away from it all. I thought the record [*Harvest*] was good, but I also knew that something else was dying. I became very reclusive. I didn't want to come out much.

Why? Were you depressed? Scared?

I think I was pretty happy. In spite of everything, I had my old lady and moved to the ranch. A lot of it was my back. I was in and out of hospitals for the two years between *After the Gold Rush* and *Harvest.* I have one weak side and all the muscles slipped on me. My discs slipped. I couldn't hold my guitar up. That's why I sat down on my whole solo tour. I couldn't move around too well, so I laid low for a long time on the ranch and just didn't have any contact, you know. I wore a brace. Crosby would come up to see how I was, we'd go for a walk and it took me forty-five minutes to get to the studio, which is only 400 yards from the house. I could only stand up four hours a day. I recorded most of *Harvest* in the brace. That's a lot of the reason it's such a mellow album. I couldn't physically play an electric guitar. "Are You Ready for the Country," "Alabama" and "Words" were all done after I had the operation. The doctors were starting to talk about wheel-chairs and shit, so I had some discs removed. But for the most part, I spent two years flat on my back. I had a lot of time to think about what had happened to me.

Have you ever been in analysis?

You mean have I ever been to a psychiatrist? No [*laughs*]. They're all real interested in me, though. They always ask a lot of questions when I'm around them.

What do they ask?

Well, I had some seizures. They used to ask me a lot of questions about how I felt, stuff like that. I told them all the thoughts I have and the images I see if I, you know, faint or fall down or something. That's not real important, though.

Do you still have seizures?

Yeah, I still do. I wish I didn't. I thought I had it licked.

Is it a physical or mental . . .

I don't know. Epilepsy is something nobody knows much about. It's just part of me. Part of my head, part of what's happening in there. Some-times something in my brain triggers it off. Sometimes when I get really high, it's a very psychedelic experience to have a seizure. You slip into some other world. Your body's flapping around and you're biting your tongue and batting your head on the ground but your mind is off somewhere else. The only scary thing about it is not going or being there, it's realizing you're totally comfortable in this . . . *void.* And that shocks you back into reality. It's a very disorienting experience. It's difficult to get a grip on yourself. The last time it happened, it took about an hour and a half of just walking around the ranch with two of my friends to get it together.

Has it ever happened onstage?

No. Never has. I felt like it was a couple times and I've always left the stage. I get too high or something. It's just pressure from around, you know. That's why I don't like crowds too much.

What were the sessions like for Déjà Vu? *Was it a band effort?*

The band sessions on that record were "Helpless," "Woodstock" and "Almost Cut My Hair." That was Crosby, Stills, Nash and Young. All the other ones were combinations, records that were more done by one person using the other people. "Woodstock" was a *great* record at first. It was a great live record, man. Everyone played and sang at once. Stephen sang the shit out of it. The track was magic. Then, later on, they were in the studio for a long time and started nitpicking. Sure enough, Stephen erased the vocal and put another one on that wasn't nearly as incredible. They did a lot of things over again that I thought were more raw and vital sounding. But that's all personal taste. I'm only saying that because it might be interesting to some people how we put that album together. I'm happy with every one of the things I've recorded with them. They turned out really fine. I certainly don't hold any grudges.

You seem a bit defensive.

Well, everybody always concentrates on this whole thing that we fight all the time among each other. That's a load of shit. They don't know what the fuck they're talking about. It's all rumors. When the four of us are together it's real intense. When you're dealing with any four totally different people who all have ideas on how to do one thing, it gets steamy. And we love it, man. We're having a great time. People make up so much shit, though. I've read so much gossip in ROLLING STONE alone . . . Ann Landers would blanch. It would surprise you. Somehow we've gotten on this social-register level and it has nothing to do with what we're trying to put out. The music press writes the weirdest shit about us. They're just wasting their fucking time.

There was a recent item published that CSNY had tried to record a new album but couldn't because you "felt someplace else."

Total bullshit. That's just somebody trying to come up with a good line and stick it in my mouth. "Yeah, that's kind of ethereal. Sounds like something Neil Young might say." And bingo . . . it's like they were there. We had some recording sessions, you know, and we recorded a few things. That's what happened. We went down to the Record Plant in Sausalito, rented some studio time and left with two things in the can.

What was that?

A song of David's and a song of Graham's that were great. We were really into something nice. But a lot of things were happening at the same time. Crosby's baby was about to be born. Some of us wanted to rest for a while. We'd been working very hard. Everybody has a different viewpoint and it just takes us a while to get them all together. It's a great group for that, though. I'm sure there'll come a time when we'll do something again. We really did accomplish some things at those sessions. And just because the sessions only lasted three days, people started building up bullshit stories. We all love each other, but we're into another period where we're all hot on our own projects. Stephen's on tour with his new album, Graham and David are recording and I'm into my new album with Crazy Horse. Looking back, we might have been wiser to do the album before the tour. While we were still building the energy. But there's other times to record. Atlantic still has CSNY. Whenever we record together, we do it for Ahmet, which I think is right. Ahmet Ertegun kept the Buffalo Springfield afloat for as long as it was. He's always been great. I love him. There may be a live album to come from the tour last summer too. I know there's at least twenty-five minutes of my songs that are definitely releasable. We've got some really good stuff in the can from that tour. There was some good playing.

Why did you travel totally separate from everyone else on that tour?

I wanted to stay totally separate from everything, except the music. It worked well. I left right after every gig with my kid, my dog and two friends. I'd be refreshed and feeling great for every show.

Why did you make a movie?

It was something that I wanted to do. The music, which has been and always will be my primary thing, just seemed to *point* that way. I wanted to express a visual picture of what I was singing about.

One critic wrote that the movie's theme was "life is pointless."

Maybe that's what the guy got out of it. I just made a feeling. It's hard to say what the movie means. I think it's a good film for a first film. I think it's a really good film. I don't think I was trying to say that life is pointless. It does lay a lot of shit on people, though. It wasn't made for entertainment. I'll admit, I made it for myself. Whatever it is, that's the way I felt. I made it for me. I never even had a script.

Did the bad reviews surprise you at all?

Of course not. The film community doesn't want to see me in there. What do they want with *Journey Through the Past*? [*laughs*] It's got no plot. No point. No stars. They don't want to see that. But the next time, man, we'll get them. The next time. I've got all the equipment, all the ideas and motivation to make another picture. I've even been keeping my chops up as a cameraman by being on hire under the name of Bernard Shakey. I filmed a Hyatt House commercial not too long ago. I'm set. [*laughs*] I'm just waiting for the right time.

What about a plot?

It's real simple. Maybe it's not a plot but it's a very strong *feeling*. It's built around three or four people living together. No music. I'll never make another movie that has anything to do with me. I'll tell you that. That was the only way I could get to do the first movie. I wanted to be in a movie, so I did it. I sacrificed myself as a musician to do it.

So you don't really consider the soundtrack album an official Neil Young release?

No. There was an unfortunate sequence of events surrounding *Journey Through the Past*. The record company told me that they'd finance me doing the movie only if I gave them the soundtrack album. They took the thing [the soundtrack] and put it right out. Then they told me that they didn't want to release the movie because it wasn't . . . well, they wanted to group it with a bunch of other films. I wanted to get it out there on its own. So they chickened out on the movie because they thought it was weird. But they took me for the album. That's always been a ticklish subject with me. That's the only instance of discooperation and confusion that I've ever had with Warner's. Somebody really missed the boat on that one. They fucked me up for sure. It's all right, though. We found another distributor. It paid for itself. Even though it got banned in England, you know. They thought it was immoral. There were swearing and references to Christ that didn't set well with them.

Why did you leave the ranch?

It just got to be too big of a trip. There was too much going on the last couple of years. None of it had anything to do with music. I just had too many fucking people hanging around who don't really know me. They were parasites whether they intended to be or not. They lived off me, used my money to buy things, used my telephone to make their calls. General leeching. It hurt my feelings a lot when I reached that realization. I didn't want to believe I was being taken advantage of. I didn't like having to be boss and I don't like having to say "Get the fuck out." That's why I have different houses now. When people gather around me, I just split now. I mean, my ranch is more beautiful and lasting than ever. It's strong without me. I just don't feel like it's the only place I can be and be safe anymore. I feel much stronger now.

Have you got a name for the new album?

I think I'll call it *My Old Neighborhood*. Either that or *Ride My Llama*. It's weird, I've got all these songs about Peru, the Aztecs and the Incas. Time travel stuff. We've got one song called "Marlon Brandon, John Ehrlichman, Pocahontas and Me." I'm playing a lot of electric guitar and that's what I like best. Two guitars, bass and drums. And it's really flying off the ground too. Fucking unbelievable. I've got a bet with Elliot that it'll be out before the end of September. After that we'll probably go out on a fall tour of 3,000-seaters. Me and Crazy Horse again. I couldn't be happier. That, combined with the bachelor life . . . I feel magnificent. Now is the first time I can remember coming out of a relationship, definitely not wanting to get into another one. I'm just not looking. I'm so happy with the space I'm in right now. It's like spring. [*laughs*] I'll sell you two bottles of it for $1.50.

DAVE MARSH

TONIGHT'S THE NIGHT ALBUM REVIEW

Tonight's the Dark Night of Neil's Soul

"I'm sorry. You don't know these people. This means nothing to you."
—Neil Young, in the liner note

TONIGHT'S THE NIGHT FINDS Neil Young on his knees at the top of the heap, struggling to get back to his feet. The musical difficulties of last year's *On the Beach* have been resolved as directly as possible by a return to recording with Crazy Horse and Nils Lofgren.

Yet even Crazy Horse isn't what it once was: Lead guitarist Danny Whitten died last year of a drug overdose. The track on which he appears, "Come on Baby, Let's Go Downtown," recorded at Fillmore East four years ago, serves as a metaphor for the album's haunted, frightened emotional themes. Musically, Whitten's guitar and voice complement, challenge and inspire Young. The rest of the album strains to keep up.

It does so only occasionally but the effort is quixotically exhilarating. The successes—the ironic "Tired Eyes," the deceptively sweet "Albuquerque," the thunderous "Lookout Joe" and the two versions of the title song—are Young's best music since *After the Gold Rush*. Lofgren's guitar and piano are forceful and direct, Ralph Molina's drumming apt on both the rockers and the weepers (the latter driven by Ben Keith's steel guitar). Young's playing, on piano, harp and guitar, is simple but constantly charged.

The album shares with *On the Beach* a fully developed sense of despair: The stargazer of "Helpless" finds no solace here. The music has a feeling of offhand, first-take crudity matched recently only by *Blood on the Tracks*. It's almost as though Young wanted us to miss the album's ultimate majesty in order to emphasize its ragged edge of desolation. "Borrowed Tune," for example, is set against Young's stark harp and piano. The tandem guitar and bass on the opening version of the title song sounds like the crack of doom itself and Young's singing—especially on the concluding version—alternates between sheer panic and awful Old Testament threat. "Tonight's the night," he shouts, begs, moans and curses, telling the story of roadie Bruce Berry, who OD'ed "out on the mainline." Sometimes it feels as though

Young is still absorbing the shock of his friend's death, sometimes as though he is railing against mortality itself, sometimes as though he's accepted it. But never as though he believes it.

More than any of Young's earlier songs and albums—even the despondent *On the Beach* and the mordant, rancorous *Time Fades Away*—*Tonight's the Night* is preoccupied with death and disaster. Dedicated to the dead Berry and Whitten, its cover, liner and label are starkly black and white. The characters of the songs are shell-shocked, losers, wasted, insane, homeless—except for the ones who are already corpses. The happiest man in any of them, the father in "New Mama," acknowledges that he's "living in a dreamland." Ultimately, he, too, is tracked down by the ghosts from outside as he sits staring out at his frozen lake.

Young is simultaneously terrified by this pernicious landscape and fascinated by the disgust and lust it evokes. The only resolution seems to be ennui and the ritual of the music, which pounds incessantly, until the sanity of everything, including (or maybe especially) the singer and the listener, is called into question. Tonight's the night, all right, but for what? Just another kick?

Searching for a way to make sense of it, a lost Raymond Chandler story, "Red Wind," offers a clue: "It was one of those hot, dry Santa Anas that come down through the mountain passes and curl your hair and make your nerves jump and your skin itch. On nights like that every booze party ends in a fight. Meek little wives feel the edge of the carving knife and study their husbands' necks. Anything can happen." This is desert music, for certain, and the roughest part of the desert at that.

What finally happens, in "Tired Eyes," is material for a novel; in fact, as Bud Scoppa has pointed out elsewhere, the similarity to the plot of Robert Stone's *Dog Soldiers*—a novel that shares Young's obsession with heroin and the refuse of the war—is startling. "Well, he shot four men in a cocaine deal," Young sings matter-of-factly. "He left 'em lyin' in an open field / Full of old cars with bullet holes in the mirrors."

The whole album has pointed to this, song after song building the tightness with the endless repetition of phrases—musical and lyric—until the rasp of the guitars on the rockers and the sweetness of the singing on the weepers begins to grate, aching for release. Young's whole career may have been spent in pursuit of this story—remember the sinister black limousines lurking in the shadows of "Mr. Soul" and "Broken Arrow"?— but it is only now that he has found a way to tell the tale so directly.

Much has been made of Young's turn from pretty melodies on the last three albums. On this album, there are hints of the same kind of beauty that, overused, finally bloated *Harvest* with its own excesses. "World on a String" and "Roll Another Number" wouldn't have sounded out of place on that album, except that they would have exploded its pretensions.

If the songs here aren't pretty, they are tough and powerful, with a metallic guitar sound more akin to the abrasiveness of the Rolling Stones than the placid harmonies of CSNY. The melodies haven't disappeared (as they seemed to on *On the Beach*), but they are only sketched in, hints of what could be.

There is no sense of retreat, no apology, no excuses offered and no quarter given. If anything, these are the old ideas with a new sense of aggressiveness. The jitteriness of the music, its sloppy, unarranged (but decidedly structured) feeling is clearly calculated. The music draws us in, with the wonderful guitar line crashing through the ominous "Lookout Joe," with the steel guitar on "Albuquerque," the almost folkish suggestion of melody that drives "Tired Eyes" but—and here is where it is new—it also spits us back out again, makes us look at the ugliness on the surface and beneath it.

Yet the musical change doesn't reflect a similar toughening of subject matter, though that is what the casual listener might think. The tensions have always been there, only now they are unrelieved. To suggest, as some have, that Young's current music is an apology for the sweetness of his success—much less to suggest that he has only recently discovered a world in opposition to the rock scene—is to ignore the bulk of his work. The titles alone tell the story: "Broken Arrow," "Out of My Mind," "Everybody Knows This Is Nowhere," "Only Love Can Break Your Heart" (with no hint that anything can mend it again), even "Helpless." "Ohio," Young's other great CSNY contribution, speaks explicitly of the same horrors: "What if you knew her and found her dead on the ground / How can you run when you know?" Finally, those four dead in "Ohio" equate directly with the four dead coke dealers in "Tired Eyes": casualties in different battles of the same war.

All of this is half incoherent because all of the names Young could put to it are clichés. It is the measure of Young's achievement that when he sings, so calmly it's spooky, "Please take my advice / Open up the tired eyes," it brings this message home to us in a new way. Suddenly the evil is no longer banal but awful and ironic, in simultaneous recognition that the advice is silly, or that if taken, it might not help or it might only aid in enlarging the wounds.

Crying over the death of his real and imagined friends, Neil Young seems at once heroic and mock heroic, brave and absurd. He leaves us as he found us, ravaged but rocking.

THE TOP 100
THE BEST ALBUMS OF THE
LAST 20 YEARS
TONIGHT'S THE NIGHT

I N 1987, ROLLING STONE asked seventeen rock writers to submit nominations for the 100 greatest albums of the last twenty years—albums initially released between 1967 and 1987. Neil Young's *Tonight's the Night* came in at Number Twenty-six.

#26 *Tonight's the Night,* Neil Young

The haunting *Tonight's the Night* is Neil Young's most personal, stirring work. Crazy Horse guitarist Danny Whitten had died of a drug overdose in 1972, sending Young into a murky depression. The sessions for this LP were the first time Young and the band had got back together. The album "is like an OD letter," Young told ROLLING STONE in 1975. Bruce Berry, a Crosby, Stills, Nash and Young roadie, had also died of an overdose, and Berry's brother Ken ran the studio where most of the tracks were recorded.

Young said the band—which included drummer Ralph Molina, bassist Billy Talbot and guitarists Nils Lofgren and Ben Keith—would get high, drink tequila and play pool until midnight, then start playing. "We all got high enough," he said, "right out there on the edge where we felt wide open to the whole mood. It was spooky. I probably *feel* this album more than anything else I've ever done."

Although the results are sometimes sloppy and often bleak, the dark, country-flavored music has an undeniable cathartic power. From the casual piano tinklings that open the title song to the last crashing chord of its reprise at the album's end, the listener is drawn in to commiserate.

Young's emotional rawness translates into a loose boldness. On "Tired Eyes," which concerns four dead coke dealers, his vocal is half spoken narration, half layered harmonies; on "Borrowed Tune," he is upfront about appropriating the melody of the Stones' "Lady Jane" because he feels "too wasted to write my own."

As Young himself said, "If you're gonna put a record on at eleven in the morning, don't put on *Tonight's the Night.* Put on the Doobie Brothers."

Recorded at the Fillmore East, New York City, 1971, and at Studio Instrument Rentals, Hollywood, California, and Broken Arrow, California, spring 1973. **PRODUCERS:** David Briggs, Neil Young, Tim Mulligan and Elliot Mazer. **ENGINEERS:** Elliot Mazer, David Briggs, Tim Mulligan and Gabby Garcia. **RELEASED:** June 1975. **HIGHEST CHART POSITION:** Number Twenty-five. **TOTAL U.S. SALES** [as of 1987]: 436,082. Reprise Records.

■ **RANDOM NOTES** (November 20, 1975)

Neil Young was operated on in L.A. October 13 for the removal of "an object" on one of his vocal cords, according to manager Elliot Roberts. Roberts called the operation successful, though plans for a November acoustic tour by Young have been scratched. "Neil has no plans other than to get healthier and write," said Roberts, adding that Young won't tour again until next summer. Young's throat had been bothering him during the last year, and for one month recently he had been unable to talk, having to answer his phone by whistling.

BUD SCOPPA

ZUMA ALBUM REVIEW

Neil Young and Crazy Horse Still Lookin' for a Love

"It's another rock & roll album. A lot of long instrumental things . . . It's about the Incas and the Aztecs. It takes on another personality. It's like being in another civilization. It's a lost sort of form, sort of a soul-form that switches from history scene to history scene trying to find itself, man, in this maze. I've got it all written and all the songs learned. Tomorrow we start cutting them. . . . We're gonna just do it in the morning. Early in the morning when the sun's out . . ."

—a typically ironic Neil Young describing *Zuma*

NEIL YOUNG'S NINTH SOLO album, *Zuma,* is by far the best album he's made; it's the most cohesive (but not the most obvious) concept album I've ever encountered; and despite its depths, *Zuma* is so listenable that it should become Young's first hit album since *Harvest.*

One of the most fascinating aspects of Young's masterwork is the context in which it appears. In recent months, rock & roll has become terribly vital again, not just because of the emergence of major new figures, but also because of the rebirth of old heroes. Despite their dark scenarios, Dylan's *Blood on the Tracks, The Who by Numbers* and Young's awesome combination punch, *Tonight's the Night* and *Zuma,* crack with naked, desperate energy in a partly familiar, partly novel form of rock & roll (a "soul-form" as Young describes it) invented simultaneously by these three great artists out of emotional as well as aesthetic necessity. And as serious as their albums are, all but Young's self-proclaimed "horror album" are thoroughly accessible.

If *Tonight's the Night* was bleakly, spookily black, *Zuma*—Young's "morning" album—is hardly suffused with sunlight and flowers. Apparently, tempered gloom is the brightest this love- and death-haunted epileptic genius can manage these days. But if, as a stubbornly solitary Young proclaims in "Drive Back," he wants to "wake up with no one around," in "Lookin' for a Love" he's still holding on to some hope of finding that magical life- and self-affirming lover who can make him "live and make the best of what I see." Young doesn't shrink from the paradox, he embraces it like the lover he imagines.

There are real lovers pictured throughout *Zuma* too, but all have been lost. Like the love-scarred Dylan of *Blood on the Tracks* and the new "Sara," Young is struggling to get a grip on himself, to "burn off the fog" and see what went wrong with his loves and his dreams. Out of these agonized, bitter and painfully frank confessions he manages to reach both a new, honest lovingness and—even more important—the revelation (first glimpsed years ago in "The Loner") that neither his wings nor his woman can carry him away. For Young this insight holds both terror and liberation.

For this struggle, Young wheels out all his familiar heavy artillery: Prominent are his recurring metaphors of birds in flight and boats on the water, his compulsive truthfulness, his eccentrically brilliant (and seemingly intuitive) narrative style, his effortlessly lovely melodies and his cat-in-heat singing. Components of every one of Young's earlier albums (especially *Everybody Knows This Is Nowhere* and *After the Gold Rush*) jostle their way into the agitated synchrony of *Zuma*.

But what finally causes the album to burst into greatness is the presence of Crazy Horse, which has finally found in rhythm guitarist Frank Sampedro an adequate replacement for Danny Whitten. Sampedro's majestic rhythm work urges Young to what is clearly the most powerful guitar playing he's ever recorded. His guitar lines snake through Sampedro's chordings with the dangerous snap of exposed wires crossing. Young's solos throughout more than match the eloquence of his lyrics, transmitting anguish, violence, joy and longing.

With Crazy Horse providing both firepower and stability, Young is at his best: boundlessly inventive and determinedly multileveled. As he attacks, Young manages to work in oddly playful references to other songs ("with little reason to believe" in "Pardon My Heart"; "Whatever gets you through the night / That's all right with me" in "Drive Back"), cryptic comments ("I don't believe this song" in "Pardon My Heart"; "I might live a thousand years / Before I know what that means" in "Barstool Blues"), dramatically forceful incongruities (the cheery "la la" backing vocals in Young's loss-wracked "Stupid Girl"), novel structural devices (two simultaneously sung but completely different verses vying for attention in "Danger Bird"; the unresolving verses and chords of "Pardon My Heart") and brilliantly, uniquely ironic expressions (the whole of "Lookin' for a Love" and "Barstool Blues").

Of the nine songs on *Zuma*, five are hot, stormy rockers, three are gorgeous, hazy ballads and the last, "Cortez the Killer," is an extended narrative tale that packs equal wallop as a classic retelling of an American legend, a Lawrencian erotic dreamscape and Young's ultimate personal metaphor. This song, perhaps Young's crowning achievement, builds with gathering intensity through several minutes of tense, deliberate playing before Young's voice strikes the first verse:

> *He came dancing across the water*
> *With his galleons and guns*
> *Looking for the new world*
> *And that palace in the sun.*

> *On the shore lay Montezuma*
> *With his coca leaves and pearls*
> *In his halls he often wandered*
> *With the secrets of the worlds.*

The secret of the album, indeed of Young's work in its entirety, is encapsulated in this confrontation: force and wisdom, innocence and aggression, love and death are the issues and the stakes. And the climax is inevitable, but not before Young succumbs for a single verse to a direct comment on the classic struggle:

> *And I know she's living there*
> *And she loves me to this day*
> *I still can't remember when*
> *Or how I lost my way.*

In the brief final ballad, "Through My Sails," Young (joined by Crosby, Stills and Nash), soaring on wings that have "turned to stone," lands finally on a shoreline where he transforms his wings into sails and sings, "Know me / Show me / New things I'm knowin'." Then off he sails.

Perhaps some sunlight does break through on this one.

MARSHALL KILDUFF

SHOW CLOSE TO HOME—NEIL YOUNG SAYS NO

W HEN NEIL YOUNG, among the shyest of stars, showed up at a meeting of the San Mateo County Planning Commission— well, something had really gone wrong.

So thought Monte Stern, the soft-spoken, twenty-three-year-old heir to the Sears, Roebuck fortune. He'd spent a year and $13,000 trying to win over county officials and neighbors to his plan for outdoor concerts on a 600-acre ranch he'd leased in the mountains fifty miles south of San Francisco.

The locals, though, had lined up against him, predicting that the idea would flop economically and also lead to trespassing, traffic and fire dangers.

Into all this came Young—who owns the Broken Arrow Ranch a few hollows away from Stern's place—to tell the county fathers what he thought.

"He really surprised me," said Don Woolfe, the county planning director. "Here comes this big rock star in an old jacket and Levi's. You'd think he's going to support this idea. He makes a fair living at these outdoor concerts, my daughter tells me.

"So he tells the commission how rock concerts are his business and how he's played at about fifty or sixty of them in fifteen countries. But then he describes the drug overdoses he's seen backstage and out in front in the crowd, and how if fifty guys want in, they'll come in whether you have cops or not.

"It was all very interesting," Woolfe added.

Paul Grushkin, a project director of Stern's J.P. Productions who has served as copromoter for the concert plan, said that Young's performance "came off mighty weird to me."

"I've never seen a situation where a man speaks out against his own profession so strongly. It's pretty hard to listen to 'Sugar Mountain' after remembering what Young sounded like," Grushkin said.

Young was unavailable for comment, reportedly because of the flu, but a friend named David Klein said that Young opposed the concert because he feared for his privacy and wondered about the inevitable hassles. "You don't know what it's like at the ranch. People drive down and sit there waiting to talk to Neil about his latest album or try to hit on him for a job as a roadie. He wants to be alone there."

Others said that the ranch is a refuge for Young when he is not in Southern California. At the ranch he has a recording studio and an outdoor stage trimmed with redwood bark. Crosby, Stills, Nash and Young practiced there for their tour last summer.

■ RANDOM NOTES (February 12, 1976)

Is it rolling, Zuma?: Neil Young and Crazy Horse have done a dozen or so unannounced shows around northern California since December. But unlike Bob Dylan's Rolling Thunder Revue, Young has played for free and stuck to clubs in obscure places like Cotati and seaside Marshall (population 50). One of our correspondents made the thirty-mile trip northward from San Francisco to the Marshall Tavern. His report: "We went over hills, through fog and rain. As we rounded a bend, we found ourselves entering and leaving Marshall. We parked in the mud alongside the road and walked halfway through town (five houses) to the bar. The doors were open. Nobody was collecting money. It was warm and dry inside and everybody was drinking. The place had a capacity of 100 but it wasn't full.

"Young and Crazy Horse stepped out of their back room and descended the staircase to the stage. Young broke into 'Down by the River,' then continued with things from *Zuma*. 'Don't Cry No Tears' brought the crowd to an orgasm as the mixer cranked the volume.

"Neil came back to play an encore of 'Take Me to the Country' and 'Southern Man.' Though the band was a bit sloppy on 'Southern Man' (otherwise they played especially tight), Neil's voice was strong and clear as ever."

Afterward, our correspondent continued, Young hung around for a few beers and talked easily—although he declined to say where he'd take the Rolling Zuma Revue next.

■ RANDOM NOTES "DEEP QUOTES" (May 20, 1976)

Neil Young, on his music: "One day Neil Young will write a happy song. But I'll probably sell it to TV for a commercial."

CAMERON CROWE

CSNY: ON AGAIN, OFF AGAIN

THE WORD BEGAN TO filter out in early May: Crosby, Stills, Nash and Young were back together and secretly working on a new album at Miami's Criteria Recording Studios. And sure enough, it was true. Steve Stills and Neil Young, finishing a joint LP, had summoned their old friends to give that mythical third CSNY studio album another try.

A month later, it's as if the attempt had never been made. Stills and Young are back in the final mixdown for their album while Crosby and Nash are wrapping up their as-yet-untitled third LP. According to one source, Nash and Crosby, during a session break, flew to L.A. to catch up on lingering business commitments. When the two called Stills and Young to make plans for their return to CSNY, they were told the project had reverted back to a Stills and Young LP.

"The old magic just wasn't there," according to Michael John Bowen, Stills' manager, who was at the sessions. "It was too identifiably Stills and Young."

David Crosby confirmed the story. "I was very surprised and very sorry to see the album not happen for us. We've always said we'd be right there for Stephen and Neil and we were. I really thought there was room for all of it. But then I've always been an optimist.

"The bottom line is this," continued Crosby. "We love good music. We were happy recording with the other guys but it's not happening, so we're back making good music with our own band [Craig Doerge, keyboards; Danny Kortchmar, guitar; Tim Drummond, bass; and Russ Kunkel, drums]. And we love it."

Bowen cited poor timing as another reason the reunion—the group's fourth known attempt—failed. "This year is just too soon for Crosby, Stills, Nash and Young to resurface," he said. "This summer Steve and Neil will tour and release their album. They need to do that. That's the next stage in this cycle. Then, with that behind them, circumstances will be just right for CSNY to come back. Next year will be perfect."

Reached at Criteria last week, Stills was no less than ecstatic over his newly released *Illegal Stills* LP and the nearly finished *Stills/Young* album, due out this month. "I love the way things are working out," he said. "I was in the doldrums for a while, but I'm comin' back. I wouldn't call it a comeback, though, 'cause I never went anywhere."

It will be basically Stills' band—with Young on guitar—that will tour this summer. "The whole idea came about when Neil showed up for a couple of shows of mine in L.A. and San Francisco. We knew it felt electric and exactly right."

Young, as far back as last spring, had the idea for a Stills/Young project firmly in mind. "Stills," he said at the time, "is one guy I *always* get off with. All that shit about Young and Stills always being at each other's throats . . . that's a bunch of fuckin' shit. I really want to do an album with him."

Meanwhile, Crosby and Nash will take to the road this summer as well. "Nash and I have no desire to do the big shows," said Crosby. "We'll be doing smaller halls, the choicest places."

■ **RANDOM NOTES** (July 15, 1976)
Lynyrd Skynyrd, those Southern men who once sang that they didn't need Neil Young around anyhow, will tag along with Young and Steve Stills on some July/August outdoor dates. In real life, Skynyrd and Young are pals. "They play my kind of music," says Young. "They sound like they mean it."

DAVE MARSH

STILLS AND YOUNG PERFORMANCE REVIEW

Young's Hot, Stills's Not

Nassau Colliseum, Hempstead, New York

July 1, 1976

THE MOST TELLING MOMENT in this traveling historical revue came when Stephen Stills began to sing "Bluebird," the most beautiful and dynamic song he's ever written. The audience granted its opening chords one of the grandest ovations of the night. But Stills can no longer reach the notes and in the end, it was an embarrassment.

This tour was probably inevitable—David Crosby and Graham Nash's 1975 success made a Stills/Young pairing too lucrative to pass up. But it was never much more than a bad idea gone wrong. Though both Stills and Young remained trapped by entropy, they've evolved in strikingly separate ways: Young has found courage and even inspiration in his ennui, while Stills (on the evidence of his recent recording work) has only succumbed to his. This concert did nothing to dispel those trite categorizations, and much to reinforce them.

Young, in fact, has never seemed so animated, bouncing from one side of the stage to the other, leading the band, playing guitar and piano, singing with what amounts to abandon. But even so, he never committed himself fully to the duet idea: Aside from a single unrecorded song, the most recent material he sang was a pair of songs from *After the Gold Rush*. Some of what he did was awesome: a crackling guitar interchange with Stills on "Southern Man," a spookier than usual "Helpless," a pleasantly nostalgic "Cowgirl in the Sand." But on "Helpless" the supporting harmonies of Crosby and Nash were missed and the attempt to recapture the spirit of Buffalo Springfield, most notably with "For What It's Worth," went aground on the shoals of its own portentousness. A few songs from *Time Fades Away, On the Beach, Tonight's the Night* or *Zuma* could have redeemed the show. Those jagged, bitter songs might also have redeemed Stills during the pair's few guitar interchanges.

In the crudest sense, the Stills/Young tour is filler, occupying space between more worthwhile projects for both men. It would hardly be fair to call the show worthless, but it certainly stands as one of the season's great disappointments.

STILLS AND YOUNG TOUR CUT SHORT BY RAW THROAT

A MONTH AFTER IT HAD begun, the eleven-week-long Stephen Stills/ Neil Young band tour was over. The reason was Young's recurring throat malady, something he had had surgery to relieve just last summer.

Although the managers and promoters preferred to use the term "postponed," rather than "canceled," the tour has not yet been rescheduled. Stills will play out the three outdoor Florida shows remaining in the first leg, bravely following Lynyrd Skynyrd in their home state. "It's the least I can do," he said in Jacksonville, "to salvage the tour." Regardless of his partner, Stills will probably perform throughout the summer.

Young canceled a tour with Crazy Horse in the spring of '75 for the same reason. Shortly afterward, his throat was operated on for the removal of a growth. His first subsequent public appearance was as a surprise guitarist for a Stills concert in Berkeley's Greek Theatre in July of that year. At the time, he could communicate only with handwritten notes. The two later booked time at Criteria Sound Studios and recorded an album, *Long May You Run,* then canceled their summer 1976 solo tours in favor of a joint one.

After several weeks spent shuffling songs and arrangements, the tour had just begun to peak. Their last show was in Columbia, South Carolina, and was well received in the local media. According to several sources, Young's throat began acting up during that show and by the next concert, in Atlanta three days later, he had yielded to the illness. He immediately flew to Los Angeles for medical treatment and is now recuperating at his northern California ranch.

In Atlanta, the sudden cancellation spawned a number of wild rumors, the most widely spread of which was that Young had been killed in a plane crash. At last word, he was waiting for his doctor's diagnosis, which will decide whether the Stills/Young tour will surface again.

CAMERON CROWE

QUICK END TO A LONG RUN

In which Neil Young and Stephen Stills find that old magic and lose it all to a sore throat

FORGET THE BALDING pate and those wisps of gray. Stephen Stills and Neil Young, their hair cut summer-short, looked eerily like they did on the cover of *Buffalo Springfield Again*. But gone, at least temporarily, was the carefree abandon of those days. This was serious business.

The scheduled three-month-long Stills-Young band tour had been rolling only two weeks, and while it came close to jelling in Boston just a few days before, the show still teetered on the edge of the magic that everyone knew they were capable of.

Even before they broke into their opener, "Love the One You're With," the sold-out crowd of 20,000 at the Capitol Center exploded at the sight of Stills and Young on the same stage again. In this, the summer of Aerosmith and ZZ Top, it was nothing short of astonishing to see the sustained drawing power of two artists who have not seen a solo hit single or gold album in years.

On paper, Stills and Young's set was a fan's dream. "Love the One You're With" was followed by a verse-trading rendition of "The Loner," then "Helpless," "For What It's Worth," the title track of their forthcoming album, *Long May You Run,* "Black Queen" and "Southern Man." After a ten-minute break, Young returned alone for "Sugar Mountain," "Old Man," a superb new song called "Stringman" and "After the Gold Rush." Stills performed his own solo set of "Helplessly Hoping," "49 Bye Byes," "Word Game" and "Four Days Gone." Together they did an acoustic "Ohio," then "Buyin' Time" with the band and another new song, "Evening Coconut," "Make Love to You," "Cowgirl in the Sand" and "Mr. Soul." The encore was an electric "Suite: Judy Blue Eyes."

Aside from the power of the songs themselves, though, it was another off performance. Stills had difficulty singing on mike and sometimes even remembering words. The harmonies sounded ragged. Young, in the process of keeping the vocals faithful, became too tense to cut loose on guitar himself. In typical style, Young did not hang around afterward. He went straight from the stage to the airport, where a Lear jet would take him to Miami for a day of remixing some vocals on *Long May You Run*. "If we both go," he told Stills, "neither of us will want to come back."

Stills spent the rest of the night in the Holiday Inn bar, nursing drinks and talking with fans. Somewhere in the early morning hours, he was even coaxed onstage for jams with the house band on "The Thrill Is Gone." Less than an hour after he finally headed upstairs to retire, the morning paper's review was out. The assessment was more bewildered than negative. Like most every other review thus far, it wondered why Young had ever taken on such a project.

Neil Young refused to be quoted in connection with the Stills/Young band tour. He expressed a strong desire to just do the tour, bypass the hype and move on. He was fully aware of their ever-diverging paths, but he respects Stills as a musician . . . and worries about him. This tour, one sensed, was Young's way of helping Stills back on his creative feet. "It was," said one associate, "something Neil felt he had to do."

At thirty, Young has begun more than ever to realize his potential. Besides working on a screenplay, he writes several songs a day, has a few complete albums in the can and maintains an entirely separate career with Crazy Horse.

Stills, now thirty-one, knows full well that his solo work has lacked critical importance in recent years. "These last few years," he said, "I've been concentrating on my guitar work. I want to be considered one of the masters." As a result, the emphasis has gone off what was once Stills' strongest area—songwriting. When his last album, *Illegal Stills,* was ignored in most circles, including ROLLING STONE's review section, he was very disappointed, but he said recently, "I'll tell you something. I'm gonna keep at this until I win back every last person.

"If I'm cruddy on my own, it doesn't bother me half as much as if I don't hold my own backing up Neil. The one thing that everyone has always assumed is that there's a fundamental competition between us. In fact, it's the difference between us that makes it work. When he comes up with those killer lines, I fall on the floor just like everybody else. And when I play something that blows his mind, he falls on the floor just like everybody else. It's the ultimate complementary relationship."

The changes that that relationship has undergone must strike Young as ironic at times. Stills was the one who brought him into the Buffalo Springfield and later Crosby, Stills and Nash. Young, at that point, was little more than a hired gun—another electric guitar to toughen up CSN's sweetness-and-harmony image. Young caught on quickly. Today it's that same hired gun whom everyone expects to call most of the shots. Whenever

CSNY tries at another reformation, it is usually because Young has expressed the interest. But—and here's the snag—Neil Young is not a pressure performer. His constant frustration is that he must stand in a spotlight.

"I could have dug playing guitar with the Eagles," Young blurted late one night in the customized bus he designed himself. He jammed with the band three years ago at a San Luis Obispo benefit and never forgot how much fun he had. "I'd join any band I got off with. I'd love to play with the Rolling Stones . . . but they probably don't know my rock & roll side."

It's that same guitar player in him that brought Young back to Stills last summer. Young had just been released from the hospital after a throat operation when he dropped by a Stills concert at the Greek Theater in Berkeley on July 25. He could not speak, much less sing. "It was truly great," Stills remembered. "He was passing us notes and playing up a storm. We both got off like motherfuckers."

Young did not forget. Four months later, he "just showed up" backstage at Stills' Stanford University appearance. Young watched the show and finally wandered out for the acoustic set. When he turned up the next afternoon in Los Angeles for Stills' concert at UCLA's Pauley Pavilion— again without warning—Young was equipped with his electric Les Paul. He and Stills dueled guitars far into the night, dazzling themselves and the audience to no end. "The spirit of the Springfield is back," Stills shouted in ecstasy. The commitment had been made.

Young went on to play a few northern California bars, then visited Japan and Europe with Crazy Horse. The tour, by every account, soared beyond Young's highest hopes. "Every night was incredible," he recalled. "I really get free with Crazy Horse. They let me zoom off . . . and know me well enough to be right there when I get back. They're the American Rolling Stones, no doubt about it."

When it came to America, though, Young returned to Stills. The two flew to Miami and began work on an album. Midway into the sessions, Young had the impulse to turn it into a Crosby, Stills, Nash and Young project. Crosby and Nash agreed to give it a shot and flew down to Criteria Sound Studios to help out. For a few weeks it looked as if that third CSNY album would finally become a reality. Then, while Crosby and Nash took a break and returned to L.A. to meet the deadline for their own sessions on *Whistling Down the Wire,* Stills and Young continued working. They eventually decided to return to the original idea of a Stills/Young band. Crosby and Nash's harmonies were replaced by Stills' band.

Said Nash of the near-CSNY reunion attempt: "We probably came closer this last time than we've ever come before. Stills was amazingly loose. Neil was great. I just have to say that I deeply resent David's and my vocals being wiped off the album. That hurts me. The four of us together have a special power . . . we make people happy with our music. The fact that we deprive people of that happiness by acting like children really bothers me sometimes. I don't care what anybody says, there's room for CSNY just like there's room for anything else we might want to do."

As for another go at CSNY, Nash admitted, "I'm not closed to the idea."

Neither is Crosby. "Look," he said, "here's what it's like. If you were crawling through the desert and knew of a place where there once was a luscious fucking well . . . you'd go back to see if it was still there, wouldn't you?"

Stills, too, didn't close the door on some future reunion of the four: "The last thing I want is to have Graham Nash and David Crosby as enemies. But this Stills/Young album . . . I don't know, we just had to do it ourselves this time. No Richie Furays, no David and Grahams, no nobody between us."

After finishing everything but the final mixing of *Long May You Run,* Young and Stills took to the road together. Both canceled solo summer commitments. Although it was Stills' band (George "Chocolate" Ferry on bass, Joe Lala on congas, Jerry Aiello on keyboards and Joe Vitale on drums), the tour was the same one originally intended for Young and Crazy Horse.

Following Washington, D.C., the next show, a muggy outdoor affair in Hartford, Connecticut, was unquestionably closer to the mark. The album now entirely finished, the band relaxed into a comfortable pace. The harmonies remained ragged but by the end of the set, Young and Stills' slashing guitar work was near-flawless. Stills, just after leaving the stage, gushed: "There's no place I'd rather be than right here, playing with *that* guy."

Young caught him in a bear hug, hopped in his bus and headed for Cleveland to beat the traffic.

On board his own bus—a more standard travel-only model he rents from Young—Stills spent the ride listening to *Long May You Run.* He was proud of the album, unabashedly claiming it to be his best work in years.

"There is one very special thing that Neil and I do for each other," he laughed. "Every time we play, I learn a little bit more about being real and he learns a little bit more about polish."

By the night of the Cleveland show, Stills was ready to kill. He ripped into "Love the One You're With" with an urgency that hadn't surfaced since he'd written it. Young responded with a blazing solo in "The Loner." Stills came back with a chilling delivery of "For What It's Worth" . . . and on it went. Suddenly, they were beyond the smiles and the backslapping.

The Stills/Young band bore down for a snarling night of what they'd all been waiting and hoping for. The magic.

Standing offstage during Young's solo act, Stills was enjoying the long overdue taste of victory. What happened? "Neil crawled all over me," Stills chirped. "He snapped me awake. I guess I was flaking it a little bit, so he jumped on my ass."

After the show, Young was similarly jubilant. Alive and animated, he told Stills not to consider the Cleveland show a peak. "Think of it," he coached, "as a new standard. Something you can't dip below."

Visiting the hotel bar before hitting the open road for Cincinnati, Young raised a toast. "Here's to the return of Stephen Stills."

The next night in Cincinnati, Young let Stills run with the ball. Stills delivered. The roughest part of the set for him—following Young's show-stopping "After the Gold Rush" with his own acoustic set—was a breeze. Stills sat down and began gently playing the chords to "Helplessly Hoping." When it came time for the vocal, gone was the whiskey wheeze of old. Singing slowly and into the microphone, Stills let the audience fill in the lilting harmonies themselves.

Young studied the sight, glowing like a proud father. "Now," he told the writer, "you have something to write about."

It seemed the proper place to bow out and do just that.

THREE CONCERTS LATER, it was over. Pittsburgh, Greensboro and Charlotte had been good shows—great by some accounts—and Young was reportedly pleased with each one. By Atlanta, though, a recurring throat illness had silenced him. Young flew home to California, was told to rest by his doctors, and went into seclusion at his northern California ranch. Rumors immediately pegged the tour's cancellation as intentional, and Young hasn't taken any phone calls or had any visitors.

Stills' reaction to the aborted tour: "I learned a lot and had a lot of good times. I don't think they're over, and I'm just not going to let this set me back."

In the meantime, both have canceled all appearances this summer. Young has a tentative ten-date tour with Crazy Horse scheduled for November, just about when he'll release his next album, planned as *Chrome Dreams*. Stills, recently sued for divorce by wife Veronique Sanson, is planning a fall tour with stalwart guitarist friends Chris Hillman and George Terry.

After that, Stills may well take a few years off to write a book and relax. "My hearing has gotten to be a terrible problem. If I keep playing and touring the way I have been," Stills shrugged, "I'll go deaf. I want to take care of myself and be around for a while. . . ."

Whether Young has fulfilled or abandoned his drive to revive the affiliation with Stills is unknown. With *Long May You Run* just out, Stills is confident that he has not seen the last of Young.

KEN TUCKER

LONG MAY YOU RUN ALBUM REVIEW

L ONG MAY YOU RUN is like an old *World's Finest* comic book: the team-up of Superman and Batman always drained each of his most interesting characteristics. Like Superman, Stephen Stills is a rather muscular lunkhead of a personality; Neil Young's Batman is less heroic— shadowy and darkly mortal. The music on *Long May You Run* is a collection of each man's puffier and less autobiographical new material.

Young contributes five compositions, Stills four, and each track is solely its author's creation; there is little collaboration here, even few vocal duets (not that the combination of Young's yowl and Stills' sonorousness is a special treat).

For both, this is a less personal project, and the straightforwardness such objectivity provokes makes the album very accessible. Less a series of inner explorations than of California observations, *Long May You Run* includes a diatribe about a hotel, "Fontainebleau," proof that Neil Young can be entertainingly misanthropic about almost anything. There also are no fewer than three songs about the beach, Young's "Midnight on the Bay" and "Ocean Girl" and Stills' "Black Coral"; "Long May You Run" even includes a sarcastic reference to the Beach Boys. Weaker moments include "Guardian Angel," Stills' cautionary tale about protective spirits set to cocktail jazz, and the sappy, singalong title tune.

Both authors are plagued by bloated images and occasional simple-mindedness: the chanted refrain to Young's "Midnight on the Bay" consists of "Midnight on the bay . . . sure feels good to me"; in "Black Coral" Stills feels content " 'cause heaven just might be the sea."

But Young plays some fine raw guitar on "Ocean Girl" and especially "Let It Shine," and avers, in a non sequitur in this song of religious romance, "My Lincoln is still the best thing built by Ford." And "12/8 Blues (All the Same)," a rigorous song about obsessive love—always Stills' most rewarding theme—contains his best writing in a good while.

In terms of their recent solo output, *Long May You Run* represents a holding action for Young (nothing nearly as potent as any song on either *Zuma* or *Tonight's the Night*), and an encouraging boost for Stills (all his stuff here is superior to the criminal *Illegal Stills*). It's not an important record, but it's certainly interesting.

■ RANDOM NOTES (June 16, 1977)

Neil Young will be doing several dates this summer with Linda Ronstadt, Waylon Jennings and Jessi Colter. Young has also finished a new album called *American Stars 'n Bars*, which includes a nine-minute tune called "Will to Love" that portrays Young as a salmon fighting his way upstream. He's backed by Crazy Horse and the Bullets (vocalist Nicolette Larson and violinist Carole Larson from Crystal Pistol, and sometimes Ronstadt).

"I've reached a point where it feels good to be working in harmonies again," says Young. "And these girls inject a whole new vibe into it. Me and Crazy Horse are going to be on our best behavior—real gentlemen."

PAUL NELSON

AMERICAN STARS 'N BARS
ALBUM REVIEW

Neil Young's Solitary Journey

RIGHT NOW, I THINK it would be just about impossible to overrate Neil Young. In the last few years he has wed the most avant-garde styles to the corniest of archetypes—and deliberately ignored the public's penchant for pasteurized product by rampantly (im)perfecting Bob Dylan's crude but spontaneous recording technique. Seething with psychic dynamite, his raw and passionate electric-guitar playing boasts a tactility and uniqueness unmatched by any guitarist since Jimi Hendrix. Young has written songs as sensitive and beautiful as any by the most fragile and aesthetic singer/songwriter, yet he has played life-and-death rock & roll with the delirious ferociousness of the Rolling Stones at their most sordid and seedy. Of course, he has been misunderstood too quickly.

Since *After the Gold Rush* (1970) and *Harvest* (1972), many erstwhile admirers have filed strong charges of morbid self-indulgence and drugged-out incomprehensiveness against the later LPs. In the *New York Times,* John Rockwell, in a highly favorable review, characterized Young as "the quintessential hippie-cowboy loner, a hopeless romantic struggling to build bridges out from himself to women and through them to cosmic archetypes of the past and of myth." Well, no.

Unless one understands the "On the Beach"/"Motion Pictures"/"Ambulance Blues" trilogy from *On the Beach* (and "Don't Be Denied" from *Time Fades Away*), one simply cannot write intelligently about Neil Young. But when one understands these songs, one begins to perceive the exciting possibility that perhaps Young is rock & roll's first (and only?) post-romantic. That he knows something that we don't, but should. Indeed, I suspect that Young took one of the longest journeys without maps on record, never even slowed up at the point of no return, but somehow got back anyway, a better man with all senses intact. When nearly overwhelmed by marital difficulties and the death of friends, he apparently looked into himself and managed an instinctive or willed act of Jungian purification that put him somewhat safely on the far side of paradise, if not paradox. I'm not saying he's happy, but who the hell is happy? For Young, being a postromantic probably means he still loves the war, but knows exactly how and where to invest his combat pay—he may lose it, but never hopelessly. Romanticism is a foreign country; they do things differently there. It's a nice place to visit, but I wouldn't want to live there. Too homicidal.

Having gotten through the more self-destructive aspects of romanticism, Neil Young certainly takes full advantage of his revisiting privileges, pointing out the highlights and contradictions of his itinerary to all who will listen. Perhaps only a man who has known the answers can really see both sides of the questions. At any rate, Young's Mona Lisa smile from the barroom floor on the curious *American Stars 'n Bars* isn't so much arrogant ("If you can't cut it / Don't pick up the knife") as it is inclusive ("I know that all things pass / Let's try to make this last"). So inclusive, in fact, that the album can almost be taken as a sampler, but not a summation, of Young's various styles from *After the Gold Rush* and *Harvest* (much of the country rock) through *On the Beach* (the incredible "Will to Love") to *Zuma* ("Like a Hurricane" is a worthy successor to "Cortez the Killer" as a guitar showcase), with a lot of overlap within the songs.

If one can divide *American Stars 'n Bars* into major and minor Neil Young, I think that it breaks down this way: "The Old Country Waltz," "Saddle Up the Palomino," "Hey Babe," "Bite the Bullet" and "Homegrown" are excellent examples of country rock at its most pleasant and muscular. While these songs abstain from cloyingness and retain the artist's characteristic idiosyncrasies (Young is nothing if not quirky), they lack the necessary resonance to stand up to the LP's four masterpieces.

In "Hold Back the Tears" and "Star of Bethlehem," two songs about how it feels when you've just been left and didn't want to be, a corrosive view of love metamorphoses into hopefulness ("Hold back the tears and keep on trying / Just around the next corner may be waiting your true love"), with a final metaphor equating the inevitability of the quest for a meaningful relationship with the apotheosis of the religious experience.

Which leads right into the shining "Will to Love," a song that flies into the face of reason by flaunting the seemingly ridiculous—the thoughts of the singer as a salmon swimming upstream—in order to gain the truly sublime. And it works. (When was the last time you heard something like *this* on record?) Starting with a typical Young epigram ("It has often been my dream / To live with one who wasn't there"), the song moves from the manic to the depressive (the two lines about "a fire in the night") to a combination of both ("Now my fins are in the air / And my belly's scraping on the rocks") before homing in on the universal plight ("I remember the ocean from where I came / Just one of millions all the same . . .") and promise (". . . but somewhere someone calls my name").

If Young's triumph is that he will never lose the way to love, his need to locate that special someone can certainly cause tribulations. "Like a Hurricane," with its gale-force guitar playing, is a perfect either/or, neither/ nor description of a modern-day Gatsby caught between the tangible idea of transcendental love and the intangible reality of it. Everything is "hazy," "foggy," lit by "moonbeam" and "the light from star to star."

> *I am just a dreamer*
> *But you are just a dream*
> *And you could have been anyone to me*
> *Before that moment you touched my lips*
> *That perfect feeling when time just slips*
> *Away between us and our foggy trip*

The first three lines imply that the singer's need to invent someone to love may be far greater than the someone he finds. One can infer from the last three lines that the feeling gained from the *creation* and the chance taken is undoubtedly worth it, no matter what the cost. Is there a happy ending? I don't think so. "I want to love you / But I'm getting blown away," Young sings. It's like *Key Largo* with feedback.

Although he may be circling in a peculiar and seemingly haphazard manner (some claim he has as many as nine unreleased albums), Neil Young has a very good chance to be the most important American rock & roll artist in the Seventies. Bruce Springsteen, Jackson Browne and others must be considered, of course, but I don't know anyone who goes after the essences with as much daring as Young. I don't know anyone who finds them like he does, either.

■ RANDOM NOTES (September 8, 1977)

While ex-partners Crosby, Stills and Nash were recapturing the national limelight, Neil Young went off in the opposite direction to join the Ducks—temporarily at least. Published reports to that effect upset Young's regular backup band, Crazy Horse, so a source close to the reclusive singer is now saying Young will "definitely not be quacking on a permanent basis."

Young was serious enough about the band to have rented a beach house in Santa Cruz, about seventy miles south of San Francisco, to rehearse. Consisting of Young's old friend Jeff Blackburn (once of Blackburn and Snow) on rhythm guitar, Bob Mosley (once of Moby Grape) on bass and Johnny Craviotto (who has toured with Ry Cooder and Arlo Guthrie) on drums, the Ducks played local bars, charging no more than $2.50.

The Ducks had a set of about fifteen songs, mostly by Blackburn and Mosley, with just a handful by Young: "Mr. Soul," "Ready for the Country" and "Long May You Run."

"This band isn't just me and some other guys who back me up," Young had said before splitting town to avoid curiosity seekers and to placate Crazy Horse. "I just play my part. It kind of reminds me of when I was with the Buffalo Springfield. It feels good to be part of this group, like being in a band for the first time."

And where was it all going? "We don't want to plan ahead," Young had said adamantly. "I think we've all been planning ahead too much already. We'll just give it a chance and see what happens."

■ RANDOM NOTES (July 13, 1978)

The theme of Neil Young's film-in-progress, *Human Highway*, is still a mystery, but his five-night solo acoustic stand at San Francisco's Boarding House, which found him "wired for sound—and that's not all," revealed a healthy, duded-up and inspired singer/songwriter whose documentary aspirations may be dangerously close to those of Bob Dylan's. (One source said, a little mournfully: "He liked *Renaldo and Clara*. . . . He didn't think it should be cut.")

Young played a song, "Out of the Blue and into the Black," dedicated to Johnny Rotten. One of the lines was "better to burn than to rust." He recorded it with the New Wave group Devo. New songs that impressed included "Comes a Time" (title track for his again-delayed next album, which had been billed as *Give to the Wind*), "Thrasher" and "Already One," a tune for his son. Actress Sally Kirkland, in what was apparently a scripted moment, stepped onstage and hung onto Young like a groupie. One whisper said the movie would be about "the people who follow him around."

YOUNG'S *GIVE TO THE WIND* DUE

THE NEW NEIL YOUNG album, *Give to the Wind,* has finally been set for release on May 15. Recorded late last year in Nashville, the LP utilizes many of the same session musicians who assisted Young on *Harvest.* Largely acoustic, the album is an impassioned return to the folk and country themes of earlier albums.

Young, who appears in *The Last Waltz* singing "Helpless," has lain low since his '76 tour with Crazy Horse. His only stage appearance has been a one-shot benefit at Bicentennial Park in Miami Beach last November, when he showed up with his entire twenty-four-piece Gone with the Wind Orchestra, featuring fiddle, steel guitar, four acoustic guitarists and a female accompanist, Nicolette Larson, on vocals. After an hour-and-a-half set that debuted most of his new material, Young closed with a tribute to Lynyrd Skynyrd—his own version of "Sweet Home Alabama."

Give to the Wind has been delayed by art and sequencing of cuts, no surprise to Young aficionados. Young has been traveling North America in his customized bus, visiting family in Toronto and sightseeing with his son, Zeke. Plans for a major concert tour were recently canceled, and instead, Young will make his "summer tour" a four-day stint at San Francisco's 200-seat Boarding House.

New song titles include "Already One," "Motorcycle Mama" and "Human Highway."

PEGGYLEE BELLAS

NEIL YOUNG'S *HUMAN HIGHWAY*

NEIL YOUNG HAS started filming a documentary-style modern western entitled *Human Highway* (also the name of one of Young's new songs). He will share directing and writing credits with Dean Stockwell *(Compulsion),* who will also costar with Young. Others committed to roles include Dennis Hopper, Sally Kirkland and the New Wave group Devo.

The film will be a mixture of concert footage and other scenes shot on location at Young's ranch and in Taos, New Mexico. One sequence reportedly involves an attack by robbers on Young's tour bus. Young will use no backup band in the film and will play only acoustic instruments. He will use a wireless microphone system for amplification, enabling him to leave the stage and interact with audiences or to be recorded while walking down a highway.

L.A. Johnson, who worked with Young on *Journey Through the Past,* will produce the film. Johnson's other credits include *The Last Waltz, Woodstock* and *Renaldo and Clara.* David Myers *(Journey through the Past, Marjoe, Renaldo and Clara* and *The Last Waltz)* will be chief cinematographer. The film will be shot in 16mm.

No release date has been set, and it is not certain whether a soundtrack will be released.

PAUL NELSON

NEIL YOUNG PERFORMANCE REVIEW

Young's One-Stop World Tour
The Boarding House, San Francisco
May 26, 27, 1978

WHEN NEIL YOUNG performed with Crazy Horse at the Palladium in New York City almost two years ago, he made such an impression on me that sometime during the opening show (for which I had a ticket), I knew I had to see them all. For the first time in my life, I patronized the scalpers. Though the tickets cost something like thirty bucks apiece, they were the only way to get in, and I just couldn't let the music stop. Here was rock & roll so primal and unexplainable that I simply wanted to let it wash over me, pulse through me. When Young wandered out and began to play songs like "Cortez the Killer" and "Like a Hurricane" on his black electric guitar, I figured I'd at last found the perfect target for that most overused of adjectives: *mythic*. For once, none of the answers mattered, because the questions themselves formed such complete and satisfying entities—entities that had long crossed the border of Freudian logic and were now headed out toward the farthest of the far countries. *Neil Jung,* I wrote in my notebook. A not-inappropriate pun.

At his recent five-night gig at San Francisco's Boarding House (a club that seats fewer than 300), Young played four acoustic guitars, harmonica and piano. There was no backup band. Surprisingly, the lack of electricity diminished neither his rock & roll effectiveness nor his enormous mystique, though it did make clear his folk-music roots. ("Sugar Mountain," in fact, almost sounded like a summary of how, for some, folk music leads naturally into the perhaps more lethal art of rock & roll. After he'd sung it, someone in the audience said, "That song's about being twenty." No, I thought to myself, that song's about *not* being twenty.) At any rate, Neil Young's "1978 world tour"—he plans to spend the rest of the year working on his second movie, *Human Highway,* much of which was filmed at these concerts—proved that he doesn't need anybody but himself up there, that he can rule a stage through the sheer force of his will. *Strength,* I wrote in my notebook. Pure strength.

B EFORE THE FIRST set, I notice I'm not the only fanatic who's flown all the way across America just to hear Neil Young. John Rockwell from the *New York Times* is here, and he seems as obsessed as I do. As does Cameron Crowe from ROLLING STONE's Los Angeles office. While we're waiting, we trade stories, the best of which are that Young once wrote, recorded, but didn't issue an album made up entirely of songs whose *titles* other people had made famous ("Born to Run," "Sail Away," "Greensleeves," etc.), and that he's got well over 175 songs in releasable form—nearly twenty LPs' worth. There are three large wooden Indians on the dimly lit stage. We sit and stare at them for a while. They seem to say it all.

When Young appears onstage—he doesn't ever seem to walk on: All of a sudden, he's just *there*—he announces, "It's good to be back on the boards again, as Mick Jagger said in 1967." He pauses for a moment, looks down, then fixes the crowd with a benevolent, behind-blue-eyes stare. His eyebrows are so black he looks like a cartoon varmint trying to emulate the barrels of a shotgun. "Just think of me as one you never figure," he says. My God, the guy can read minds, I think. Not only that, but he's his own best critic.

True to his word, Young does a lot of things no one can figure. Technically, he's literally wired for sound with a set of complicated electronics that enable him to move about freely without any visible microphones. (Once, when something goes awry in the control room, he emits static and sputters like the Six Million Dollar Man-gone-bad.) Musically, he plays impeccably—and *in tune.* And with *Comes a Time,* his new record, due out soon, you'd expect him to do quite a few songs from it, right? Wrong. He does three: the title tune, the lovely "Already One" (about Carrie Snodgress and their son, Zeke) and "Human Highway." He doesn't sing that many old favorites either, though "Birds," "After the Gold Rush," "Sugar Mountain," "Down by the River," "Cowgirl in the Sand" and a Buffalo Springfield song called "Out of My Mind" invariably bring the house down.

Instead, Young stalks the stage like a slightly seedy James Stewart/Henry Fonda type—moving in arhythmic bobs and weaves, he sometimes seems to be performing a near-tribal dance—and guides us through a raft of new (or at least unreleased) material: "Out of the Blue and into the Black," "Thrasher," "Shots," "Pocahontas," "Powderfinger," "Sail Away," "Ride My Llama" ("an extraterrestrial folk song"), "The Ways of Love." Of these, I'd bet *at least* two are masterpieces. "Out of the Blue and into the Black" is about—well, here are some of the words:

My my, hey hey, rock & roll is here to stay
It's better to burn out than to fade away . . .
The king is gone but he's not forgotten
This is the story of Johnny Rotten . . .
Hey hey, my my, rock & roll can never die
There's more to the picture than meets the eye . . .

And "Thrasher"—a complex and incredibly touching song about friendship, duty, work and death, I'd guess, after four listenings—sounded even better, especially on the twelve-string guitar.

In the manner of the best of the traditional blues singers, Neil Young seems totally alone onstage in a way that almost no contemporary performer ever does. But he's not foreboding, and you don't feel shut off. Head down, chin tucked into his shoulders like a boxer, he peers out at you with those all-knowing eyes filled with humor and flashes that beatific, silly grin. Like Muhammad Ali, he may well be the greatest. But we'll never know until we hear those 175 or so unreleased songs, will we? How about it? I'm ready and raring to go.

CAMERON CROWE

GETTING INTO NEIL YOUNG'S BIZARRE ACT

THE SIGN—CRAZY NEIL—has hung outside Neil Young's dressing room for several tours now. Down the hall it's YOUNG HORSE. Almost ten years after "Cinnamon Girl," Neil Young and Crazy Horse are back on the road with a show like no other in rock & roll.

Young has always denounced the impersonal feel of big halls, so as a partial solution he's changed the scale for this tour. The set is a huge bandstand complete with oversized amps, man-sized glass of water, four-foot harmonica and a towering "microphone"—all erected in front of the audience by scurrying, hooded figures with gleaming red eyes.

The house lights dim and we hear Jimi Hendrix' Woodstock version of "Star-Spangled Banner" over the sound system, then the Beatles' "A Day in the Life." Suddenly Neil Young bolts up from atop one of the massive amps where he has been "sleeping." Picking up a guitar and singing by way of a wireless mike, he wanders childlike around the surreal bandstand playing acoustic songs spanning his entire career, from "I Am a Child" to "Comes a Time." He crawls back into a sleeping bag and the "road-eyes," as he calls them, prepare for an electric set with Crazy Horse.

While the equipment is being set up, the sound system booms announcements from the stage at Woodstock (remember "There's some brown acid out there that is not specifically . . . too good"). The fully scripted show has the unmistakable feel of a dreamlike retrospective of Young's last twelve years.

I catch up with the always elusive Young in the lobby of his New York hotel:

"Neil," I say, "for the first time you seem to be tying together onstage all the directions of your career into a kind of futuristic/nostalgic statement."

"Can't find a newspaper in this town," he says.

I try again backstage at Madison Square Garden, just after his second sold-out performance:

"Neil," I venture, "this show would surprise anybody expecting the old laid-back image."

"The songs all fit a certain mood. Frank, Billy and Ralphy [Crazy Horse] are playing really great."

The next night at Nassau Coliseum: "Neil, the playing of stage announcements from Woodstock . . ."

"I have an idea for the show," he says. "It's a parody of when I used to wait for everyone to be quiet before playing. Well, just as the show is about to start, this popcorn vendor is making all this noise toward the front of the stage: 'Hey, get your popcorn.' The stage announcer comes out and says that Neil Young won't come out until everyone is quiet and that *vendor* leaves. But the vendor doesn't leave, he makes more noise. The kids start getting pissed off, then the vendor jumps onstage." Young laughs. *"I am the vendor."*

"Incredible," I say. "But the concept of this show and the road-eyes?"

"Want some participatory journalism? You're going to work tonight. Larry, Jeannie . . . fix him up."

My transformation into road-eye takes several minutes. Young enthusiastically explains the duties: as a road-eye I can do anything as long as I crouch and move with "urgent fervor." For the second half of the set I am to change into an elderly professor, the free-roaming assistant to Doctor Deaf (coproducer David Briggs). This way, I can take notes in character.

Wandering around onstage during a performance is an education. You hear deafening, echoing applause, but it's impossible to see the audience, save for the first seven rows. Those rows are all too clear. You can see the guy and his date trying to light a roach, acid casualties fluttering their hands, guards goosing young girls who've rushed the stage and mesmerized faces wondering exactly what Young is up to this time. Young, grinning as if he's finally at home onstage with his assortment of road-eyes, doctors and professors swirling around, has never played with so much passion.

The month-long tour will be captured in Young's upcoming movie, *Human Highway*—which is a good thing because it shouldn't go unrecorded. In the warm words of a fellow road-eye, as we were erecting the giant microphone in front of 16,000 screaming fans, "He's the only guy I would wear this goddamn hood for . . . he's the only guy that would *ask*."

JOHN ROCKWELL

NEIL YOUNG AND CRAZY HORSE PERFORMANCE REVIEW

Theatrics Belittle Neil Young and Crazy Horse
Madison Square Garden, New York City
September 28, 1978

IN 1972 NEIL YOUNG had a Number One album with *Harvest*. The experience horrified him, and he turned to defiantly raw, personal and commercially marginal music making. But what he's lost in sales, he's gained steadily in critical reputation, so much so that for some of us he counts now as the single most important figure in Seventies rock.

Recently, Young has begun to relax a bit about softer sentiment, suggesting the possibility of revitalized commercial strength at no cost to his serious credentials. The purely folkish side of his music has always been centrally concerned with love, to be sure, even if the spare instrumentation, crude recording and that quavery voice kept him far from the middle of the road. But the new *Comes a Time* album was cut mostly in Nashville, with pervasive, female harmony singing (Nicolette Larson), smooth country sessionmen and even a string section.

For a while, Young considered a large-scale tour this past spring with Larson and the Nashville musicians. But it proved unwieldy to coordinate the session players, and so finally Young decided to tour with Crazy Horse, and it was this pairing that showed up for two nights at the Garden in late September.

The reversion to Crazy Horse may well have allayed Young's guilt that he had drifted back too close to the commercialism of *Harvest* with *Comes a Time,* but it caused problems. Crazy Horse has always been an extremely crude outfit, and it's never made much of an impact apart from Young. Combined on this tour with an unusually loud and distorted sound system, the band bludgeoned many of Young's best songs into rough reductions of their recorded originals—even when the originals were also with Crazy Horse. There's a thin line between noble primitivism and simple ineptitude, and too often Crazy Horse crossed that line.

There were other problems, too. Young had given a lot of thought to the need for theatrics in a large-scale concert setting, and his choice reflected a shrewd anticipation of the sort of audience this tour seems to be attracting—young, male and raucous. The stage was dwarfed by props designed as oversized amplifiers and speaker banks, with the roadies dressed in the brown robes and beady red eyes of the Jawas of *Star Wars*. Young was literally uncovered "sleeping" on an amp, and his childlike costume and the outsize props reinforced the aura of boyish wonderment; his first two selections were "Sugar Mountain" and "I Am a Child." The concert as a whole played with concepts of maturation, Sixties idealism and the loss inherent with growth.

But even while one could applaud the cleverness of Young's theatrics, their actuality looked a little silly and self-conscious; as his film *Journey Through the Past* suggested, Young is no more sure-footed than Dylan when he tries to extend his art from the musical to the theatrical and visual. The very staginess of all those Jawas scurrying about undercut the honesty that lies at the heart of his music.

Still, the concert was both a commercial success and appreciably superior to Dylan's current offerings. There was still enough subtlety, sophistication and haunting emotionality in the acoustic material, and enough biting passion in the best of the electric songs, to reaffirm Young's permanent place in the past decade of rock & roll.

DAVID FRICKE

THE 20 GREATEST CONCERTS

Neil Young and Crazy Horse U.S. Tour
September–October 1978

As part of its twentieth-anniversary celebration, ROLLING STONE commemorated the greatest live rock performances of the last two decades. ROLLING STONE editors' criteria: "the most exciting, musically outstanding and historically significant concerts." According to David Fricke, "Our selection highlights the lasting impact and pivotal artistic contributions of the musicians . . . captured in their finest performances."

NEIL YOUNG WAS ON A SAILING holiday with his family, skating over the blue Pacific waves in his schooner, when it hit him. "I started thinking of this idea," he says. "Some kid has a dream that he could be in a rock & roll band. He's a little kid, so everything's bigger than life—all of the gear is so huge. So he's asleep on top of this big amplifier, and he wakes up and sings a couple of acoustic songs about being young. Then he comes down off the amp and starts walking around, getting more knowledge, thinking about more worldly things."

For twenty-two performances during the fall of 1978, that dream became reality, sort of. Every night on Neil Young's all too brief but truly memorable *Rust Never Sleeps* tour, that guitar-toting tot—played by Young himself—woke atop a giant Fender amplifier and found himself on a fairytale bandstand populated by elfin "road-eyes" in oversize monk's cowls who moved the giant equipment and danced madly in the wings. Stage announcements from the Woodstock festival came over the P.A. like voices from a mythic rock & roll past ("Hey, if you think really hard, maybe we can stop this rain!"). And when pint-size Neil wasn't happily strumming songs of childhood and innocence like "Sugar Mountain" and "I Am a Child," he made a joyful noise with his electric guitar, wreaking megadecibel havoc on "Cinnamon Girl," "Like a Hurricane" and "Cortez the Killer" with the help of his faithful crunch-rock trio Crazy Horse.

THE '78 *RUST NEVER SLEEPS* tour, which spawned two records (the electric half of the *Rust Never Sleeps* album and the double *Live Rust*) as well as a feature-length concert film, was a delightful combination of mischievous surrealism and Neil Young's greatest hits, a dramatic confirmation of both Young's songwriting achievements and his love of offbeat rock & roll theater. But Young's *Rust Never Sleeps* fantasy of a young boy in love with this wild new sound also symbolized everything that was right about rock at a time when everything about the music seemed wrong. In a pop world bloated by disco and fatuous arena rock, little Neil and his band cut away the crap and reveled in the essentials. *Rust Never Sleeps* was Young's demonstration of faith in the true power of rock & roll—that with a great song and a band of good buddies, anybody could move the earth.

It was easy to miss the point of the show, and at the time, some critics did. The original ROLLING STONE review of Young's September 28 show in New York was headlined THEATRICS BELITTLE NEIL YOUNG AND CRAZY HORSE. Young insists that the staging was crucial to the realization of the dream. The Woodstock announcements, for example, "were like part of a storybook for the kid, like a rock & roll bible," he explains. "It was like all this history was happening all over again for him." Indeed, Young took his scenario a step further in 1986 with a tour called In a Rusted Out Garage, in which little Neil and Crazy Horse "rehearsed" nightly in a fictional suburban garage stocked with some of the old *Rust* props. "Where *Rust Never Sleeps* was the dream, the garage was the reality of the same kid, working hard to get that big gig," he says.

Young admits that *Rust*'s skyscraping-amplifier motif actually served a very practical purpose. When he and Crazy Horse first set up their equipment in rehearsal, "we could see that it was really ugly," he says. "We had so much shit onstage. I just thought, Well, it sounds like one big amp. Why don't we just make it look like one?" The road-eyes were, of course, modeled on the hobbitlike Jawas from *Star Wars*. "The *Star Wars* thing had just started, and that was a big thing for kids," Young says. "I took everything that would affect a child at that time and jumbled it together." But Young's favorite part of the *Rust* show was when Crazy Horse—bassist Billy Talbot, drummer Ralph Molina and guitarist Frank Sampedro—plugged in a third of the way through, turning songs like "The Loner" and "Welfare Mothers" into glorious displays of fuzz-tone fireworks. "The thing about *Rust* that I'm happiest about is it put Crazy Horse in its true perspective. I talk to a lot of musicians who say, 'Why do you bother to play with these guys? They make mistakes, the rhythm is uneven. . . .' I don't care. All I care about is the groove and whether we're having a good time.

"We don't want to be good," he adds, cackling with impish delight, quoting little Neil's theme song from In a Rusted Out Garage. "It's just not in our plan."

GREIL MARCUS

COMES A TIME ALBUM REVIEW
Neil Young Harvests Another Gold Rush

N*EW MUSICAL EXPRESS* recently carried an item noting that Neil
Young had been awarded a gold record solely for the number of
test pressings he'd racked up for *Comes a Time*— well, you never
know. As with so many other Young productions, *Comes a Time* was less
released than drawn out. I seem to remember hearing radio ads for it last
spring, though since no one was sure of the title at that time (*Gone with the
Wind* was on the boards for a while), the snatches of song were simply
announced as from "the new Neil Young album." I lost count of how
many times Young was reported to have rejected the vinyl Warner Com-
munications had in mind, or how many changes the cover art suffered
before Young settled on an ordinary Huckleberry Neil photo for the front
and a paste-on sheet of titles for the back. And that's not even to mention
what the four producers (including Young) and ten engineers presumably
went through. It must have taken forever to get the sound unbalanced
properly.

All of which ensures a certain disappointment—in *this* case—because
Comes a Time is neither a knockout punch like last year's *American Stars 'n
Bars* nor a wildly idiosyncratic, cracked triumph/disaster like *Zuma* or *On
the Beach*. A restrained and modest set of love songs that traces a long affair
from first light to final regrets, *Comes a Time* is a singer/songwriter's offering,
more like *After the Gold Rush* or *Harvest* than any other Young LP—though
without most of the cloying innocence of those two enormously popular
records. It's a pleasing, clearly commercial piece of work that's defended
from slickness by Young's insistence on playing out of tune, skewing the
levels of the vocals (Nicolette Larson is sometimes given a true screech) and
singing without much affectation. *Comes a Time* isn't deep, it's not threatening, and Young can't have intended it to be: he can dive deep and make
his threats stick when he wants to. Rather, the album is meant to be straight
and honest—folkish, like Young's small-club "World Tour" at the Boarding House in San Francisco last May. The clatter and clash of Young's best
music (from "Cowgirl in the Sand" to "Like a Hurricane"), the jagged,
tearing emotion that explodes even out of the messy rehearsal tapes for

"Alabama" and "Words" (released on *Journey Through the Past*) is missing, or muted.

The music doesn't press; it's comfortable. There's a moment halfway through "Look Out for My Love" when the guitar turns into a fiddle and the passion rises like an omen—but it's a moment, no more. "In the field of opportunity / It's plowing time again" are fabulous lines—I laughed out loud when a friend quoted them to me a few months ago—but here Young has taken the glee out of them. Their ribaldry is muffled by a hokey hillbilly arrangement, and what should have been an outrageous double-entendre just sounds contrived when Young refuses to stick to his musical concept, singing "plowing" instead of the "plowin' " his country mode is begging for. The LP includes a traditional amount of traditional Neil Young sappiness, as when he wonders why the world spinning round doesn't make the trees fall down.

Comes a Time comes across despite all this, partly because we know Young never has and never will make a record without glaring flaws (think of the endless "Will to Love" on *American Stars 'n Bars*), and because the dose of personality it contains is bracing. Young long ago gave up trying to sing properly; his last real attempt to do so (*Neil Young,* his first solo album) is made up of better songs than is *Comes a Time*. But it sounds stiff and emotionally compromised by comparison. Here, even on the more standard compositions, his voice wars with the facelessness of the material: it breaks, surges, drops back on itself. If at first the new LP seems all smooth surface, Young's voice cracks that surface and carries you through the tale he's telling, even warning at one point that he'll soon be boring you, yet never making good on that promise. When Young closes out his story with Ian Tyson's "Four Strong Winds," there's a real sense of time having passed, of choices made and chances blown: The wistfulness of Tyson's song doesn't survive Young's refusal to cater to its prettiness.

It's still pretty—Meat Loaf could sing "Four Strong Winds" and it'd probably still be pretty—but it's also knocked off the pedestal that has always been part of the tune's package. Young sings as if he's talking to a real person, not as if he's engaging in a precious reverie with himself. The unpleasantness—i.e., the utter conventionality—of the composition falls away, and the pressed-flower poetry of the chorus dissolves into something like plain talk. I found myself thinking of Bob Dylan's "If You See Her, Say Hello" and "Shelter from the Storm."

For all its clichés, though, "Four Strong Winds" stands out *here* because it's a carefully crafted song, crafted to stick in your mind, and Young's own songs on *Comes a Time* aren't and don't. They're incidents on an album and they work as such, but dropped onto other records, they'd be forgettable.

(Save for "Field of Opportunity," which, despite all I've said against its performance, is just too neat an idea to fade from memory.) There's a dogged retreat from musical intensity on the new disc: nothing to match the chorus of "Helpless" or the shivery hesitations of "Tonight's the Night." The terrible drama of Young's guitar—a quality, based in the ancient modal figures of mountain music, that always suggests dread and courage—is present only in fragments and distant echoes. It's those echoes that save *Comes a Time* from the little-boy-lost conceits of *Harvest* and *After the Gold Rush,* and the fact that they're no more than echoes may make this LP just as commercially potent. If so, commercial success will continue to give Young the freedom he has fought for, won, used and stood up to better than any rock & roller of the decade.

Junking covers and test pressings, suggesting new art and then junking that too, ending up with out-of-phase singing and worse, is all part of that freedom—a way of testing it, pushing it, seeing what one can get away with in the corporate world on which Young's music rests. Though *Comes a Time* seems like a move toward easy acceptance and the act of a man who knows it's time to tidy up his economic base, those unbalanced vocals and flat notes might be seen as the flip side of fiddling with the record company: a way of testing the audience, keeping it just a bit off guard—reminding those who'll love *Comes a Time* because it can be mooned over that something a lot rougher, who knows what, is certain to follow.

SALLEY RAYL

MALIBU FIRE TAKES ROCK STARS' HOMES

IT WAS ALMOST TOO much of a coincidence. As Neil Young, appearing with Crazy Horse on October 23 at the Inglewood Forum, sang "I was standing in a burned-out basement," the opening lines to "After the Gold Rush," his Zuma Beach house was burning to the ground.

That day, Southern California was besieged by four major fires and twelve smaller brush fires, now known as the Black Monday fires. But the Agoura/Malibu blaze that leveled Young's house was by far the most devastating. Possibly the area's worst in terms of property loss, the Agoura/Malibu fire also gutted the homes of the Band's Garth Hudson, actresses Katharine Ross and Ali MacGraw and comedian Buddy Hackett. Propelled into a storm by sixty-mile-per-hour winds, the flames spewed balls of fire and brush that ravaged some 28,000 acres of land. Though there were fifty to sixty injuries reported, only one death was recorded.

It has been more than a year since Neil Young has lived in his two-story Zuma Beach house, once owned by F. Scott Fitzgerald and something of a landmark. "It was such a shame," says neighbor Rick Danko. "Neil shared that house with so many people. It was just one of those magical places. But somebody found the original blueprints so perhaps it can be built back to specification."

■ **RANDOM NOTES** (December 28, 1978–January 11, 1979)
Several tapes cut in 1965 by a group called the Mynah Birds—including Neil Young, his Buffalo Springfield buddy Bruce Palmer and Rick James—may be too sketchy to add up to an album for Motown Records, which recently discovered the tracks in their archives.

CAMERON CROWE

NEIL YOUNG: THE LAST AMERICAN HERO

It was supposed to be something holy, *for God's sake, when old Ernie sat down at the piano. . . . I swear to God, if I were a piano player, or an actor or something, and all those dopes thought I was terrific, I'd hate it. I wouldn't even want them to clap for me. People always clap at the wrong things. If I were a piano player, I'd play it in the goddam closet.*
—HOLDEN CAULFIELD, *The Catcher in the Rye*

MY PARENTS OCCUPIED the bedroom directly above mine while I was growing up. Luckily they were heavy sleepers, and loud music late at night didn't seem to bother them much—unless, of course, it was the high-pitched guitar or vocal work of Neil Young. On such occasions, my mother would trudge downstairs, rap at the door and stand there with a look that suggested the wrath of every deprived sleeper over the ages.

"Are we going to listen to this man baying at the moon all night?" she would invariably ask, on behalf of my father and herself.

There was a time, sure, when I tried to explain to them what it was to be a Neil Young fan. "How important is an in-tune vocal?" . . . "But it's *great* when he hits the same note thirty-eight times in 'Down by the River.' " Here was an *artist,* as opposed to an entertainer. Here was someone who would never turn up hawking his wares on some talk show.

Young's popularity would soon speak for itself. In 1972 my parents would hear "Heart of Gold" played in the supermarket, find it tuneful, and begin to see things differently. When Young announced he would be playing San Diego, our hometown, on a rare concert tour, it became a family outing. My sister, my teenage cousins visiting from Kentucky, my parents and I all went to the show.

Young appeared right on time, nervously walking out in front of the screaming crowd, one arm upraised. He looked skittish and tired as he picked up a guitar and began to sing an acoustic song, one of the first he ever wrote, called "Sugar Mountain." The audience rushed the stage, shouted for the electric songs and Young called his band out onstage. But instead of Buffalo Springfield chestnuts and standards like "Down by the River," they played a set of reckless new music, causing no small tension in the arena.

Then, during the final song of the evening, the pressure seemed to cause Young to crack. He began to shout, "Wake up San Diego. Get up San Diego. . . ." A few minutes later, the houselights were turned on and the hall was filled with an eerie silence.

"He acts like a drunken monkey," said one of my cousins. The rest of the family didn't say much. We didn't talk about Neil Young for the next few years.

Recently, I found myself back in the same old room late one night, typing this article and listening to Neil Young records, when a familiar knock came at the door.

"Well," said my mother with a note of sentimentality. "A *survivor.*"

THE FACT THAT NEIL YOUNG can barely relate to his successful current album, *Comes a Time,* is typical of his career, and perhaps one of the reasons he *is* a survivor. He's thirty-three and he's spent twelve years in the forefront of the most fickle of businesses, shattering expectations. "It's in the middle of a soft place," he says of the album. "It was made to come out a year ago and got hung up with pressing problems. I hear it on the radio and it sounds nice. . . . But I'm somewhere else now. I'm into rock & roll."

Held up because Young had approved a faulty test pressing of the album, and then bought back $160,000 worth of the already printed record because of his mistake, *Comes a Time* is a complacent Neil Young album. In the time that it took for the LP to come out, something in music changed. Much of the music made by artists who came to popularity in the Sixties and Seventies began to fall on deaf young ears.

"I first knew something was going on when we visited England a year and a half ago," says Young. Sitting in the half-light of his ranch home in northern California after the end of his *Rust Never Sleeps* tour, Young speaks with an urgency. "Kids were tired of the rock stars and the limousines and the abusing of stage privileges as stars. There was new music the kids were listening to. As soon as I heard my contemporaries saying, 'God, what the fuck is *this*. . . . This is going to be over in three months,' I knew it was a sure sign right there that they're going to bite it if they don't watch out. And a lot of them are biting it this year. People are not going to come back to see the same thing over and over again. It's got to change. It's the snake that eats itself. Punk music, New Wave. You can call it what you want. It's rock & roll and to me, it's still the basis of what's going on."

Young had given up on touring and was working on his second movie, a comedy/fantasy/musical called *Human Highway,* in which he plays a folk singer named Neil Young, when his friend Dean Stockwell (who plays Otto, the manager, in the film) told him about the New Wave band, Devo. Young knew immediately that this was the band he wanted for a nightmare episode in the film. He even had the song they would play together, the new one called "Out of the Blue" that he'd written with the Sex Pistols in mind ("It's better to burn out / Than it is to rust").

Members of Devo were flown in from their base in Akron, Ohio, to shoot the nightmare sequence in front of an audience at the San Francisco punk club Mabuhay Gardens. Devo introduced Young as "Grandpa Granola," and played the song live and in a local studio before flying back to Akron. Later, listening closely to the tape, Young heard two of the members chanting the phrase, "Rust never sleeps."

He called them in Akron. "What is 'Rust never sleeps'?"

Two of the members of Devo, it turns out, used to be in advertising. They had devised the phrase during a campaign for the rust-remover Rustoleum and decided it fit the song. To Young, it fit his very career, and his battle against the dreaded, creeping disease of trying to make a good thing last. Suddenly, Young once again felt the pull of the road, felt the pull of rock & roll. He booked a six-week tour with Crazy Horse, plotted a fully scripted show with filmmakers/directors L.A. Johnson and Jeanne Field, and took off on *Rust Never Sleeps*.

"I knew I had to get out there and rock," he says. "But I also knew that I couldn't see myself out there doing it the way it had always been. Standing out there with a microphone. It's got to continue to be as new as when it started.

"The music business is so big these days, I feel dwarfed by it. I mean, I put out a record and, you know, it does okay. Somebody like Foreigner or Boston, they come out with a record and sell ten times as many as I do. I think that's great. But I still feel like this . . . little guy."

A set was designed in which huge amps and a huge microphone were constructed before the audience's eyes by Young's roadies. Now they were Road-Eyes, dressed in blackface and hoods not unlike *Star Wars* Jawas. (When Young explained the concept to his puzzled crew, he instructed them to "wave yourself goodbye for a few hours then move with fervor and purpose." Young himself would play a child dreaming about rock & roll.) Beginning the shows with "Sugar Mountain," he moved through a cross section of old and new songs, ending with a phenomenally loud set with Crazy Horse. "I wanted people to leave saying that Neil Young's show was the loudest fucking thing they'd ever heard." It was a heavy-metal tour de force, and somewhere in the middle of the tour, *Comes a Time,* Young's most subdued album since *Harvest,* was finally released.

"You know," says Young, confidently, "I do the same thing over and over and over again. It has a slightly different look to it every time. This tour seemed to wrap something up. It's a retrospective, but it's looking back on right now. I think I broke through to another arena; now, people won't be surprised if I enhance the program with actors and diverge totally away from music, then come back out of it into music again. It's making rock & roll more visible to me."

He is struck with an idea. "I'm lucky," says Young. "Somehow, by doing what I wanted to do, I manage to give people what they don't want to hear and they *still* come back. I haven't been able to figure that out yet."

I FIRST MET NEIL YOUNG in 1973, on a bus to San Luis Obispo. He had come along to play guitar with the Eagles at a small benefit for the Indian community there. Young sat playing banjo, a grinning cipher in reflector shades. I was instructed not to talk to him, that he had nothing to say.

After the show—which climaxed with a fiery "Down by the River" that Young and the Eagles still talk about—Young plopped down in the seat next to mine. His shades were off, and his eyes were dark, sunken shadows below an Indian-like forehead. But they were mischievous, adolescent eyes. Dennis the Menace eyes.

"Hey," he said, "Bernard Shakey." We shook hands, and he began to tell me that he was an amateur filmmaker, that he was working on his first film (he was finishing *Journey Through the Past* at the time) and was a little nervous about it. He talked excitedly, punctuating his words with a smirk. "Tough business. I'd hate to go back to shooting Hyatt House commercials."

I turned to look out the window, remembering my impression of Neil Young as a depressed loner. Now here he was—a joker. I turned back around. He was gone, of course, and I was right back where I started.

Young must have remembered the conversation or enjoyed my gullibility. Two years later, when he was releasing his most antipop album, *Tonight's the Night,* I received a phone call saying that he was ready to do an interview.

There was a listening party in Los Angeles, his first-ever such media function, and we made plans over beers to meet at manager Elliot Roberts' office. I arrived the next morning to find Young, cheerfully cordial, discussing the album with three hungover disc jockeys. "I just wanted to obliterate everything that I was, you know," he was saying, "and wipe the slate clean."

After the conference, Young remained on a sofa drinking orange juice and playing with his dog, Art ("Art is just a dog on my porch"). He sized me up and smiled.

"You need some sun," he said. "You look like people expect *me* to look. Let's go for a ride."

We walked across Sunset Strip and Young rented a red Mercedes convertible for the occasion of his first extensive interview in five years. A sweltering afternoon, we took a ride out Pacific Coast Highway. After a few attempts at small talk, Young turned and announced: "My uncle played ukulele. Outside of that, I don't really come from a musical family."

There was a lengthy silence. A car full of surfers made a dangerous swerve through traffic to pull alongside for a look. "Hippies," he cracked.

I asked him about his childhood, a question that met with a good two minutes of silence. I began to wonder if the interview was already over. Young was born in Toronto, the son of a sportswriter for the *Toronto Sun,* Scott Young. Young's parents split up when he was fourteen, and he moved to Winnipeg with his mother, Rassy.

"I know the newspaper business," said Young, who was a *Sun* paperboy. "I had a pretty good upbringing. I remember really good things about both my parents. I don't feel the need to communicate all that much with them. I think back on my childhood and I remember moving around a lot, from school to school. I was always breaking in." He looked over. "I liked to play jokes on people."

Jokes?

"Same old shit," he continued talkatively. "Once, I'd become a victim of a series of chump attacks by some of the bullies in my room. I looked up and three guys were staring at me, mouthing, 'you low-life prick.' Then the guy who sat in front of me turned around and hit my books off the desk with his elbow. He did this a few times. I guess I wore the wrong color of clothes or something. Maybe I looked too much like a mamma's boy for them.

"Anyway, I went up to the teacher and asked if I could have the dictionary. This was the first time I'd broken the ice and put my hand up to ask for anything since I got to the fucking place. Everybody thought I didn't speak. So I got the dictionary, this big Webster's with little indentations for your thumb under every letter. I took it back to my desk, thumbed through it a little bit. Then I just sort of stood up in my seat, raised it up above my head as far as I could and hit the guy in front of me over the head with it. Knocked him out.

"Yeah, I got expelled for a day and a half, but I let those people know just where I was at. That's the way I fight. If you're going to *fight,* you may as well fight to wipe who or whatever it is *out.* Or don't fight at all."

He looked over again, offering me a vision of my own amazement in his shades.

"Few years later, I just felt it," he concluded cheerfully. "All of a sudden I wanted a guitar and that was it."

IN HIS MIDTEENS, NEIL YOUNG hit the Winnipeg dance-band circuit with his band, the Squires, and his own songs—stinging instrumentals heavily influenced by the Shadows and the Ventures. Then came the Beatles and Bob Dylan, and Young started to write lyrics.

"I never forgot," he says, "that every time a new Beatles or Dylan album came out, you *knew* they were way beyond it. They were always doing something else, always moving down the line."

Moving back to Toronto, Young soon took up a twelve-string acoustic guitar and tried folk singing around the coffeehouses. He made friends easily with other musicians like Stephen Stills, Joni Mitchell and Richie Furay, who were traveling along the same path. Mitchell wrote "The Circle Game" for him after hearing "Sugar Mountain," which was about growing too old to get into the local teen club.

Rock & roll, meanwhile, was booming. One of the biggest bands around Toronto was a group called Ricky James and the Mynah Birds. "We played rock and blues," James, now a disco star, recalls in Los Angeles. "I remember our first gig," continues James. "When Neil took his first solo, he was so excited he leaped off the stage, the plug came out and nobody heard anything."

The Mynah Birds broke up after a flirtation with Motown when James, AWOL from the navy, was arrested. Their young career at a standstill, James and Young spent a teary afternoon promising each other that they would form another band after James returned. "It was heavy, man," recalls James. "I had really gotten close to the cat. He was never very healthy—he got bad epileptic fits sometimes—but he had balls like you wouldn't believe."

After a while, money ran out and Young had to sell the Mynah Birds' equipment. Typical of his sense of humor, he used the money to buy a long, black Pontiac hearse and headed for Los Angeles with Mynah Birds' bassist Bruce Palmer. Neither had working permits or the proper papers. "But if you were looking for a break," says Young, "the great Canadian Dream is to get out. So we came down anyway."

They were lumbering down Sunset Boulevard when the Ontario license plates were spotted by two folkies Young had met up in Canada. Stephen Stills and Richie Furay pulled Young and Palmer over. There, on the street, they talked of their stalled careers. Stills and Furay's folk group had broken up, Stills had even failed an audition to join the Monkees because of his teeth. They decided to form a group, later adding Dewey Martin on drums. They named themselves after a steamroller, the Buffalo Springfield.

THE BUFFALO SPRINGFIELD were largely a West Coast phenomenon for most of their stormy two-year existence. Around Los Angeles, where their single, "For What It's Worth," became an anthem for the budding hippies battling cops on Sunset Strip, they were a sensation—a tougher, younger brother to the Byrds. Their live shows centered around incredible lead-guitar battles between Stills, the fair-haired, bluesy Southerner, and Young, the dark and fiery "Hollywood Indian" who was always either quitting or rejoining the group. Their fans split into camps and argued for years about why the group broke up.

"Stills and I have always gotten along," explained Young on his bus during his 1976 tour, as we headed for a show in Madison, Wisconsin. "I just had too much energy and so much creative flow coming out that when I wanted to get something down, I just felt like, 'This is my fucking trip and I don't have to listen to anybody else's.' I'd do what they wanted with *their* stuff, but I needed more space with my own. And that was a constant problem in my head. So that was why I had to quit. Then I'd come back 'cause it sounded so good. I just wasn't mature enough to deal with it. Everything was going much too fast."

By late 1968, the intense chemistry of the group had lit a fire under all its members. Everyone had scattered in different directions, leaving bassist and then engineer Jim Messina to assemble the band's third and final album, *Last Time Around,* at Sunset Sound studios. While Young was recording, though, Joni Mitchell was down the hall, beginning her first solo album produced by her then-boyfriend David Crosby.

"I don't really want to go down there," said Crosby at the time. "That guy Neil Young is strange."

Mitchell turned to her manager. "Elliot," she said, "you have to meet Neil Young. You'll love his sense of humor."

The possessor of a mercurial wit, Brooklyn-born Elliot Roberts immediately hit it off with Young. "Everybody was intimidated by Neil," says Roberts. "I heard all these stories—Neil had left the band twice. . . . Everyone was always on eggshells around Neil. Say the wrong word, he's gone. That is all I ever heard. Well, I found it easier to deal with Neil than Stephen. I used to tell people the funny things Neil had said. They'd say, 'Neil?' "

After the Springfield's demise, Roberts became Young's manager, and launched him on a solo career. Roberts tested Young's appeal by getting him a guest appearance during a Dave Van Ronk show at a Pasadena nightclub. "We stayed up all night because we were so thrilled he didn't get booed off," recalls Roberts. "He hated his voice and thought all his songs were depressing."

"AFTER THE SPRINGFIELD," Young said during that ride on his tour bus, "I wanted to get out to the sticks and think everything over." Along with his wife, Susan, Young moved into a spindly house high atop a hill in Topanga Canyon. After finishing his first solo album, *Neil Young,* in a local studio—which, these days, he fondly characterizes as "overdub city"—he built his own studio in his garage.

"The problem was, I needed a band again," Young said. "I met these guys that were, to me, the American Rolling Stones. There has never been a bad night with them, to this day. Crazy Horse."

Danny Whitten was the leader of Crazy Horse. A husky, blond guitarist/surfer, the intensely sensitive Whitten wrote all his songs about the same sixteen-year-old girl who had broken his heart. He had moved to California from back East with Ralph Molina and Billy Talbot, as part of a vocal group called Danny and the Memories.

"You had the impression," Elliot Roberts recalls, "that he had been through a lot and was very soulful. Whatever very soulful is, he had it. Very strong guy, but you could see that you say the wrong word and you'd slap him in the face. We all liked Danny. He was obviously very talented and Neil was drawn to him instantly."

Young met Whitten through a mutual girlfriend while he was still with Buffalo Springfield, and they began playing together. Whitten's guitar playing cut slashing patterns across Young's. After working on the first Buffalo Springfield album during the day, Neil fell into the habit of dropping by Talbot and Whitten's house in Laurel Canyon at night. "We used to have a great time," remembers Talbot, "sitting around, singing 'Mr. Soul' in D-modal tuning—all four of us singing harmony."

Young eventually enticed Whitten, Talbot and Molina to come up to his Topanga home/studio and record some "strange songs" he'd written while being laid up with the flu. "In a single day," Talbot says, "we did 'Cinnamon Girl,' 'Down by the River' and 'Cowgirl in the Sand.' There wasn't much need to discuss it. . . ."

Everybody Knows This Is Nowhere—still Neil Young's favorite of all his albums—was finished in two weeks. He and his new band toured small halls as Neil Young and Crazy Horse, and together they built a lasting reputation for hard, metallic rock. Young would spin off on searing guitar solos during which he wildly tipped back and forth on his heels. Because he acted so quickly, Young was never considered as a leftover piece of the Buffalo Springfield for long.

Neither was Stephen Stills, who had meanwhile teamed with David Crosby and Graham Nash to record *Crosby, Stills and Nash.* When the trio finished their album and realized they needed another guitarist to hold up

the instrumental end of things on the road, Stills visited Young. Just beginning his career with Crazy Horse, Young knew he had a decision to make.

"I decided to do both," Young has said. "The obligation with Crosby,
Stills and Nash wasn't going to be that heavy, a few songs and lead guitar."
It became much, much bigger than that. Or, as Billy Talbot says, "Neil
joined up with those guys, man, and everything went crazy."

Young punched the clock twice a day for a year, touring with Crosby,
Stills, Nash and Young, then Crazy Horse, then CSNY again. "I never
really fit into CSNY as well as Joe Walsh does with the Eagles," he explains.
"Everybody had a different viewpoint on what's happening and it takes a
whole lot to get them all together. It's a great group for that. Four totally
different people who all know how it should be done, whatever *it* is."

Young went straight from *Déjà Vu,* the first CSNY album, into recording his own third solo album, inspired by actor Dean Stockwell when he
unraveled a screenplay idea of his. It was about three lives—one of them a
moody musician—on the day that a mythical tidal wave swallowed
Topanga Canyon and was called *After the Gold Rush.* The apocalyptic theme
influenced the bulk of material for Young's album of the same name.

"The film fell through," says Young, "and there I was with a record.
So I put it out. Would have made a great movie."

It was a more poetic album than *Everybody Knows This Is Nowhere,* due
in part to the fact that the tenacious, black Les Paul guitar he played
throughout the previous album had been lost. "I took it to this store to be
repaired," says Young. "I came back to pick it up the next week and the
store was gone."

Young chose an enigmatic cover for the album, a solarized shot of him
passing an old lady on his way to a CSNY show in New York City. It
symbolized his own passage, his breakup with wife Susan and a farewell to
the Topanga house that had already started to become overrun with fans ("I
came home to find people I didn't know in my bedroom"). The album
captured a huge audience for Young as a solo artist, and that success brought
more changes than he could have ever planned for.

"By the time Young did *After the Gold Rush,* he'd fired us," says Billy
Talbot. "Danny was doing . . . you know."

Talbot jabs his arm.

"I was really suprised when Danny became a junkie. There was no
reason. In those days, people just started shooting right up. Didn't snort
nothin'. He just shot some speed, the next day some smack and from then
on, he was a junkie. He was always a strong person and he was also a strong
junkie. Did more than anyone else, they tell me."

For all his disheveled looks and maybe-I-know-where-I-am-maybe-I-don't stage presence, Neil Young is not a drug case. For a long time, according to friends, he would ask, "Is this hard grass," before accepting a joint. ("When I get high," he says, "I'm a basket case.)" He has never taken acid and never tried heroin. And Whitten's strong aura of junk scared Young considerably—in fact, he wrote "The Needle and the Damage Done" for him.

W ITH *AFTER THE GOLD RUSH* just released, Neil Young embarked on a solo acoustic tour of small halls, performing the best of his old work and a slew of new songs, written about his new ranch in northern California and a new love. During a stopover in Nashville to tape *The Johnny Cash Show,* he began recording a followup to *After the Gold Rush.* Spiriting away the show's other two guests, Linda Ronstadt and James Taylor, he recorded "Old Man" and "Heart of Gold," with Taylor on banjo, at a local studio. But a lingering back ailment worsened as he continued on the tour, and after it ended, Young suffered a slipped disk on his left side. He underwent operations and a long confinement on his ranch. Doctor's orders allowed him only four hours a day on his feet.

"I tried to stay away from the success as much as possible," Young says. "And being laid up in bed gave me a lot of time to think about what had happened. I thought the popularity was good, but I also knew that something else was dying. I became really reclusive.

"There was a long time when I felt connected with the outer world 'cause I was still looking. Then you get everything the way you want it. You stop looking out so much and start looking in. And that's why in my head I felt something change; I was thinking about all these things. I was lying on my back for a long time. It affected my music. My whole spirit was prone."

The lethargic downbeat of much of *Harvest,* Young's next album, was partially a result of the sedation he was under during much of the recording. Released in February of 1972, it was the biggest-selling album of that year and influenced an entire genre of country rockers.

Young's back gradually improved; he began writing and playing electric guitar again, and used some of his wealth from *Harvest* to finance his movie, *Journey Through the Past.* In the fall of 1972, Young decided it was time to end the seclusion and undertake his biggest tour yet—three months long and recorded every night for a live album (*Time Fades Away*) of new material. Jack Nitzsche, the producer of his first solo tracks, was on piano; the Nashville rhythm-section core from *Harvest*—Kenny Buttrey on drums, Tim Drummond on bass and Ben Keith on steel guitar; and the rumored-to-be-healthy-again Danny Whitten on lead guitar. A huge crew of technicians was brought in, and the mammoth tour began rehearsing at Young's Broken Arrow ranch.

Danny Whitten was the last to show up, still in the full throes of kicking his habit "city style"—with numbing quantities of booze and drugs. The band started rehearsing, and Whitten soon stopped and propped himself up with his guitar. "You guys are really great," he gurgled in wonderment. He looked at the sheet music Young had studiously written out for the musicians. "Hey Neil, where's my music *stand*?" he demanded and broke up laughing. "Hey, Jack! Play 'Be My Baby.' "

Whitten was driven to the airport, given a plane ticket and fifty dollars. Arriving in L.A., he used the money to score a dose of pure heroin. Danny Whitten shot it up and died that night.

"NEIL WAS PRETTY STRANGE on his big tour," recalls former tour manager Leo Makota. "He'd already been through heavy changes with Danny, then Neil tells him to go and Danny reads that as him just not having it anymore . . . and kills himself. It's like playing God. And are you ready to play God? But that was just one thing that happened.

"Neil was trying to get a certain sound out of the band that he apparently could never find. The band would jam at sound checks in the afternoons and sound great. Then they'd come in and do the show at night and never make it. Neil's mood never seemed happy or comfortable. So you have a situation where everybody is trying to please him and nobody really pleased him."

One reason, conjectures Makota (who is now a carpenter), is that everyone got a little money-hungry seeing those full houses every night. The band revolted, wanting more dollars and a percentage. Makota himself tried negotiating for a bigger crew price. "I admit," says Makota, "we should have just done the job that was at hand."

The revolt took Young by surprise. "It turned him against everything," Elliot Roberts recalls. "He didn't know how to handle his friends constantly hitting on him for more money. He rebelled against the success, started to see what it did to people. I was afraid to leave. I knew if I left, Neil was gone."

Meanwhile, puzzled audiences were treated to ragged versions of his new songs. ("Every time I go out on the road," Young says now, "the album that just came out is behind me. I don't want to lose the time frame to old material.") Young took to drinking tequila to relax. All those expectant faces waiting for "Heart of Gold" began to look, as he would later write, like an ocean of shaking hands that grab at the sky. They were his demons. And, in Cleveland, he began to scream at them. "Wake up, Cleveland. Get up. . . ." The rest of the tour was biding time.

He returned to the solitude of his ranch, bewildered, saddled with problems from *Journey Through the Past* and deeply upset. "For the first time in my life," he says, "I couldn't get anything to turn out the way I wanted." It was the beginning of a time he would later call his Dark Period.

THERE WAS A BRIEF try at a CSNY reunion in Hawaii in the summer of 1973, but Young left the proceedings because he was "too tired to start another cycle." Causing no small resentment within the group, Young returned to Los Angeles, where he found another person close to him had OD'ed—CSNY guitar tuner Bruce Berry. For the first time since Danny Whitten's death, Young rounded up the remainder of Crazy Horse, and they started recording at a small rehearsal room. The sessions began after midnight, after everyone had drunk enough tequila and played enough pool to do songs in memory of Whitten and Berry. According to Ralph Molina, "a picture began to develop . . . and it became *Tonight's the Night.*"

An album in which tuneful vocals, commercial choruses and artistic humility took a back seat to raw emotion, *Tonight's the Night* was rejected by Warner Bros. in 1974 when Young, wearing wraparound, razorback shades, brought the tapes to the executive offices. "I always noticed that Otis Redding would fuck up words on his records, but he'd just keep on going . . . if the spirit was there," Young explains today. "Not everyone, however, shares that particular philosophy."

Young then recorded a slightly more conventional work, *On the Beach,* but not before taking his rejected album on the road throughout Europe. He assumed the character of a sleazy Miami Beach emcee, a chatterbox of Vegas-type one-liners, and directed the band through a tequila-soaked show.

"I slipped out of myself," Young recalls, "and into something easier for me to take . . . that would destroy what everybody thought I was. I don't like to be prejudged before I do something. I don't like people to say it's going to be this, and have them be right. I might have been really slapping the audience in the face with some of the shows, but they had their minds totally turned around and that's more than you can say for most concerts. It was really healthy for me. I was the same person for too long.

"We tried to put on the entire show for under fifty dollars. 'Everything is cheaper than it looks,' was our motto. We hung one light bulb behind the stage. We did everything that we could to get as far out on the edge and try to play our music and to get it loose. I took the Eagles on tour with me—they thought I was pretty crazy. They were a good, clean country group back then, and they sounded like what a lot of people would have expected me to sound like after hearing *Harvest.* They think, 'We're gonna have an evening of really fine country-flavored rock & roll and folk rock.' And then we just came out and . . . took 'em all to Miami Beach."

Returning to the States in the wake of a massive critical backlash against him, Young, in a characteristic turnaround, agreed to a huge CSNY summer tour of stadiums. He traveled separately, in a Winnebago, leaving immediately after the show to keep his participation strictly musical. At every turn, though, there were accusations that CSNY had reunited only for the money.

"There's no question that we got paid a lot of money for doing it," says Young. "But there's no question that we were all there and delivered every night. It was just that we were playing these huge fucking places where we could get people to come in like cattle and fucking see us from half a mile away and listen to you squeak. If the wind was blowing the wrong way, they couldn't even hear you do that. It's a huge money trip, which is the exact antithesis of what all those people are idealistically trying to see in their heads when they come to see us play. So that's where the problem is. It costs a lot of money to put the show on. I don't know where it goes. All of it doesn't go where it's supposed to."

The last CSNY show was at Wembley Stadium in England in September of 1974. "Sometime," says Young, "we'll do something again in some combination."

After a brief vacation, Young returned to Los Angeles to begin another album, this one meant to be "the other side of *Harvest*." The resulting LP was full of the beautiful, melodic ballads his audience had been clamoring for. But the songs were mostly self-pitying, metaphorical details of the breakdown of his most recent relationship. Called *Homegrown,* the completed album depressed an entire room full of Young's friends when he played it for them. Someone turned the tape over and played the other side, a resequenced version of the *Tonight's the Night* material for a possible Broadway musical. The room began to party again. Rick Danko, of the Band, challenged Young to put *Tonight's the Night* out instead. He did.

The album was initially panned by many critics, but by the end of that year, *Tonight's the Night* turned up on the best-ten lists of the same critics for whom Neil Young had once symbolized a near comatose laid-back chic.

Says Young today: "It took two years to make it sound like it was made in one night. Everyone thought we'd done this great work. And it still didn't sell. For me, a perfect album."

IN THE SPRING OF 1975, daylight seemed to be breaking through on Neil Young's artful decline. He recovered the missing Les Paul played on *Everybody Knows This Is Nowhere* and Billy Talbot called to say he might have finally found a Crazy Horse guitarist worthy of Danny Whitten. Young turned up at Talbot's Silver Lake home with guitar in hand and heard Frank Sampedro for the first time. Staying for a week, Young played with the refurbished Crazy Horse and wrote material for *Zuma*.

"*Zuma* was breaking free of the murk," says Young. "My best records are the ones with Crazy Horse. They're the most fluid. *Zuma* was a great electric album coming from a place where pop leaves rock & roll."

After finishing the album, Neil Young and Crazy Horse toured the world. "We played England, Japan, everywhere except America," says Talbot. "It was an idyllic time, man, Neil was just *sparkling*. We had a band again. I heard us playing like I knew nobody else could play. I remember in Rotterdam, coming offstage and seeing Paul McCartney standing there. We'd just finished the set, the four of us are running through this wind tunnel to get back to the dressing room, and McCartney's just standing there. He nods at me like, you know, musician to musician. I just kept thinking . . . four of us. Four of *them*. Have we got a band or *what?* I don't think we've come down from that tour yet.

"I have this tape from Japan. Compared to this tape, *Zuma* sounds like a bunch of guys sleeping in big, fat armchairs, smoking pipes. Whenever I feel down, I listen to that tape."

Sampedro shakes his head. "Some shows Neil gets crazy with the guitar," he smiles. "Way crazy."

During a break before the world tour was to continue throughout America, Young found time to begin a long-discussed album with Stephen Stills in Miami. After the project (*Long May You Run*) was completed. Young took Stills and band on the tour that had been originally planned for Crazy Horse.

"Stephen asked Neil to do it," says Elliot Roberts, "and Neil said yes. He loves Stephen. They're the oldest of friends . . . and think about it. In ten years, you'll be happy to see anybody you've known that long."

But after mixed reviews and the onset of a throat ailment, Young left the tour in Atlanta, with a telegram saying: "Dear Stephen, funny how some things that start spontaneously, end that way. Eat a Peach, Neil."

NEIL YOUNG, WHO WRITES virtually all the time, can look back and find all the movements of his life and career documented in his songs, some more cryptically than others. "My songwriting process has never changed," he explains briefly, as if talking too much about it might betray the muse. "I never try to write. I know when it's there. I hear a bell ringing in my head and I just leave . . . but I don't try. Sometimes three months can go by. . . ."

Some artists, I point out, have been known to get writer's blocks that last for years.

"Well, if that happens to me," says Young, "I'll take up gardening."

One afternoon during a tour several years ago, Young sat in his manager's hotel room. The phone kept ringing, tour crew members bustled in and out . . . and through it all, Young sat on the bed with his son Zeke, peacefully watching the news.

The broadcast was interrupted by an emergency bulletin. Pat Nixon had suffered a stroke, an announcer said over a filmed report of the sad and beaten Richard Nixon tearily moving through the hospital's revolving doors. After a time, Young got up and disappeared into his bus in the parking lot. Onstage several hours later, Young played the song he had written:

Hospitals have made him cry
But there's always a freeway in his eye
Though his beach got too crowded for a stroll.
Roads stretch out like healthy veins
And wild gift horses strain the reins
Where even Richard Nixon has got soul.

The song was at first called "Requiem for a President." Young later changed the name to "Campaigner," and placed it on his three-record retrospective album, *Decade*. "Guess I felt sorry for [Nixon] that night," he said of the song while traveling on his bus the next year, just as 300,000 copies of *Decade* were being prepared for release within the week. "That album was a chance to use some of the unreleased material. Hopefully it's a greatest-hits album that's more like an album." Young laughed. "Should be timeless."

I wondered when he'd decided his first decade was over. He thought about that.

"Well," he said, "I'm not sure it's over."

He was silent for a long while. I drifted back to a bunk to watch television. Young joined me after a few minutes and stared at the screen intently.

"Listen to me," he said, eyes riveted to the tube. "What if I just save *Decade* for a year, then put out a new album. The new stuff sounds so good—I've got this song called 'Hurricane' that just *soars*—I think I'd feel better releasing something new. It's not time to look back yet."

I looked over at Young, who had obviously made up his mind and was now fully enjoying *The Boy in the Plastic Bubble*. A few minutes later, Young went to the front of the bus to make a call on a mobile phone. "Elliot?" I could hear him say. "Here goes another album. . . ."

In two short days, Warner Bros. President Mo Ostin and Executive Vice-President Ed Rosenblatt had flown to the next stop along the tour to discuss delaying *Decade* with Young. Neil played them most of an album he'd already recorded and titled *American Stars 'n Bars* ("because one side is about American folk heroes and the other is about getting loose in bars"). They honored his wishes to postpone *Decade* a year in favor of the new album.

By the time *American Stars 'n Bars* was released four months later, Young's prolific songwriting nature had completely altered the album to include a side of new music "written fast and in the spirit of country music," performed with Crazy Horse and the Saddlebags—singers Nicolette Larson and Linda Ronstadt.

Several of the still-unreleased original songs from *Stars 'n Bars*—"Powderfinger," "Captain Kennedy" and "Sedan Delivery"—were sent to Lynyrd Skynyrd for possible use on their *Street Survivors* album. None of the songs fit the tone of the album but singer Ronnie Van Zant was saving "Powderfinger" for a future LP at the time of his fatal plane crash. Van Zant and Young had sent messages of mutual admiration for each other, but Young never got to tell the man who wrote "I hope Neil Young will remember Southern Man don't need him around anyhow" that "Sweet Home Alabama" was one of his favorite songs.

"I'd rather play 'Sweet Home Alabama' than 'Southern Man' anytime,' Young says. "I first heard it and really liked the way they played their guitars. Then I heard my own name in it and thought, 'Now *this* is pretty great. . . .'"

IN THE SUMMER OF 1977, a rumor shot through California music circles that Neil Young was appearing nightly in the bars around Santa Cruz. It was disregarded by most as typical gossip, but a trip up the coast one Friday night found a crowd milling around the entrance to a small bar called the Catalyst. The marquee simply read: DUCKS. Inside, the place was filled with the dull roar of zoo people quacking and blowing duck calls.

After a while, out wandered four musicians. On lead guitar was Young, his painter's hat pulled down low. The Ducks opened with a scorching version of "Mr. Soul" and played through an hour of simple, hard Chuck Berry-esque rock & roll. The songs, only a few of which were Young's, celebrated trucks, girls and bars. The Ducks became a secret, local institution. For a buck, you came in and Neil Young burned up the frets, then joined you at the bar for a drink.

Young had turned up in Santa Cruz to visit an old friend from the Springfield days, singer/songwriter Jeff Blackburn. Once part of the San Francisco duo Blackburn and Snow, he'd been playing around the quiet coastal town with a band that included ex-Moby Grape member Bob Mosley and drummer Johnny C. Craviotto. When the group lost its lead guitarist, Young joined up. They decided to call themselves the Ducks and within weeks every duck call within miles had been purchased.

"These guys play some great music," Young told one local. "Sure they want to go out and do something, but all I want to do is play some music right now, and not go out and do anything. You see, I haven't lived in a town for eight years. I stayed on my ranch for about four years and then I just started traveling all over, never really staying anywhere. Moving into Santa Cruz is like my reemergence back into civilization. I like this town. If the situation remains cool, we can do this all summer long."

This exchange was later written up as a front-page story in a local newspaper. Crowds began to arrive from everywhere. Record companies even sent scouts. Word got out about the house that the band lived in. There was a robbery. And one day Neil Young disappeared again.

"I still have the team spirit," said Jeff Blackburn when I called him recently. "It's almost hard to comprehend it ever happened. We all knew Neil had commitments and everything. . . . I guess we were in the fairy tale and unable to see out of it."

After the Ducks episode, Young had taken his son Zeke for a cross-country ride in his tour bus. They ended up in Nashville and Young decided to begin his next record there. Young rounded up a crew of sidemen that included country session musicians who had never played anything resembling rock, a singer—Nicolette Larson—he had worked with on *American Stars 'n Bars,* and six acoustic guitarists. Young began his most accessible and ultimately best-selling album since *Harvest.* "I was feeling pretty sunny," he recalls.

Nicolette Larson had kept a tape of some of the material from when she and Young first met and sang together at her friend Linda Ronstadt's house. When the phone call came from Nashville, she was ready. Young barely had to show her the songs before they were singing the duets that appear on the album.

The Gone with the Wind Orchestra, as the entire conglomeration of twenty-two musicians was called, lasted throughout the album and for one live performance, on Young's thirty-second birthday, at an outdoor benefit for children's hospitals in the Miami Beach area. Young rehearsed the outfit in a Nashville storefront and flew everyone to Florida where, sharing the windy stage with Larson, he played what could well have been his purest and most note-perfect performance ever. The show ended with Young playing part of Lynyrd Skynyrd's "Sweet Home Alabama," which he dedicated to "a couple of friends in the sky."

A visit to Young's house in Zuma Beach a month later found him and Larson in floppy sweaters before the fireplace—Ma and Pa Kettle at home. Young made some coffee, put on the tape, and they sang with themselves while *Comes a Time* played. On the living-room table was the then-current issue of *People,* with the re-formed Crosby, Stills and Nash on the cover.

"Strange seeing that," said Young. "Those three with Jimmy Carter on the inside . . . it makes me think. It's good that they're together, but it's also good to be apart too. They all must feel sometimes like getting away from it. Just like when I'm someplace and decide, 'Think I'll get on the bus and go.' I have to be able to go. . . ."

YOUNG IS IN ELLIOT ROBERTS' office a year later, rubbing the two-day beard he's grown since the end of the *Rust Never Sleeps* shows. The tour had ended in L.A., the night after a raging coastal fire had swept through Zuma Beach and gutted Young's house. All that was left was the stone fireplace.

"Beautiful house," Young says. "Burned to the ground."

I have the impression that if the house had to go, the imagery suits Young just fine. That evening a year before, listening to *Comes a Time* with him and Larson, seems like it's from another time and place entirely.

"People don't understand sometimes," he says, looking down at a pencil he's toying with, "how I can come in and go out so fast, how I can be there and want to do something and then when it's over, for me it's over. To other people it's just a beginning. Sometimes that's hard for people to take. I can see how that would be. I just don't like to stay in one place very long. I move around, I keep doing different things. . . ." He looks up. "Just different things."

It must be difficult, I wonder, to decide which impulses to follow.

"I only follow the ones I get," says Young. "And if it makes me laugh . . . I *know* it's a good one. Basically I've had a really good time, even though my songs have mostly expressed the down side. I like that there's a lot of humor in rock & roll now. A lot of people take me so *seriously*. They don't know what to do with me not taking myself so seriously anymore. I guess it's just that a lot of people from the Sixties and early Seventies . . ." the old smirk . . . "just aren't that funny."

To many of his own fans Neil Young is still the antithesis of humor. He is the disheveled loner, a space case, a drug casualty. . . .

"Burned out," adds Young helpfully. "Weird. I think I have a pretty healthy image. Just gives me a chance to catch everybody off guard."

"Two times I've had to call Neil with reports of his death," says

Roberts. "One time his father called me. Said that he'd read in the AP that Neil died and was it true. Another time Warner Bros. called me and said was there any truth to Neil's demise in Paris. Both times they were 'drug accidents.' "

"Right," says Young. "I was traveling on the highway and was hit by a huge drug truck."

One of Young's long-standing jokes is that he's saving his best material for his "Bus Crash" album. The few who have heard samplings of Young's tape vaults—songs that didn't fit into the flow of his albums, entire unreleased works, live tapes, Buffalo Springfield tapes—agree that some of his most compelling performances are among the unreleased material.

"All those songs," he says, "they're still there. They're there. And they're in an order. They're not gone. But, you know, they're old songs. Who wants to hear about it. They're depressing. They are. It's like ancient history to me. I don't want to have to deal with that stuff coming out."

"Until," I ask, "you're not around to deal with them coming out?"

"That's right," he says. "Then they're there. I think every artist plans the future like that. I have things in a certain order, so that if anything ever happened to me it would be pretty evident what to do."

A FEW DAYS LATER, photographer Joel Bernstein and I are to meet Young and his new wife, Pegi, at Elliot Roberts' home in the wilds of northern California. The screen door opens and a disturbed-looking, wild-eyed Neil Young bolts in.

"Did you read," he all but hisses, "that article in *Time* magazine about me and Bob Dylan. I'd like to make a *comment* about that."

The *Time* writer had caught both Young's and Dylan's shows when they recently played Madison Square Garden back to back, and compared the artists according to their most current tours. The verdict was that Dylan had slipped into the billow sleeves of middle age and now "sometimes looks as if he is auditioning for the *Gong Show.*" Young, on the other hand, "kept closer to the ground than Dylan and sneaked into rock's pantheon like a highwayman."

"Show me this *pantheon,*" says Neil Young, pacing around his neighbor's kitchen, insulted that he could be pitted against his own mentor. "I don't want to have to read that shit in *Time* magazine. That's irresponsible journalism. Disco attitude. Somebody somewhere is going to believe it. I did not see Dylan's show—but to think that all he's given, all he's meant to us . . . you can't cancel that in one night. . . . I don't know how to feel." He sits down at a table, clasping his hands. "I don't think I want to comment at all."

We talk of other things during the night, but the *Time* article seems to run through all of Young's thoughts. To him it represents another wave of popularity, the kind that wrenched everything out of control for him before. I remind him of something he once told Peter Frampton, after meeting the English guitarist in New York when Frampton was suffering his own critical drubbing. It is the mystique that gets written about, not the music.

"Well," says Young, staring strangely at the tape recorder whirring a few feet away from him, "as soon as you start talking about mystique, you have none."

I knew then what would happen.

A few days later Young would call and ask that this article not be published. It had happened before. It had happened after the ROLLING STONE interview in 1975, but I had gone out of town to write the article and missed the nervous messages. It had happened after the Stills and Young tour when Young called to say he'd "been thinking a lot about maybe not having an article come out" and it happened after the 1976 tour when "the time wasn't right." It is hard to argue with a man whose emotions have served him so well.

"I've got a job to do," Young had said at his ranch. "The Eighties are here. I've got to just tear down whatever has happened to me and build something new. You can only have it for so long before you don't have it anymore. You become an old-timer . . . which . . . I could be. . . . I don't know.

"After all, it's just me and Frank Sinatra left on Reprise Records."

PAUL NELSON

RUST NEVER SLEEPS ALBUM REVIEW

Neil Young: Every Promise Fulfilled

FOR ANYONE STILL passionately in love with rock & roll, Neil Young has made a record that defines the territory. Defines it, expands it, explodes it. Burns it to the ground.

Rust Never Sleeps tells me more about my life, my country and rock & roll than any music I've heard in years. Like a newfound friend or lover pledging honesty and eager to share whatever might be important, it's both a sampler and a synopsis—of everything: the rocks and the trees, and the shadows between the rocks and the trees. If Young's lyrics provide strength and hope, they issue warnings and offer condolences, too. "Rust never sleeps" is probably the perfect epitaph for most of us, but it can also serve as a call to action. On 1974's *On the Beach,* the singer summed up a song ("Ambulance Blues") and a mood with the deceptively matter-of-fact phrase, "I guess I'll call it sickness gone." On that same LP, he felt such a renewal of power that he delivered, in "Motion Pictures," what may be the most boastful and egotistic line in all of rock & roll: "I hear the mountains are doing fine." *Rust Never Sleeps* makes good on every one of Young's early promises.

As you can see, we're dealing with omniscience, not irony, here. Too often, irony is the last cheap refuge for those clever assholes who confuse hooks with heart, who can't find the center of anything because their edges are so fashionably fucked up, who are just too cool to care or commiserate. Neil Young doesn't have these problems. Because he actually knows who he is and what he stands for, because he seems to have earned his insights, because his idiosyncratic and skillful music is marked by wisdom as well as a wide-ranging intelligence, Young comes right out and says something—without rant, rhetoric, easy moral lessons or any of the newest production dildos. He doesn't need that crap. This man never reduces a song to the mere meaning of its words: he gives you the whole thing, emotions—and sometimes contradictions—controlled but unlimited. For my money, Neil Young can outwrite, outsing, outplay, outthink, outfeel and outlast anybody in rock & roll today. Of all the major rock artists who started in the Sixties (Bob Dylan, the Rolling Stones, the Who, et al.), he's the only one who's consistently better now than he was then.

Though not really a concept album, *Rust Never Sleeps* is about the occupation of rock & roll, burning out, contemporary and historical American violence, and the desire or need to escape sometimes. It's an exhortation about coming back for those of us who still have that chance—and an elegiac tribute to those who don't. That much is pretty clear. But unlike most of Young's records, this one's a deliberate grab bag of styles, from sensitive singer/songwriter seriousness ("Thrasher") to charming science fiction ("Ride My Llama") to country rock ("Sail Away," a gorgeous *Comes a Time* outtake sung with Nicolette Larson) to an open embrace of the raw potency of punk (the hilarious and corrosive social commentary of "Welfare Mothers"). Side one is awesomely acoustic: ostensibly a folkie showcase, it's actually a virtuoso demonstration of how a rock & roller can switch off the electricity and, through sheer personal authority and force of will, somehow manage to *increase* the voltage. Side two is thunderous Crazy Horse rock & roll, but its opening song, "Powderfinger," is, oddly enough, the LP's purest folk narrative. And, to prove that he's more than just a contender, Young punches out one tune, "My My, Hey Hey (Out of the Blue)" or "Hey Hey, My My (Into the Black)," both ways.

Rust Never Sleeps leads off with "My My, Hey Hey (Out of the Blue)," and you can tell in an instant—by those haunted, ominous low notes played on the bass strings of the guitar, by the singer's respectful and understated vocal, by the lyrics' repetition—that this song lies not far from the heart of the matter. The heart of the matter here is death and desperation. And commerce. While "out of the blue and into the black" is a phrase that's filled with mortal doom, "into the black" can also mean money, success and fame, all of which carry a particularly high price tag. "My my, hey hey," Young sings, the line both fatalistic and mocking, "Rock & roll is here to stay." Elvis Presley and the Sex Pistols are introduced:

> *The king is gone but he's not forgotten*
> *This is the story of a Johnny Rotten*
> *It's better to burn out than it is to rust*
> *The king is gone but he's not forgotten.*

Though Young believes "Rock & roll can never die," he knows that a lot of people in it can—and do. Fast. Hence, the final admonishment: "There's more to the picture / Than meets the eye."

The autobiographical "Thrasher" (the threshing machine as death symbol) follows, and it's about rock & roll destructiveness, too—this time in the guise of the easy living that can lead to artistic stagnation. But even as the singer chronicles the downfall of many of his friends and fellow musicians, he makes the decision that it won't happen to him:

> *They had the best selection, they were poisoned with protection*
> *There was nothing that they needed, they had nothing left to find*
> *They were lost in rock formations or became park bench mutations*
> *On the sidewalks and in the stations, they were waiting, waiting*
> *So I got bored and left them there, they were just deadweight to me*
> *Better down the road without that load.*

Written partly in the florid and flowery style of mid-Sixties rock "poetry" and beautifully played on the twelve-string guitar and harmonica, "Thrasher" is a very complex composition that dwells deeply on the ties and boundaries of loyalty, childhood memories, fear, drugs, the music business, taking a hardheaded stand and art itself. When the latter is threatened, Young sings:

> *It was then that I knew I'd had enough, burned my credit card for fuel*
> *Headed out to where the pavement turns to sand*
> *With a one-way ticket to the land of truth and my suitcase in my hand*
> *How I lost my friends I still don't understand.*

If those lines remind you of the "On the Beach"/"Motion Pictures"/ "Ambulance Blues" side of *On the Beach,* they're supposed to. That song cycle was also about survival with honor.

Taken as a unit, "My My, Hey Hey (Out of the Blue)" and "Thrasher" almost suggest a paraphrase of the frontier father's warning to his son in side two's "Powderfinger": rock means run, son, and numbers add up to nothin'. But Young isn't that preachy. If he's strong enough to leave, he's strong enough to stay and work, too. He's able to adapt ("I could live inside a tepee / I could die in Penthouse thirty-five"). He'll bury his dead and maybe even drop a ghastly joke about it: "Remember the Alamo when help was on the way / It's better here and now, I feel that good today." Though his profession may be dangerous, it can also be glorious, and in the end, he's proud of it ("Sedan delivery is a job I know I'll keep / It sure was hard to find"). With Crazy Horse in *Rust Never Sleeps'* ferocious finale, "Hey Hey, My My (Into the Black)," Neil Young makes rock & roll sound both marvelously murderous and terrifyingly triumphant as the drums crack like whips, the guitars crash like cannons and the vocal soars above the blood-red din like the flag that was still there. *"Is this the story of Johnny Rotten?"* the singer asks. Yes and no. If we can't beat it, we can sure as hell beat it to death trying, he seems to be saying.

I'd be the last person in the world to claim that "My My, Hey Hey (Out of the Blue)"/"Hey Hey, My My (Into the Black)" and "Thrasher," two of the album's best tunes about rock & roll, have any direct connection with "Pocahontas" and "Powderfinger," *Rust Never Sleeps'* pairing about America. Of course, I'd be the last person in the world to deny it, too.

"Pocahontas" is simply amazing, and nobody but Neil Young could have written it. A saga about Indians, it starts quietly with these lovely lines:

> *Aurora borealis*
> *The icy sky at night*
> *Paddles cut the water*
> *In a long and hurried flight*

and then jumps quickly from colonial Jamestown to cavalry slaughters to urban slums to the tragicomic absurdities of the present day:

> *And maybe Marlon Brando*
> *Will be there by the fire*
> *We'll sit and talk of Hollywood*
> *And the good things there for hire*
> *And the Astrodome and the first tepee*
> *Marlon Brando, Pocahontas and me.*

With "Pocahontas," Young sails through time and space like he owns them. In just one line, he moves forward an entire century: "They massacred the buffalo / Kitty corner from the bank." He even fits in a flashback—complete with bawdy pun—so loony and moving that you don't know whether to laugh or cry:

> *I wish I was a trapper*
> *I would give a thousand pelts*
> *To sleep with Pocahontas*
> *And find out how she felt*
> *In the mornin' on the fields of green*
> *In the homeland we've never seen.*

Try reducing *that* to a single emotion.

Like the helicopter attack in Francis Coppola's hugely ambitious *Apocalypse Now,* the violence in "Powderfinger" is both appalling and appealing—to us and to its narrator—until it's too late. In this tale of the Old West, a young man, left to guard a tiny settlement, finds himself under siege and can't help standing there staring at the bullets heading his way. "I just turned twenty-two / I was wonderin' what to do," he says. Between each verse, Neil Young tightens the screw on his youthful hero with some galvanizing guitar playing, while Crazy Horse cuts loose with everything they've got. The tension is traumatizing, our empathy and fascination unbearable. And Young refuses to let us look away.

"When the first shot hit the dock I saw it comin'," the boy says. We hang with him. And underneath the lyrics (in critic Greil Marcus' classic description), there's "that string of ascending [guitar] notes cut off by a deadly descending chord—fatalism in a phrase." The hero acts: "Raised my rifle to my eye / Never stopped to wonder why." Young pulls the trigger. The narrator says: "Then I saw black and my face splashed against the sky."

The song doesn't even end there. Instead, the dead boy adds another verse:

> *Shelter me from the powder and the finger*
> *Cover me with the thought that pulled the trigger*
> *Just think of me as one you never figured*
> *Would fade away so young*
> *With so much left undone*
> *Remember me to my love, I know I'll miss her.*

The king is gone but he's not forgotten. This, too, could be the story of a Johnny Rotten. Hey hey, my my. Rock & roll can never die.

Neil Young should have the final word on his music, his future and *Rust Never Sleeps.* These lines from "Thrasher" make a magnificent credo:

> *But me, I'm not stopping there, got my own row left to hoe*
> *Just another line in the field of time*
> *When the thrasher comes I'll be stuck in the sun like the dinosaurs in*
>   *shrines*
> *But I'll know the time has come to give what's mine.*

THE TOP 100
THE BEST ALBUMS OF THE
LAST 20 YEARS
RUST NEVER SLEEPS

I N 1987, ROLLING STONE asked seventeen rock writers to submit nominations for the 100 greatest albums of the last twenty years—albums initially released between 1967 and 1987. Neil Young's *Rust Never Sleeps* came in at Number Sixty-six.

#66 *Rust Never Sleeps*
Neil Young and Crazy Horse

Hey hey, my my, rock & roll will never die—at least not as long as rockers like Neil Young keep making comebacks like *Rust Never Sleeps.* The result of a 1978 tour in which he premièred and recorded the basic tracks live, the album followed years of lackluster, indifferent records from Young. It didn't come as a complete shock—this guy could never be trusted to follow the expected path in anything, including artistic decline—but it was a delightful surprise, a half-acoustic, half-electric work that showed Young working with the depth of a veteran and the vigor of a youngster.

A collection of complex fables about the moods of Americans facing an uncertain, threatening future, *Rust Never Sleeps* took most of the themes that had occupied Young since the late Sixties and put them in an unexpectedly succinct, cogent package. Whether you'd been drawn to Young because of the folksy, homespun feel of his acoustic songs or the undisciplined thrash of his electric workouts, you found something to like: the unaccompanied ballads on side one are among his loveliest, the rockers on side two his roughest.

The acoustic side opens with "My My, Hey Hey (Out of the Blue)" in an unadorned form that makes it sound like a folkie's smart, affectionate salute to the Sex Pistols and the spirit of rock. "Thrasher" is a vivid, haunting ballad about—choose one—uncontrolled technology or Crosby,

Stills and Nash. The next three songs—"Ride My Llama," "Pocahontas" and "Sail Away"—explore Young's longtime fascination with open space and noble savages. The images were indelible, but just as crucial was the dry wit.

Flip the record over, and you found Young taking Johnny Rotten's rage to heart and playing what might have been the most shattering hard rock of his life. "Welfare Mothers" and "Sedan Delivery" are abrasive barn burners, while the remarkable "Powderfinger" sets out to capture the feeling of being outnumbered, adrift and doomed and makes its points with overwhelming power. Finally, there is "Hey Hey, My My (Into the Black)," in which he revamped the album's opening song and played it with barely controlled fury. The two dramatically different versions of that song are united by Neil Young's simple belief in the mythologizing, transforming power of rock & roll—a power he'd never before harnessed this fully.

Recorded at various concert locations in 1978. Mixed at Gold Star Studio, Los Angeles, and Broken Arrow, California, **PRODUCERS:** Neil Young, David Briggs and Tim Mulligan. **ENGINEERS:** Tim Mulligan and David Briggs. **RELEASED:** June 1979. **HIGHEST CHART POSITION:** Number Eight. **TOTAL U.S. SALES** [as of 1987]: 1.5 million. Reprise Records.

TOM CARSON

LIVE RUST ALBUM REVIEW
Neil Young Unleashes a Live One

BECAUSE NEIL YOUNG is so ambitious, his career has sometimes seemed frustratingly incomplete. He's as much a master politician as David Bowie—always deftly changing masks, from sensitive folkie to screeching rock & roller, from child of the Sixties to dour Seventies revisionist, from reckless romantic to sardonic critic of his own culture. And his success at it is all the more remarkable because he works in a folkie-hippie, romantic-sentimental idiom in which any kind of role playing risks crossing the line into a fatal loss of emotional credibility. But there hasn't been any one record, or one role, that's been able to fuse all the dialectical opposites of his character into a single statement that would define not only the artist but his audience as well—though Young's heroic sense of himself won't settle for anything less.

The last two years have seen Young's best work. In late 1978, *Comes a Time* so purified and refined his folk roots that the album became a perfect, stylized miniature, beyond persona. Then, in mid-1979, came *Rust Never Sleeps,* an LP that was *all* persona: jangled, chaotic, intense and filled with a desperate urgency that Young hadn't shown in quite some time. For him to release *Live Rust* so hard on the heels of *Rust Never Sleeps* is a way of further stepping up the pressure. Though Neil Young is aiming at a larger target now, he's gone to a live recording here for the same reason he did on 1975's *Tonight's the Night.* He wants its jarring, journalistic impact to jolt his audience with the immediacy of the historic moment.

History is evidently much on Young's mind—the fact that it's the tenth anniversary of Woodstock matters a great deal to him. He first made his legend as an elegist for the Sixties, and one reason why his *oeuvre* during the long period of willful obscurantism that followed *Harvest* (1972) didn't loom as large as it should have was that he hadn't found another theme of commensurate scope. For Young, 1979 represents the end of another epoch, and this seems to have spurred him into action. What he's trying to do on *Live Rust* is to set himself up as a rock & roll Tiresias, sounding warnings for the future, and to somehow tie his songs of the last ten years into a vast and singular history of the times. *Live Rust* covers almost every aspect of Young's career, and it's all been arranged and presented as a sprawling epic of disillusion and loss. It's rock & roll as emotional superspectacle—wildly ambitious and wildly successful.

Though *Live Rust,* like *Rust Never Sleeps,* begins with an acoustic side and then explodes into rock & roll, what was counterpoint on the earlier album is a progression here. By following "Sugar Mountain" and "I Am a Child" with "After the Gold Rush," Young equates the real childhood in the first two numbers with the symbolic childhood of the Sixties. "Comes a Time," though it's out of chronological order, dovetails perfectly into this sequence, because it's the artist's answer song, eight years later, to "After the Gold Rush"—conciliatory where the other is absolute, stoically mature where the other alternates between youthful idyll and equally youthful bitterness. The message is obvious: Innocence is a passing season, and tougher tests are ahead.

Throughout the LP, Young is playing off dualisms of young and old, time and change. He lashes together intimately personal compositions with broader social canvases, questioning his own past even while he tries to make it stand for ours. Over and over, early tunes are given new meaning by their juxtaposition with later ones, and by the arching, mythic context. Sometimes an old song is used as an artifact: On its own, for instance, "The Needle and the Damage Done" is a slight, rather self-righteous condemnation. But here, sandwiched between the belligerent, overheated romanticism of "The Loner" and the wistful "Lotta Love," and introduced by a fatuous snippet of Woodstock tape, it's simply another journalistic snapshot and all the more powerful because of it.

By mating *Zuma's* "Cortez the Killer" with *Rust Never Sleeps'* "Powderfinger," Neil Young undercuts his particular romantic feel for the American frontier with an acerbic awareness of just how that frontier got started in the first place. Within "Cortez the Killer," Young manages an amazingly daring transformation by singing the line, "He came dancing across the water," in reggae patois—thus not only connecting a story of colonialist exploitation with present-day Third World politics, but also aligning himself with the single most politically radical music being made today. Other times, a composition's meaning is changed by a new emphasis in the performance: By making the phrase, "Hard to find a job," the focal point of "Sedan Delivery," hitting it again and again over a galvanizing guitar riff, the singer converts the song from a gnomic fantasy to a recession anthem.

Young made his breakthrough with rock & roll as pure sound on 1975's *Zuma* after learning how to use raw noise on *Tonight's the Night,* but even so, you aren't prepared for the reach and depth of the playing on this record. It's sweeping and majestic, filled with ragged strength. Instead of speeding up the tempo on the long rave-ups, Young and Crazy Horse slow it down to an almost funereal pace, leaving plenty of space between the drawn-out, corrosive guitar notes and muffled, thudding drums. Then they startle you with a sudden burst of dirty noise. The entire last two sides of *Live Rust* coalesce into one dark, enormous dirge. It's so massively stately that you get the feeling of huge mountains on the move. And yet, in "Cortez the Killer" and the shimmering "Like a Hurricane," the guitars almost seem to float, only to rush down like a river of molten lava for "Hey Hey, My My (Into the Black)."

On *Rust Never Sleeps,* "Hey Hey, My My (Into the Black)" erupted out of nowhere, as stark as a telegram. Here, it's the logical culmination of everything that *Live Rust* has been leading up to. It's rock & roll treated the way a Southerner might view the Civil War—indeed, it seems to hearken back in spirit to the Band's "The Night They Drove Old Dixie Down" far more than it does to Danny and the Juniors' "Rock & Roll Is Here to Stay." "Hey Hey, My My (Into the Black)" is both a chilling tone poem to death, with Young's vocals valiantly striving to reach you across long stretches of empty space, and a grimly defiant ode to survival. When Neil Young sings, "The King is gone but he's not forgotten / Is this the story of Johnny Rotten?," it's clearly Rotten he's mourning, not Elvis Presley: Rotten embodied the extreme that Elvis had retreated from long before, the extreme that Young himself is now trying to sustain.

"Tonight's the Night" follows. It seems like a natural coda and takes on added resonance. Instead of being about Bruce Berry and Danny Whitten, "Tonight's the Night" sounds and feels like an elegy to all the dead that stretch back to the beginning of the album, and all the way back through the Seventies.

The evocation of that journey is Neil Young's final achievement. The current catch phrase among music-industry flacks is "a preview of the Eighties." It'll probably be applied to this record as well, perhaps with some justice. But the real message of *Live Rust* is that the rites of passage of the last ten years, going on even today—and tonight—are what's important.

1979 MUSIC AWARDS

February 7, 1980

The fourth annual readers poll drew 6,500 ballots, up 20 percent from last year. And virtually every winner from last year was deposed. The big winner in 1979 was Neil Young, who tied the Who for Artist of the Year, won as Songwriter and Male Vocalist and had the Best Album, *Rust Never Sleeps*. The Who, who put out two soundtracks—*Quadrophenia* and *The Kids Are Alright*—and who performed sensationally on a tour of the U.S., also won Band of the Year.

READERS PICKS:

ARTIST OF THE YEAR
Neil Young
The Who
Supertramp
Bruce Springsteen
The Cars

BEST ALBUM
Rust Never Sleeps
  (Neil Young)
Breakfast in America
  (Supertramp)
In Through the Out Door
  (Led Zeppelin)
Slow Train Coming
  (Bob Dylan)
Candy·O (The Cars)

SONGWRITER
Neil Young
Bob Dylan
Elvis Costello
Bruce Springsteen
Paul McCartney

MALE VOCALIST
Neil Young
Bruce Springsteen
Bob Dylan
Robert Plant
Van Morrison

CRITICS PICKS:

ARTIST OF THE YEAR
Neil Young

BAND OF THE YEAR
The Who

BEST ALBUM
Rust Never Sleeps
  (Neil Young)
Armed Forces (Elvis
  Costello)
Into the Music (Van
  Morrison)
Tusk (Fleetwood Mac)
Squeezing Out Sparks
  (Graham Parker)
Fear of Music (Talking
  Heads)
Bad Girls (Donna Summer)
Labour of Lust (Nick Lowe)

JOHN PICCARELLA

HAWKS & DOVES ALBUM REVIEW
Neil Young Takes a Close Look at America

BACK IN THE FIRST few days of the Eighties, a friend and I were arguing about whether or not the Clash had already made the album of the year, *London Calling*. I said: "Maybe Neil Young will surprise us again and get even better." My friend said: "Yeah, he could. But he'd have to make a political record, and I don't know if that's possible in this country right now." *Hawks & Doves* may not be the LP of the year (it's only thirty minutes long!), but it *is* an American political album. And like most Neil Young discs, it's not what you expected—or rather, as usual, not what he was doing last year.

Though there are several Sixties superstars who sailed through the Seventies intact, who else in the history of rock & roll has so improved with age? Who else has remained vital without ever really becoming slick? The astonishing thing about Young's recent strength is his added reach. In 1978 he made his first perfect record. Elegant and carefully crafted (for once), *Comes a Time* also signaled maturity. Few American artists survive youthful fame to outdo themselves, but like a great author with many masterpieces behind him, Neil Young settled into the confidence of his craft and did it better. He'd had five or six careers by then: the Buffalo Springfield; the early superstar solo years; Crosby, Still, Nash and Young; the dark period culminating with *Tonight's the Night;* the mid-Seventies triumphs as a revitalized rocker. But apart from an occasional sociopolitical narrative ("Southern Man," "Cortez the Killer"), Young's songwriting, even at its best, was claustrophobic—and I mean *phobic!* With *Comes a Time,* he achieved distance and an ease of expression. And in 1979, his best year ever, he took bold strides toward his audience, summing up his career with a brilliantly organized concert movie (*Rust Never Sleeps*) and two closely related albums (*Rust Never Sleeps* and *Live Rust*).

"My My, Hey Hey (Out of the Blue)"—or "Hey Hey, My My (Into the Black)"—was probably his first anthem. And *Rust Never Sleeps* was the first Neil Young record that was more about the world than about the artist. "Powderfinger" and "Pocahontas" fused personal visions of fear and desire to the sense of American history that's always come and gone throughout

Young's work. But more important, the imagistic wealth of "Thrasher" and the wisecracking, working-class rocker pose of "Welfare Mothers" and "Sedan Delivery" utilized his narrative gifts to define the sociology of his generation.

Though it's something of a musical throwback (Young has once again abandoned Crazy Horse for his stable of country musicians), *Hawks & Doves* is the sequel to the broadened vision of *Rust Never Sleeps*. Yet stylistically, as its title and cover art clearly indicate, it's the sequel to *American Stars 'n Bars,* too. Like that LP, *Hawks & Doves* has a strange mixed bag of a first side and a tight set of electric country-rock on the second. But it also preserves the acoustic-electric division of *Rust Never Sleeps* and *Live Rust.*

Every track on *Hawks & Doves* sounds like an instant classic built on the barest materials: one good hook or simply a mood. The disc's title provides a concept that almost covers the contents. Initially, this theme seems to divide the album's main characters. "Little Wing," a gorgeous fragment of an opener, is unquestionably a dove: "She comes to town when the children sing / And leaves them feathers if they fall." "Captain Kennedy," who closes side one, is an obvious hawk: "And when I get to shore / I hope that I can kill good." Yet musically speaking, the hawks might be the electric numbers and the doves the acoustic—just to mix things up. In another extension of the title imagery, the songs on the first side borrow, at least in atmosphere, from "Birds" on *After the Gold Rush* to *Zuma*'s "Danger Bird." But in *Hawks & Doves'* two longest and strangest compositions, "Homestead" and "Lost in Space," the metaphoric consistency collapses. And it's within this enigmatic chaos of images that the record begins, paradoxically, to come together.

The long-awaited sequel to "The Last Trip to Tulsa," "Homestead" is an eerie, elliptical and surreal narrative in which the moon, a man's shadow and a flock of prehistoric birds accompany a naked rider on a seven-minute journey through his head in search of some cosmic telephone connection. These images hang over him like omens of a fate that never arrives. The LP's major song, "Homestead" casts a peculiar light on the apparently freewheeling hoedowns of side two. "Lost in Space" starts as if it's the album's one personal tune: "Live with me," Neil Young sings. It ends similarly with "Look at these blues / The deep sea blues." But between the lines is a dream scene that suggests the nature of the unnamed fate in "Homestead." The quiet acoustic mood of "Lost in Space" turns weird when a waterlogged chorus of children asks: "What could be stranger than the unknown danger / That lies on the ocean floor?"

Each short song on side two is centered on a hook that offers a snippet of proverbial working-class fortitude. Linked by guitar and fiddle riffs that jump from cut to cut, these compositions form a suite about contemporary middle-American attitudes. The side opens with "Staying Power" ("We got stayin' power you and I / Stayin' power through thick and thin"), which is followed by "Coastline" ("We don't back down from no trouble / We *do* get up in the morning"). In the rollicking "Union Man," Young, in mock seriousness, allies himself with the American worker. Pretending to chair a union meeting, he calls for a vote on an important item of new business: "LIVE MUSIC IS BETTER! bumper stickers should be issued!" As far removed from proletarian reality as the No Nukes movement, this reminds me of Ronald Reagan's ironic bid for blue-collar support when he declared he led the first strike of his union back in Hollywood.

Rufus Thibodeaux' fiddle begins "Comin' Apart at Every Nail" with the same riff that closes down "Union Man" as the recession hits home:

> *It's awful hard to find a job*
> *On one side the government, the other the mob*
> *Hey hey, ain't that right .*
> *The workin' man's in for a helluva fight*
> *Oh this country sure looks good to me*
> *But these fences are comin' apart at every nail.*

In "Comin' Apart at Every Nail," the dread of the first side becomes an explicit threat of war, and the record ends with the title track collecting all the ambiguities of being part of the problem. Built on an irresistible "YEW-ESS-AAY" hook, "Hawks & Doves" sounds celebratory and mournful at the same time: "Ain't gettin' old / Ain't gettin' younger though / Just gettin' used to the lay of the land." Through a series of casual ironies, Young subtly hammers home the feeling that in this election year, faced with the most dismal political choices of our lives, we make up the midsection of the electorate: "Got rock & roll / Got country music playin' / If you hate us / You just don't know what you're sayin'." And the chorus—"Ready to go / Willin' to stay and pay / U.S.A! U.S.A! / So my sweet love / Can dance another free day / U.S.A! U.S.A!"—only underlines the complacency.

In the offhand, half-informed rhetoric of the average citizen (that includes you, me and him), Neil Young has articulated the tone of the body politic. But if *Hawks & Doves* is a major statement, it's also an understatement. Another throwaway masterpiece, dashed off like most of his LPs— like a letter, letting you know what he's thinking, for the moment. So this year, after the apocalyptic dread of side one, the present-day, shit-kicking urban cowboy of side two looks like an endangered species. And if you think that Young's portrayal of life-before-wartime America misses the supposed vitality of the New Wave, then you've got it backward. He mourned the death of Johnny Rotten *last* year.

■ **RANDOM NOTES** (April 16, 1981)

It was three A.M. at the Ritz in New York, and headliner Ian Lloyd and most of the audience (including Graham Parker and Cheap Trick vocalist Robin Zander) had split—when who should toddle in but Neil Young and his wife, Pegi. Since the Danny Shea Band (incorporating such local studio pickers as Rob Stoner and G.E. Smith) was onstage whipping up an impromptu Mike Bloomfield tribute, Young obligingly strapped on a Gibson electric and led the group through a sloppy but spirited three-song set that included the Jimmy Reed staple, "Baby, What You Want Me to Do," another tune that fell into the "slow blues" category, and a rollicking Chuck Berry medley of "Sweet Little Rock & Roller" and "Maybellene." Young may have had an unspoken dedication for the Reed number: actress Sally Kirkland, who recently slapped him with a $2 million lawsuit in connection with injuries she allegedly suffered on the set of Young's as-yet-to-be-released film, *Human Highway*.

JOHN PICCARELLA

RE-AC-TOR ALBUM REVIEW

★ ★ ★ ★

Neil Young Checks in with Another Winner

ANOTHER INSCRUTABLE Neil Young album! Never repeating himself, Young continues to toss off records like drawings from a sketch pad—each one faster, less filled in, less fussed over than the last, but each also bearing an unmistakable master's touch and a fresh vision.

Proceeding as he has since *Rust Never Sleeps* to observe America, Young renders the country in precise media catchphrases and slogans that he then anchors to the most fundamental blues-based forms. He still prefers, as he has from the beginning of his solo career, to uncover a new format each time. Neil Young has always shuffled three basic styles—bandless folkie, sweet country rocker and hard blues rocker—with the unpredictability of a three-card-monte dealer. So it's fitting that the electric Crazy Horse session we expected after *Rust Never Sleeps* comes now, *after* the folk-to-country turnaround of *Hawks & Doves*. We're caught off guard again. And, of course, *Re-ac-tor* is different from anything Young's ever done.

Re-ac-tor is the one and only Neil Young LP (sue me if I'm wrong) on which he's backed by Crazy Horse throughout. (Yeah, I know *Everybody Knows This Is Nowhere,* but I dare you to find a rhythm section in "Round and Round." Besides, that disc featured guest musicians and was made a dozen years ago.) Just as *Hawks & Doves* built on *Rust Never Sleeps* thematically but was also a throwback, formally, to *American Stars 'n Bars, Re-ac-tor* continues *Hawks & Doves'* working-class, mid-America sketches as well as its deceptive brevity and flag-detail album-cover design. (*Re-ac-tor* replaces *Hawks & Doves'* red, white and blue lone star and bars with red and black triangles and circles in a kind of nuke-hawks-and-solar-doves motif.) Yet the new work, in its total embrace of the rock & roll mode, is also the flip side of *Comes a Time,* the only other of Young's last half-dozen or so records that seems an undisturbed stylistic whole. *American Stars 'n Bars, Rust Never Sleeps, Live Rust* and *Hawks & Doves* each pitted A side against B side.

Note: In 1981, ROLLING STONE *began using the star rating system; it was discontinued in 1985 and brought back in 1988.*

Re-ac-tor, however, is all noisy electric social comment, while *Comes a Time* was all quiet acoustic personal expression. And though *Re-ac-tor,* with "Shots" as its finale, climaxes as noisily as either of the *Rust* LPs, the music here is carefully crafted studio raunch, whereas *Comes a Time*'s was carefully crafted studio prettiness.

Re-ac-tor's title, apart from its obvious nuclear meaning, seems to characterize both Young's role as keen-eyed but offhand observer and the band's explosive commitment to rock out. But while Crazy Horse follows the gargantuan live-blues attack of the electric *Rust* sides, the production is tidier and the organizational values somewhat more formalized. This group's unique professional primitivism combines volume and distortion levels worthy of Blue Cheer with the structured tightness of Creedence Clearwater Revival. Neil Young's lyrics and lead guitar come in small spurts and serve a general overriding rhythmic intent. While previous extended guitar pieces, from "Cowgirl in the Sand" to "Like a Hurricane," framed journeying solos with verse and chorus forms, "T-Bone," the longest track on *Re-ac-tor,* simply alternates its single verse with short guitar breaks for more than nine minutes. "Got mashed potatoes / Ain't got no T-Bone" may seem like a silly thing to say over and over, but the phrase locks right into the record's unifying theme like a rocking comic mantra.

Re-ac-tionary Reaganomics divide the LP's images and characters: hawks and doves are now haves and have-nots—the black (profit) and red (loss) of the album cover's colors. This dichotomy takes many forms. In "Opera Star," it's the highbrows or cultural haves against the rocking have-nots. In "Surfer Joe and Moe the Sleaze," it's winners versus losers, with the leisure class ("We're all going on a pleasure cruise") as spectators, who are neither. The song's Los Angeles decadence and its combination of vague plot with proper-name details recall Steely Dan's cynical insider's view of luxury. Side one's closing cut, "Get Back on It," introduces the rhythms and images of transportation that pervade side two. In "Southern Pacific," mandatory retirement robs a Mr. (Casey?) Jones of his job on the railroad, leaving him both a have (pension) and a have-not (dignity). In "Motor City," a have who owns three cars thinks he's a have-not because one car's breaking down, one's stolen and the third, an army Jeep, doesn't have all the options.

Riddled with machine-gun fire and high-shriek-to-deep-fuzz guitar jumps that recall Jimi Hendrix in his "Machine Gun"/"Star Spangled Banner" style, "Shots" offers a panoramic view of America building up and tearing down. Ripped by the violence of the music, the men, women and kids here are trying to patch up sand-castle securities, while the real forces at work are guns, machines and lust. Each verse ends with the phrase "in the night," lending the whole scary montage the shifting psychological impact of a dream. On these fuzzy borders between supply and demand is where Young means to evoke the Serenity Prayer, printed in Latin on the back of the record: "God grant me the serenity to accept the things I cannot change, courage to change what I can, and wisdom to know the difference." It's this important "wisdom to know the difference" that the singer's after as he "keep[s] hearing shots."

These are clear, harsh, lowest-common-denominator visions of the country in trouble. Young's just rocking out, you say? Maybe, but fatalistic resignation appears in the very first tune, in which "Some things never change." In *Re-ac-tor*'s funkiest cut, "Rapid Transit," media phrases like "Mmmmmmelt-down" and "Ppppppublic Enemy" are stuttered into sound. Above all, what Young continues to do with vigor and genius is to create powerful moods. These fast-edit intensities, fashioned from limited materials, broken pieces of American language and American music, are totems of contemporary crisis. And if they seem to be just marking time, that's because in Neil Young's apocalyptic nightmares, marking time is a profound and terrible activity.

PARKE PUTERBAUGH

TRANS ALBUM REVIEW

★ ★ ★ ★

Neil Young's Computer Love

"WELL, MR. WEIRD IS AT it again" was one of the first reactions I heard to the synthesized sounds and Vocoderized vocals that typify a lot of the material on Neil Young's new album, *Trans*. With Young, one learns to expect the unexpected, but this record is as drastic a break from career form as David Bowie's kiss-off to his Thin White Duke persona with *Low*. And twice as surprising, too, because Young, despite his penchant for shifting gears from record to record, has always sunk his roots deep into the good earth, the fertile loam, of the American singer/songwriter tradition. So, if Neil Young feels compelled to scramble his lyrics in computerized Morse code, running his voice through Vocoders and octave dividers, what are we to make of this brave new world that's overtaking us, turning our sturdiest songsmiths into computer clones? Has the ever-suggestible Young, in his zeal to escape the sad fate of those touring Tutankhamens (and former bandmates) Crosby, Stills and Nash, taken it too far this time?

Well, not exactly. Seems that Young was catching up with a lot of new releases around the time of *Re-ac-tor,* and one of them, Kraftwerk's *Computer World,* particularly grabbed his fancy. Indeed, a lot of *Trans* documents his impressions of the computer world that Kraftwerk celebrated so icily and nimbly on that 1981 LP. But at some later point, Young also went to Hawaii with his band of regulars—the Crazy Horse alumni, Ben Keith, Nils Lofgren, et al.—and recorded a batch of new tunes written in a more traditional vein. Material from both sessions wound up on *Trans,* and the intentional clash of styles—there is always method in Young's madness—is what makes this record such an intriguing puzzle. *Trans* commences with a false start: a perfectly innocuous love song entitled "Little Thing Called Love." The music is bouncy and bright, and the payoff is that pretty major-seventh chord stuck at the end of the chorus, which itself is a series of sweet nothings delivered in a wry deadpan: "Only love puts a tear in your eye / Only love makes you hypnotized. . . ." And so on. It's the sort of thing you could hum in your sleep, and maybe that's the point.

But no sooner does this wisp of pleasantry fade than out issues the programmed thud-thud of a computer drum, joined by an ethereal wash of synthesizer, heralding the arrival of the androids. Young sings in an electronically altered voice on the four songs that round out this side, and on side two's "Sample and Hold." It would seem to be his mission here to animate the binary world. Such compositions as "Computer Age" and "Transformer Man" sound like anthems to a microchip utopia of the future. And Young's computer cadets, which serenade us in a precious little squeak of a voice, are singularly unthreatening. It's as if by abstracting human intelligence from the emotional biases that often misdirect it, we can attain a truer ideal of perfection—electronically.

As conversant as Young has become with his new toys, and as fully as he's conceptualized his thoughts about them, it's a long way from the wide-open spaces of his California ranch to the high-tech environs of, say, Kraftwerk's West Germany. All of which means that however much *Trans* is given over to a certain stylistic mimicry—Kraftwerk writes "Computer World" and "Computer Love," Young writes "Computer Age" and "Computer Cowboy"—it's counterpointed by at least three songs in which Young plays it pretty straight. "Like an Inca," in fact, is one of the least ironic and unabashedly visionary songs he's ever written, right up there with such masterpieces as "Last Trip to Tulsa," "The Old Homestead" and "Like a Hurricane."

This incongruity between old and new modes on *Trans* is striking—sort of like seeing a satellite dish sitting outside a log cabin. Isolate the three unencoded, untampered-with songs here—"Little Thing Called Love," "Hold on to Your Love" and "Like an Inca"—and you'll get an idea of the album that might have been: buoyant, sparkling, very singer/songwriterly, much like his 1969 solo debut, *Neil Young*. (One more "love" song, "If You Got Love," was pulled off the LP at the last moment by Young—too late even to be struck from the song listings on the jacket.) The five computer tunes, on the other hand, represent a wholly different tangent. Weave the two together and bridge them with a new version of "Mr. Soul" (dusted off from Young's Buffalo Springfield days) that bows both to the deathless past and the digital present, and you have an album of colliding realities that somehow mirrors our modern age. It's the world in transition (hence the title?), a unique moment in human history in which old technologies are yielding to new ones—and where human values struggle to maintain an equilibrium with the accelerated change.

Young seems nonplussed by it all; he has no trouble accommodating the two worlds on his slab of vinyl (and, what's more, is probably amused to think of the discomfiture his new music will bring the buckskin folkies

who like him for *Harvest*). In truth, once you get past its radical sonic
veneer, *Trans* turns out to be a pretty whimsical treatise on the theme of
man-meets-machine, with Young wisecracking his way through the high-
tech numbers—note the wild coyotes who yowl on the computer cowboy's
range, and the mate-hunting automaton who sings, "I need a unit to sample
and hold / But not the angry one, a *new design, new design*"—and tossing off
the treacle of the straight love songs with casual disinterest. Along the way,
he gets off some good guitar licks—the descending riff in "Computer
Cowboy" is a killer—and he deserves a dance-club hit with "We Are in
Control," a roll call of computer insurgency that out-Krafts the krauts.

But as Young himself has sung, sooner or later it all gets real, and he gets
down to business on *Trans'* final track, "Like an Inca." The song is a
quixotic journey with the horsemen of the apocalypse across a landscape
hung heavy with an aura of impending disaster. It's built upon a slight, jazzy
riff played on a phalanx of guitars, with drums and congas adding rhythmic
spice; its breezy, Latin feel recalls early Santana. But the tune's airiness is
contrasted by a doomy, two-note synthesizer motif, and by Young's dark
prophecies: "Said the condor to the preying mantis / We're gonna lose this
place / Just like we lost Atlantis." In a voice that cracks with outrage, Young
raises the specter of nuclear holocaust ("Who put the bomb on the sacred
altar?"), but the die has been cast, and when the gypsy reads his fortune, it
comes up empty.

Throughout this album, as well as on *Rust Never Sleeps, Live Rust* and
Re-ac-tor, Young has been stumping on behalf of the musical New Wave
and the technological Next Wave. In "Like an Inca," however, he sounds
as if he wishes he were living in any time or place but the present, and the
glories of ancient civilizations fill his imagination with longing: "I wish I
was an Aztec / Or a runner in Peru / I would build such beautiful buildings /
To house the chosen few." As it is, though, when the end of this odyssey
is at hand, he finds an oddly peaceful sense of solace and resolution:

> *I feel sad, but I feel happy*
> *'Cause I'm coming back to home*
> *There's a bridge across the river*
> *That I have to cross alone*
> *Like a skipping rolling stone.*

All of which says to me that despite his tinkering around with the
hardware of the computer age, Neil Young is really still a sweep-hand clock
in a digital world, a solitary quester after truth. And he continues to tick for
all things enduring: love, humanity, dignity, strength. The good fight.

■ RANDOM NOTES NEIL YOUNG'S *TRANS* TOUR (March 17, 1983)

There's rarely been a stage show to rival the computer-video-acoustic extravaganza that is the Neil Young tour. Young has been playing two sets each concert, the first an acoustic set of material that he doesn't often perform live—including "Heart of Gold" and "The Old Laughing Lady" and video footage that's projected onto a huge screen behind the stage. The second half showcases Young's *Trans*-like synthesized music.

Wackier still is "Dan Clear," the entertainingly smarmy emcee who holds forth from a video screen whenever Young is offstage. In Los Angeles, he even interviewed Young: "What'd you think of the first half?" "I started out strong, had some trouble but finished real well."

And how about this: Young has already recorded nine new tracks for a country album—but he'll only record when there's a full moon.

■ RANDOM NOTES NEIL YOUNG COLLAPSES, TOUR ENDS (April 28, 1983)

Neil Young's U.S. tour came to a premature, though spectacular, conclusion last month in Louisville, Kentucky, when Young collapsed during the show's intermission and angry patrons reacted to the concert's cancellation by flinging folding chairs at the stage. Young had refused medical attention prior to the March 4 show at Louisville's Commonwealth Convention Center, but he appeared wan and fidgety during the opening set. After playing for about seventy-five minutes, Young went backstage, where, according to Jefferson County coroner Richard Greathouse, he passed out. "He was just totally exhausted," says Greathouse. "He was fighting off a virus, and he had done four shows in a row. So I advised him to take a complete rest—go and get lost somewhere in his motor home." Young canceled the end of his tour.

■ RANDOM NOTES NEIL YOUNG'S ROCKIN', BUT THE JOINT AIN'T JUMPIN' (August 18, 1983)

Neil Young is up to his chameleonic tricks again. Fans who were taken aback by the high-tech *Trans* tour, which crashed to a halt last March, will be even more baffled by Young's new persona: a slicked-back, greased-up rockabilly frontman. On his current tour, Young has been halting the proceedings midway and reemerging as the lead singer of a band called the Shocking Pinks. With his pink tie, black shirt and white suit, Young looks more like Slim Whitman than Gene Vincent. And though he pumps a white piano and sings with Fifties fervor, the results have been less than electrifying—at least at the tour's outset. Young's versions of "That's Alright, Mama" and "Bright Lights, Big City" were lukewarm, as were his own retro-rock compositions. "Thank you, friends," he drawled after each song to an unappreciative audience.

Nevertheless, Young seemed to relish the chance to ape his idols, and he concluded the show by climbing into an old Cadillac and lampooning a line from the King: "This leavin' the stage—it just don't *move* me!" Young's new sound will be available soon on his *Everybody's Rockin'* LP.

DAVID FRICKE

EVERYBODY'S ROCKIN' ALBUM REVIEW

★ ★ ★ ★

Retro Rock & Roll from Neil Young
and the Shocking Pinks

JUST WHEN YOU GOT used to Neil Young's Brave New World of synth pop and computer love, he jumps into a nearby phone booth, rips off his space suit and emerges as . . . the Stray Cats? With *Everybody's Rockin'*, rock's most exasperating quick-change artist bails out of the New Wave and seeks solace in his old roots by cutting ten deeply primitive rockabilly and country-blues tunes with *Sun Sessions* reverence.

Everybody's Rockin' is a spirited protest against the humorless chill of most pop electronics (never mind that Young himself stated the most eloquent case for it with *Trans*) and a celebration of Eighties dancing madness. Eight of the songs are frantic party favors, from the boozy strut of the old Bobby Freeman chestnut "Betty Lou's Got a New Pair of Shoes" to the title track's manic Chuck Berry swing. And none of them can be beat for authenticity. Tim Drummond thumps his upright bass with muscular simplicity, Karl Himmel churns up a locomotive shuffle on his snare drum, and Young, who is certainly no Jerry Lee Lewis on the piano, manages to hold his own with rolling boogie rhythms and the sloppy verve of his pounding Killer-like break on "Kinda Fonda Wanda."

Even Young's scratchy vocalizing works here, gently cushioned by sensible doses of traditional slap-back echo and the sunny gospel bop-shoo-bop of his Jordanaires-style backup vocal trio. He gives a straight but energetic reading of "Mystery Train" in a poignant bluesy whine, free of the all-too-common hiccup gimmickry. He also wisely resists camping up his tender mooing on the plaintive ballad "Rainin' in My Heart," indulging himself only on the brief makeout monologue (delivered in a low greaser moan) and wheezy back-porch harmonica solo.

Everybody's Rockin' is such a fun pill to swallow that you may not catch yourself choking on its occasional jabs of moral indignation. "When Ron and Nancy do the bop on the lawn / They're rockin' in the White House all night long," deadpans Young in the otherwise euphoric title track. And

"Payola Blues" is no joke. Young dedicates the song to pioneer deejay Alan Freed, who was disgraced in the Fifties pay-for-play scandals "because the things they're doing today will make a saint out of you." Then, over a proud rock & roll strut, he wraps up the cynicism, double-dealing and artistic narrow casting of rock radio into one bitter singalong package. "If a man is making music," Young barks at one point, "they oughta let his records play."

They probably won't play this one. But so what if it's commercial suicide? You have to admire *Everybody's Rockin'* for its nerve, and eventually you'll come to love it for its frenzied sound and playful humor.

■ **RANDOM NOTES** LEGAL BRIEFS AND ROCK & ROLL SUITS (June 7, 1984)

Geffen Records has filed a $3 million suit against Neil Young, alleging that the bizarro rocker provided two "noncommercial" recordings for the label—the techno *Trans* and the retro *Everybody's Rockin'*—that were "musically uncharacteristic" of his earlier work. The suit further alleges that Young refused to sign an official contract with the label while accepting advances in excess of $2.9 million. The suit came as a surprise to many, given the close relationship between label founder David Geffen and Young's manager, Elliot Roberts, who also handles Geffen recording artists Ric Ocasek and Joni Mitchell (neither of whose recent LPs did much business).

STEVE POND

NEIL YOUNG PERFORMANCE REVIEW
Neil Young's L.A. Hoedown
Universal Amphitheatre, Los Angeles
October 23, 1984

NEIL YOUNG'S GOT A NEW anthem, one that may shock those who fondly remember "Hey hey, my my / Rock & roll will never die." It's called "Get Back to the Country;" he closes his shows with it; and it starts like this:

> *When I was a younger man*
> *Got lucky with a rock & roll band*
> *Struck gold in Hollywood*
> *All the time I knew I would*
> *Get back to the country*

That sums up what Neil Young did this summer and fall, hitting the road with a band called the International Harvesters—long on fiddles, banjos and pedal-steel guitars—and filling his sets with country songs, twangy folk songs and even rock songs dressed up in new, rural duds.

Recent history suggests it's just a phase: Over the past couple of years, Young's blithely skipped from one style to another. After his show, however, he was adamant about sticking to country. "Country music is something I feel very comfortable with," he said, "and it's what I'm gonna be doing from now on."

During the two-hour Amphitheatre show, Young and his band hit an easygoing groove that would have sounded right at home on a Tennessee back porch. His new orientation ruled out the performance of scorchers like "My My, Hey Hey" or "Like a Hurricane," but he added a little flag waving, some tears-in-the-beer and other corn pone to a package that emphasized the country strains in such Young compositions as "Flying on the Ground Is Wrong," "Helpless," "Heart of Gold," "Sugar Mountain," "Old Man" and some new, twangier tunes.

Some of the material didn't benefit from the new context—deprived of its antidrug surroundings on the *Tonight's the Night* LP, "Roll Another Number" could be a doper's call to arms—but Young made the evening's smartest move when he turned "Powderfinger," one of his most vivid, harrowing rock songs, into a jaunty yet unsettling country workout. Although Young's shift to country encourages his fondness for lying back and taking it easy—rather than challenging his exasperating, mercurial brilliance—this show suggests things may change if he keeps working the same vein.

And Young insists he will. "It seems like rock & roll has gotten more concerned with fashion and image lately," he said. "I miss the feeling of community that rock had in the Sixties. But I got back that feeling when I started hanging out with country guys."

■ **RANDOM NOTES** BRUCE COVERS NEIL (May 9, 1985)

Bruce Springsteen often turns up onstage to jam with new acts, but this time he popped up in Sydney, Australia, during a Neil Young concert and joined in on a twenty-minute version of Young's "Down by the River." The connection was Springsteen's guitarist Nils Lofgren, who played with Young's old group Crazy Horse.

PARKE PUTERBAUGH

OLD WAYS ALBUM REVIEW

ARE YOU READY FOR the country? Neil Young posed the question way back when, on *Harvest;* now, thirteen years later, he's restated it as a command: "Get Back to the Country," he urges on *Old Ways,* with Waylon Jennings seconding that emotion. Jennings provides legitimizing C&W ballast for Young on *Old Ways,* singing and/or playing on six of ten tracks. Willie Nelson adds his unmistakable nasal quaver on another tune, a lament with the barely believable title "Are There Any More Real Cowboys?"

Lord knows Young could use the credibility, at least with the country audience, which is probably at least mildly wary of this latest incarnation of his. Still the proof is in the hearing, and this turns out to be his most carefully crafted album since *Comes a Time.* On some levels, it's even arguably conceptual, although Young's deeper musings will be missed if you listen only to the polished surface of this ostensibly purist C&W exercise. "Get Back to the Country," for instance, is more than just a rabble-rousing bluegrass breakdown; in it, Young asserts that a return to roots after his quixotic rock & roll fame was inevitable. Now he sings with an audible smirk that he's "back in the barn again" as a jew's-harp boings away idiotically. One is left wondering how seriously to take him. Not very, I'd guess. Young opens the album with "The Wayward Wind," a Number One pop-schlock hit from 1956, dressing it up in slick Nashville duds, right down to the swooping strings and corny duet vocals. But if this is a put-on, why do so many lines ring true? What is Neil Young if not "a restless wind that's born to wander"?

Both songs make references to "younger days" and being "a younger man," and in "My Boy" he addresses the subject of his son's vanishing youth, in his tenderest vocal, with an almost despondent incredulity. Could it be that he's feeling his age and that country music, with its solid grounding in the sort of adult values and verities that outlast the fires of youth, has given him a forum in which to chew on these matters? Looked at this way, "California Sunset" isn't just another drippy, fiddle-happy ode to Young's home state but a potent image of a native son whose days of roaming are behind him. And "Where Is the Highway Tonight?," with understated ensemble playing and an enticing wisp of a Fifties pop melody in the vocal, finds Young looking back and wondering, "Where are those old days and crazy nights?"

But just when you think he's ready for the old rocker's rest home, he throws in a few curves. In the title track, with Young picking slow and hard at his acoustic over bluesy accompaniment, he allows that "old ways can be a ball and chain." Come to think of it, Willie Nelson doesn't sound entirely comfortable on "Are There Any More Real Cowboys?"—which might be more tongue-in-cheek than it appears. "Bound for Glory," a story about a hitchhiker-truck-driver romance, sends up "Me and Bobby McGee." And "Misfits" is as strange as a meteor falling on the farm. It's kind of a space-age parable, retold as Indian lore to the rumble of a double bass and the tribal thump of a single drum, with the occasional apocalyptic wail of a woman's voice. So disarming is "Misfits" that you don't notice the violins. Or Waylon Jennings. Pretty amazing.

■ **RANDOM NOTES** (April 24, 1986)
Neil Young is in the studio in Los Angeles recording a new LP. Danny Kortchmar is the producer. It seems he has given up his country sound; the album rocks. Meanwhile, Young has sued the state of California for almost half a million dollars; he says he was improperly taxed between 1972 and 1975.

JIM FARBER

LANDING ON WATER ALBUM REVIEW

AFTER A SERIES OF MUSICAL one-night stands, Neil Young is finally getting serious again. His previous three albums were just dalliances—in electronic *(Trans)*, rockabilly *(Everybody's Rockin')* and country *(Old Ways)* music—none of which were terribly meaningful or deeply felt. This time, however, Young has committed himself to a sound that's truly new. He's working with electronics again, but while *Trans* used conventional computer dance beats surrounded by thick, slick synth effects, *Landing on Water* keeps its electronics in the garage. Instead of using technology to go high-tech, Young creates a rinky-tink synth sound, set off by surprisingly sparse, crisp arrangements.

On this record, Young has axed *Trans*'s Vocoder, which made him sound like a singing microwave. There are also more of his raw, bleeding guitar leads. But what's really jarring is the sound of Steve Jordan's drums. They're mixed up high to exhilarating effect. In "I Got a Problem," the drums are compellingly brash, and in "People on the Street," it sounds as if Jordan could kick through the speakers.

Young lightens things up with the pop touches in "Violent Side" and "Hard Luck Stories." To insure his patented irony, the happiest pop melodies are married to some of the album's most dire lyrics. Young may kick off the LP on an optimistic note, casting off the "Weight of the World," but the rest hits like a hurricane. Of course, Young writes bitter songs best, but while it's nice to hear him confronting life again after the relative complacency of his last two LPs, his spare lyrics are not the album's forte. None has the flaky invention of his finest, and the most interesting seem to reduce the whole Sixties movement to a "Hippie Dream."

But what Young's lyrics lack in character, the music makes up for in freshness. True, *Landing on Water* doesn't have the sweep of *Rust Never Sleeps* or *Tonight's the Night*, but it's definitely his most consistent LP of the Eighties. More important, Young has found a way to give his sound a healthy new shot of neurosis.

DAVID FRICKE

NEIL YOUNG AND CRAZY HORSE PERFORMANCE REVIEW

A Garage Band in Garage Land

Madison Square Garden, New York City

October 7, 1986

F OR MOST YOUNG ROCK & ROLL musicians, life begins in a garage. For many, it also ends there. Neil Young was one of the lucky ones. But he has not forgotten what it's like to play music every night at maximum volume for an ungrateful audience of rats, bugs and complaining neighbors while sucking in the carbon monoxide from the old man's car. Young's marathon workout at New York's Madison Square Garden with Crazy Horse, his loyal thunder-punk trio of seventeen years, was an ingenious, earnest and often hilarious theatrical tribute to the eternal struggle of garage bands everywhere.

Part of a tour titled Neil Young and Crazy Horse in a Rusted-Out Garage, the show was accurate in every detail—except size. Everything in Young's fantasy garage at the Garden was Brobdingnagian in scale. A giant lawn mower was propped up against an enormous mock guitar amp. A king-size spider dangled from the lighting rig, and a mechanical cockroach zipped back and forth across the stage.

The "hassles" Young and his aspiring combo encountered throughout the evening were more lifelike—the cranky neighbor who whined about the noise, the sleazy talent scout who talked big deal and tiny bucks. Before the show even started, Neil's "mom" grumbled about the racket while taking down the wash hanging at stage left. "I've heard them practice," she said, "and it just ain't happening."

Well, that's one mom's opinion. But when the Third Best Garage Band in the World, as they called themselves, hit the stage with the martial stomp of "Mr. Soul," they sounded like Hüsker Dü in heat. In machine-gun succession, Young and Crazy Horse (guitarist-keyboardist Frank Sampedro, bassist Billy Talbot, drummer Frank Molina) ripped through "Cinnamon Girl," "When You Dance I Can Really Love," "Touch the Night" and "Down by the River" with corrosive distortion and pig-squeal feedback.

Young, transported into some kind of crazed guitar reverie, angrily stomped the floor in midsolo, like a horse desperately trying to kick his way out of his stall.

The quiet passages had an eerie power of their own. Young's solo musings on "Heart of Gold" and "Only Love Can Break Your Heart"—the latter with uneven but nostalgically stirring harmonies by surprise guests Graham Nash and David Crosby—were a flashback to hippie innocence long gone sour.

Later, with images of dead or fading rock stars (Joplin, Hendrix, Presley, Jagger, Dylan) parading somberly on a screen behind him, Young roared into a reading of "Hey, Hey, My, My (Into the Black)" with never-say-die vehemence, leaving the feedback going full blast even after a squad of "cops"—called in by the nosy neighbor—chased Young off the stage. When he and Crazy Horse sneaked back on for one last number, they cranked up a rowdy new tune, a potential garage-band national anthem with a jokey but inspiring chorus: "That's why we don't want to be good," a no-sellout sentiment that was, still is and always will be at the heart of many rock & roll dreams. In fact, a more appropriate title for the whole show might have been simply No Surrender.

MICHAEL GOLDBERG

YOUNG REJOINS CSN

"**CROSBY, STILLS, NASH AND YOUNG** is *alive,*" Neil Young said, flushed with excitement from the group's first full-blown performance together in thirteen years. Following a stunning all-acoustic Greenpeace benefit concert in Santa Barbara, California, last month, Young revealed that he has decided to work with the group once again primarily because David Crosby has kicked drugs and is now serious about making music. The four have already started recording a new album, and its release will most likely be followed by a major concert tour beginning this summer.

"We're gonna make a great album," insisted forty-five-year-old David Crosby, standing backstage at Santa Barbara's Arlington Theatre. "We're gonna kick ass!"

"Everybody's here now," Young, forty-one, said as he relaxed with Stephen Stills in his dressing room between shows. "Can't be Crosby, Stills, Nash and Young if you don't have Crosby. . . . He was always the spiritual leader of the group. Now Crosby's back. I told Crosby six years ago, 'Get it together and I'll be there.' " He glanced over at the forty-two-year-old Stills, who added, "It feels like we're a band again."

Though still overweight (he's just begun working out with Neil Young's trainer), David Crosby seemed like a new man—alert, focused, happy—both on and off the stage. When he sang, his voice was strong and sure, hitting every note with a controlled intensity that had not been evident in years. In marked contrast to his freebasing days, when he kept himself holed up in backstage dressing rooms or on a touring bus dubbed the Lab, Crosby mingled freely between sets with backstage guests, striking up conversations, slapping old friends on the back, his face constantly breaking into a big smile. "I figure David used to live for music and drugs," said Bill Siddons, who manages Crosby and Nash. "Now he lives for music." And according to Young, Crosby will soon marry his longtime girlfriend, Jan Dance.

Crosby spent eight months in Dallas County Jail and the Texas Department of Corrections in Huntsville last year following drug and illegal-weapon convictions. During that time he successfully overcame his addiction to cocaine. He was released on August 8, 1986. As a condition of his parole, Crosby must submit to weekly drug tests. "We got David back almost from the dead," said Graham Nash, forty-five, during a separate interview. "Literally. Snatched him from the jaws of fucking hell. I've known him twenty years, and I've never known him this straight. I thought, What's a straight Crosby going to be? But he's brilliant and he's funny and he's creative. . . . This first year has been the big test. So far he's passed with flying colors."

In Santa Barbara on February 6, Crosby, Stills, Nash and Young performed two separate hour-and-a-half-long sets to sellout audiences totaling over 4,000 people. They were the first "complete shows," as Nash put it, the four musicians had played since breaking up in late 1974. Arriving a day early (Crosby cruised into town on a newly purchased Harley-Davidson), they held a hotel-room rehearsal into the early hours of the morning, then regrouped for a two-hour rehearsal the afternoon of the show. "All of those benefits we've done [Live Aid, the Bridge concert] were unrehearsed, very spontaneous," said Young during a forty-five-minute interview conducted during a plane flight back to San Francisco the day after the concert. "Some of them weren't very good. Live Aid was really a disaster. . . . This was the first time where we seriously rehearsed and learned the songs."

It showed. They immediately won over the crowd with a knockout opening segment of "Wasted on the Way," "Change Partners," "Long May You Run" and "Long Time Coming" that found their voices weaving together to produce the kind of crystalline harmonies that made them one of the biggest rock groups in the early Seventies. Then Crosby was left alone on the stage. Seated on a stool, he broke the ice by joking about how he was raised in Santa Barbara and "thrown out of every school in town." Then he addressed his recent problems. "Actually, I think you all know this," he said. "It was all too public. You all know that I got loaded for a long time and wound up very badly strung out on hard drugs. Now this is not a preach to you on drugs. Frankly, you got to figure that out for yourself. Mind you, if you look at my life you can figure it out in two seconds. . . ."

Accompanying himself with just his acoustic guitar, Crosby played a beautiful ballad about "finding your way" called "Compass," which he wrote while in prison. "I have wasted ten years in a blindfold," he began, his distinctive voice sounding particularly fragile.

Rejoined by his band mates, Crosby introduced another new one, "He's an American." More new songs followed, some by Young ("Nothing Is Perfect," "This Old House," "Long Walk Home"), one by Nash ("Try to Find Me"), along with a twelve-year-old Stills tune ("As I Come of Age"). Other highlights included "Daylight Again," "Southern Cross,"

"Suite: Judy Blue Eyes," "Southern Man," "Teach Your Children" and, toward the end of the second show, a passionate version of "Ohio" and another new song from Neil Young, titled "Mideast Vacation."

"It is different," said Crosby, speaking about the sense of excitement and commitment evident in their performance. "I guess my coming back had something to do with it. We pulled off all these new songs tonight. I can't believe it. I'm so happy."

In mid-February the group began recording in L.A. with producer Bill Szymczyk to begin a record that, if all goes as planned, will become the second Crosby, Stills, Nash and Young studio album. *Déjà Vu,* released in 1970, is the only previous studio album the four men have made together. (A live set, *4 Way Street,* and a compilation LP, *So Far,* were also issued.) Attempts in 1974 to record a follow-up ended abruptly when Neil Young, upset by arguing within the group, walked out and, as Crosby once put it, "never came back."

"To tell you the truth, when I drifted away from the group, David didn't really have a drug problem," said Young. "At least if he did I didn't know about it. David always said he'd been doing all of these drugs all the time through all of his music and everything, but I don't think so. If he was, I must have been incredibly naive. Of course I was very naive, so it's possible." He laughed. "I didn't know much about drugs during that whole period. Never taken acid or anything like that. Still never have. People have an opinion of us that really isn't based on reality. It's based on what they and their friends were doing while listening to us."

Between the four of them, there is more than enough new material for a record. In addition to the songs they performed, Crosby has another one, "The Monkey and the Underdog," while Nash has at least two others, "Clear Blue Skies" and "Before the Moon Is Full." Stills also said he has some new tunes he'll be bringing into the studio.

One possible hitch in the group's plans has come from David Geffen. Young is currently signed to Geffen Records, and Geffen doesn't want him appearing on a CSNY record unless it comes out on his label. Crosby, Stills and Nash are still signed to Atlantic. Said Nash, "When he [Geffen] wanted the CSNY record and we said no, he then said, 'It's my ball and I'm gonna take my ball and we're not gonna play football. Fuck you.' "

Though he denies using those words, Geffen is adamant about the conditions under which a CSNY record can be released. "If they want to make a record with Neil Young, that record can only be made for me," said Geffen. "Because I will not allow Neil Young to make a record for anybody [else] while he's under exclusive contract to me, for which I paid a healthy amount of money."

"I don't know how that's going to work out," said Young wryly, "but I'm sure that the record companies, in their wisdom, will figure out a way for Crosby, Stills, Nash and Young to make another record. It's not my problem. We're gonna make a record anyway. No one can stop us from doing what we want. And then when it's done, it's done. Whatever happens to it after that, that's a business deal."

Nash thinks Geffen will relent since Young only owes two more albums to complete his contract: "Neil is about to hand in a record with Crazy Horse. And when you only have one record left to deliver, you have a lot of bargaining power. Because your contract is virtually up. Neil could go in and do 'My Way' six different ways and hand it in. I think if Geffen pisses him off, he's liable to do it."

But it was CSNY's bright future, not problems with Geffen, that Young was contemplating as he glanced out the airplane window at the California coast below. "There's a very strong chance of the group being better and stronger and perhaps bigger than it ever was before," he said. "There's really an audience out there for CSNY. We could have a huge tour, and if we make a great record . . . We really don't think that *Déjà Vu* and the first album [*Crosby, Stills & Nash*] were really as good as we're capable of doing. There's a lot more depth and rawness and a lot more funk and soul in this band than has ever been heard on record.

"We see ourselves as being able to do this for another twenty years," Young later said. "We don't see that it's over. With us, we can go away for four or five years and come back and our audience is still there. We don't have to stay with what's happening. Because we're happening. We're not in that race. We're in our own slot. I just don't feel competition from anyone. Who's competing with us? If the Beatles were playing today, that would be something that we would think about. Are we doing something as hip as what the Beatles are doing? What else is there?"

MICHAEL GOLDBERG

CSNY REUNION ALBUM STALLED

THE EAGERLY ANTICIPATED Crosby, Stills, Nash and Young reunion album is on hold. Neil Young will not be able to participate in the album until an arrangement is worked out with his current label, Geffen Records.

David Crosby, Stephen Stills and Graham Nash have spent about ten days in the studio; they will not resume recording until September, after an extensive summer tour. CSN's management expects a new album to be released by the end of the year, though Young's participation is anything but certain. "My guess is that if we reenter the studio in September, we'll finish by Christmas," says Bill Siddons, who manages Crosby and Nash. "The only open question is what Neil's involvement will be, if any." David Geffen, president of Geffen Records, remains adamant that he will allow Young to appear on the album only if it is released on his label. Young owes two albums on his Geffen contract; Crosby, Stills and Nash are signed to Atlantic Records. "I'd say it's seventy-thirty against [Young's being involved]," says Siddons. "It's possible that Elliot [Roberts, Young's manager] will find out a way to work something out directly with David. . . . I have to believe that people as smart as that can find a way to make something that offers so much potential for everyone happen."

There is a slight possibility that Young will join Crosby, Stills and Nash for some of the dates on their summer tour, which begins on July 2 in Binghamton, New York.

STEVE HOCHMAN

LIFE ALBUM REVIEW

THROUGHOUT NEIL YOUNG'S ERRATIC solo career, the one constant has been Crazy Horse. Despite all the experimentations with country, technopop, rockabilly and whatever else might have struck Young's fancy at any given time, there's always been something reassuring about the solid rock he makes with his home team. It's the albums with Crazy Horse—*Everybody Knows This Is Nowhere, After the Gold Rush, Tonight's the Night, Zuma,* side two of *Rust Never Sleeps, Live Rust* and the overlooked *Re-ac-tor*—that are the core of an impressive, if not always successful, body of work.

Life, the first album from Young and Crazy Horse since 1981's *Re-ac-tor,* reaffirms the power of that chemistry. Aside from a few aberrations—the overlong "Inca Queen" and side two's leadoff pair of grungy garage anthems ("Too Lonely" and the willfully, pointedly bad "Prisoners of Rock 'n' Roll")—Young and company play with a fervor and mind that belie the on-again, off-again nature of their collaborations. (And anyway, what's a Neil Young album without a few aberrations—especially ones that emphasize such Young trademarks as sloppy arrangements and awkward lyrical and vocal phrasing?)

"Long Walk Home," which picks up where "After the Gold Rush" left off, the rocking "Cryin' Eyes" and the closing elegiac ballads, "When Your Lonely Heart Breaks" and "We Never Danced," rank among Young's best songs. Even the somewhat politically muddled numbers—"Mideast Vacation," "Around the World" and "Long Walk Home" (with its annoying bomb effects)—get by on the strength of their music, which at times approaches Pete Townshend territory in its power and elegance. Flat-out rage, youthful buoyancy and unadulterated tenderness are the musical language of *Life.*

To call this a comeback would be to dismiss unfairly the four albums Young recorded on his own following *Re-ac-tor.* But on the whole, *Life* is his strongest work thus far this decade and another notable entry in the catalog of one of America's most distinctive and important rockers.

MICHAEL GOLDBERG

NEIL YOUNG BOWS BLUES BAND

THE LATEST BEND IN Neil Young's musical road is a sharp turn to the blues. The iconoclastic rocker's recording and performing career—which has rambled from folk to hard rock, L.A. psychedelia to rockabilly, technopop to country, hippie guitar jams to punk—recently entered new territory when he unveiled a crackerjack ten-piece electric blues band billed as the Bluenotes for a ten-date, two-sets-a-night West Coast tour.

Over the years, Young has periodically abandoned the arena circuit for short club tours that allowed him to stretch out on different material. "It's just a fun thing to do," Young told the longtime Bay Area disc jockey Paul "Lobster" Wells—a friend of Young's who acted as MC for the shows—in an interview for radio station KSJO.

"We'd been on the road for two years," Young said, "and I just decided that was it. I wasn't going to play my hits; I didn't want to play any more coliseums. So we got together the Bluenotes—six horns and Crazy Horse— and we just played these cabarets and clubs." Young insisted that the advertisements for the shows feature the Bluenotes, with no mention of his own name.

Judging from a ninety-minute show at the Old Fillmore, in San Francisco, the Bluenotes' performances were highlighted by Young's tour de force blues guitar. Using the moniker Shakey Deal—and dressing like an R. Crumb-style hippie bluesman, in black fedora, shades, seedy sport coat, white shirt and tie—Young abandoned the role of hard-rock primitive that characterizes his arena-show persona and was transformed into a sophisticated blues chameleon. He gave stylistic nods to Albert King, Jimmy Reed, B.B. King, Buddy Guy, Freddie King and Michael Bloomfield. Yet the show proved to be more than a mere exercise in music history, as Young brought the passion typical of his rock performances to his new blues.

Young offered up a baker's dozen of basically unknown blues songs, which he says were written throughout his career, with at least one number dating back to his teens. Opening with "Big Room," the Bluenotes' shows included "Find Another Shoulder," "High Heels," "Hello Lonely Woman," "Ain't It the Truth" and "Your Love."

The band also performed "One Thing," "Bad News," "Don't Take Your Love Away," "Sunny Inside," "Life in the City" and "Soul of a Woman." The audience's favorite, though, was an anti-corporate-sponsorship number, "This Note's for You," in which Young spat out lines such as these: "Ain't singing for Miller / Don't sing for Bud / Don't sing for politicians / Ain't singing for Spuds."

All of the shows were recorded by the Record Plant's twenty-four-track mobile studio. Whether the performances will surface on an album is unclear, however, since Young habitually records all of his shows.

Young's manager, Elliot Roberts, says Young's next album will not be an all-blues affair, although it could include a few songs from the Bluenotes' repertoire. Young recently ended a stormy relationship with Geffen Records, which released him from his contract. Roberts says negotiations to re-sign Young to Reprise Records—the label where he enjoyed his greatest success, with albums such as *Everybody Knows This Is Nowhere, After the Gold Rush* and *Harvest*—have nearly been completed.

Young's new contract will also allow him to record a Crosby, Stills, Nash and Young album this year, something he was prevented from doing under his Geffen contract. Last year Young was adamant about wanting to record and tour as a member of CSNY, and he may tour with them this summer.

"There's a lot more depth and rawness and a lot more funk and soul in this band than has ever been heard on record," Young said last February following a spirited CSNY performance in Santa Barbara, California. "There's a very strong chance of the group being better and stronger and perhaps bigger than it ever was before."

But first, Young intends to record a new solo album. "It'll be a rock & roll album, because he's doing it with Crazy Horse," says Roberts. "He's got a lot of new songs, and he's excited about making a record for Reprise."

As for the Bluenotes, Young just may hit the road again with them for some encore performances. As he told the audience at a club in San Jose, California, "The Notes will be back!"

DAVID BROWNE

THIS NOTE'S FOR YOU ALBUM REVIEW

★ ★ ★ ½

Neil Young's Blues Revival

Y**OU COULD HEAR THE** groans all the way back east. Last fall, Neil
Young began a string of unannounced gigs in California clubs,
fronting, of all things, a large, horn-heavy band called the Bluenotes. It seemed like the final insult, the depressing cap to a decade in which
one of the foremost singer/songwriters reduced his career to one attention-
getting gimmick after another: synth rocker one minute, rockabilly cat or
right-wing honky-tonk balladeer the next. Shying from the bitter and often
scathing dissections of stardom and the music business that characterized his
best Seventies work, the Neil Young of the Eighties instead opted to
become his generation's consummate weirdo, trivializing his monolithic
accomplishments and putting his future in question.

This Note's for You, the album that is the result of this spurt of activity,
seems on first listen another false step, another byway Young can use to
duck the nagging issue of artistic commitment. Opening with a walking bass
line and a swaggering blast of horns that wouldn't sound out of place on
The Tonight Show, "Ten Men Workin' " introduces both the band and the
record's motif: "We are men at work, we got a job to do," sings Young.
"We gotta keep you rockin' to keep your soul from the blues." In comparison, the semistoned mumbling that began *Tonight's the Night* and the
sweeping strings on "The Wayward Wind," the opening cut of *Old Ways,*
seem downright orthodox.

At this point, loyal Young fans who still remember *Everybody's Rockin',*
his 1983 neo-rockabilly toss-off, may be tempted to leave the room. They
do so, however, at their own risk. *This Note's for You* is not merely the most
spirited work Young has done in some time. A recasting of his considerable
strengths in the unlikeliest of settings, it is also his first conceptually successful record of the Eighties. (It may be a coincidence, but the album also
marks Young's return to the reactivated Reprise label, where he enjoyed his
greatest artistic and commercial successes.) Most important, from his re-
charged guitar chops to the juke-joint stomp of the Bluenotes—a nine-

piece band that includes a six-man horn section and two longtime Young band mates, Ben Keith on alto saxophone and Crazy Horse's Frank Sampedro on keyboards—*This Note's for You* is a rediscovery of the joys of spontaneity and, especially, the benefits of being Neil Young.

Those elements have been in short supply in Young's recent work. The brooding *Landing on Water* (1986) focused on human breakdown, failure and renewal, but its AOR sound depersonalized the effort. Last year's *Life,* his reunion with the loyal Crazy Horse, tackled more globally oriented topics, but the lugubrious arrangements all but obliterated the band's impact. Like his previous left-field musical forays, these were dead-end moves: aural sensations that ultimately couldn't compensate for the lack of musical direction.

With *This Note's for You,* one can simply revel in the album's raunchy, robust big-band swing and the blues-band gestures—off-key call-and-response vocals from the band, solid shuffle rhythms and the corniest of saxophone solos. The songs, all Young originals, rework the standard clichés: "Well I lost my job thinkin' about you / Now there's another man workin' in my place"; "Well my money's gone / And so are you." But Young's gloriously atonal guitar playing shows that this is no Ry Cooder-type archival study. Spitting off spare leads in "Ten Men Workin' " and "Married Man," Young proves himself a more than capable blues guitarist; the barrelhouse rocker "Hey Hey" employs a relentlessly sloppy slide guitar that takes on the whole horn section and wins.

Young is clearly having fun with the blues concept, as when he rebuffs a barroom temptress in "Married Man" and, on "Hey Hey," good-naturedly sings, "Get off that couch / Turn off that MTV." The downright bouncy and unexpectedly sentimental "Sunny Inside" features a swell of horns that would have made Blood, Sweat and Tears blush. At the very least, the album reveals that Young has regained his offbeat sense of humor. In "This Note's for You," a swipe at corporate sponsorship that's also the album's most urgent rocker, he spits out, "Ain't singin' for Pepsi / Ain't singin' for Coke / I don't sing for nobody / Makes me look like a joke." With twisted glee in his voice, in the next verse he adds, "I won't sing for politicians / Ain't singin' for Spuds."

But the album truly shines when Young slows down the pace and turns inward. Both "Coupe de Ville" and "Can't Believe Your Lyin' " forsake huffing and puffing in favor of an intimate after-hours setting, with brushed drums, muted trumpet and Young's own light picking. "Coupe de Ville," which recalls the moroseness of such Young angst chronicles as "On the Beach," is a lilting, melancholy ballad in which he quietly pleads to his departed lover: "I got a right in this crazy world / To live my life like anyone else." "Twilight," a dreamy tale of heading home that features menacingly ticking drums and an understated vocal, is even better.

Moments like those make it easy to forgive the album's failings. With his quivering tenor, Young—surely one of our whitest rock & rollers—is only slightly more effective as a blues singer than he was as a synth popper on *Trans* or as a honky-tonker on *Old Ways*. And anybody worried about his right-wing tendencies won't be comforted by "Life in the City," an alarmingly paranoid view of society's problems ("People sleepin' on the sidewalks on a rainy day / Families livin' under freeways, it's the American way").

Like every one of Neil Young's abrupt shifts in musical direction, this one leaves nagging doubts. Is it all a shuck? Maybe. With a Crosby, Stills, Nash and Young reunion in the works, will the Bluenotes go the way of the Ducks, the Shocking Pinks, the International Harvesters and other ad hoc Young bands of the past? Probably. Yet the renewed energy and purpose heard in *This Note's for You* provide hope for the future. Whether the album signals the beginning of another golden era for such a frustratingly erratic musician is open to question. But for the first time in a long while, the question has finally been raised.

■ **RANDOM NOTES** NEIL YOUNG'S ONE-MAN COMMERCIAL BAN (May 19, 1988)

Neil Young blasts rock & roll's cozy relationship with Madison Avenue on the defiant title track of his new album, *This Note's for You*. "It's just my statement on me and the conglomerates," Young says. "I can't sell my voice and my melodies to some company and then turn around, sing a song from the bottom of my heart and expect anybody to believe it." Young's audiences apparently agree with his sentiment, greeting the song enthusiastically at his shows. "Never in my life have I had a song that people reacted to so instantaneously," he says. "People just start cheering and singing when we play it. Everybody loves it."

Since finishing *This Note's for You*, Young has started work on a new Crosby, Stills, Nash and Young album. So far, the band has recorded eight songs in a barn at Young's ranch, outside San Francisco. "It sounds great—I love it," he says. "There's an incredible energy among the four of us." The CSNY album should be out later this year. Meanwhile, Young has several other projects in mind, including a summer tour with his new band, the Bluenotes; a cable-TV special called *Muddy Track*, about a 1987 tour with Crazy Horse; and *Decade 2*, a follow-up to his previous career chronicle.

JAMES HENKE

NEIL YOUNG: THE ROLLING STONE INTERVIEW

"YOU DON'T MIND DOING this on the move, do you?" Neil Young asks as he slides behind the wheel of his 1950 Plymouth Special Deluxe, one of the roughly thirty-five cars in his ever-expanding collection.

Spring has barely arrived, but the temperature in the hills south of San Francisco has already hit the nineties, and Young is dressed accordingly—his shirt is open, and he's wearing a pair of frayed cutoffs, sneakers and blue shades. Bits of gray have streaked his familiar sideburns and shoulder-length hair, but Young still looks very much as he did seventeen years ago, when he moved up here to redwood country and bought what he now calls Broken Arrow Ranch.

The ranch was one of the rewards of Young's first burst of success. *After the Gold Rush,* the third solo album he recorded after leaving Buffalo Springfield, reached the Top Ten in 1970, and both *Déjà Vu* and *4 Way Street,* recorded with David Crosby, Stephen Stills and Graham Nash, hit Number One. For a while, CSNY seemed like the American Beatles, and Young was their John Lennon, the passionate, slightly eccentric rocker who gave the group its edge.

But CSNY self-destructed, and after reaching Number One in 1972 with *Harvest* and the single "Heart of Gold," Young moved away from the mainstream. "This song put me in the middle of the road," Young wrote about "Heart of Gold" in his liner notes to his three-album retrospective, *Decade.* "Traveling there soon became a bore so I headed for the ditch. A rougher ride but I saw more interesting people there."

By 1979, when Young last sat for an in-depth interview with ROLLING STONE, he had reached another peak, both critically and commercially, with the country-tinged *Comes a Time* and the punk-inspired *Rust Never Sleeps.* *The Village Voice* named him Artist of the Decade, and there was every reason to think he'd continue to maintain a high level of success in the Eighties.

But Young signed to David Geffen's newly formed Geffen Records early in the decade, and the pairing proved to be a frustrating one for both sides. The five albums Young recorded for the label rank as the worst selling of his career. His intermittently brilliant but quirky stylistic experiments—techno-rock on *Trans* (1982), rockabilly on *Everybody's Rockin'* (1983) and country on *Old Ways* (1985)—caused even his staunchest supporters to lose their patience.

Young insists that the label is the real villain behind that slump, and he even claims that his best work during the period was never released. Geffen, for its part, refuses to respond to Young's allegations. "I don't want to get into a pissing match with him," says label president Ed Rosenblatt.

No matter who was at fault, Young is clearly delighted to be back on Reprise, the Warner Bros. subsidiary he was with in the Seventies. He is also determined to prove that Geffen—which at one point even sued him for deliberately making noncommercial records—was wrong. But in typical Neil Young style, his first album for Reprise—though his strongest, most consistent effort in years—is hardly a sure commercial bet. *This Note's for You* features Young and the Bluenotes, a horn-powered nine-piece band; they work up a sweat on ten blues tunes inspired by such early Young faves as Jimmy Reed and John Lee Hooker. And the album's title cut finds Young railing against rock & roll's increasing involvement with Madison Avenue.

"There's a line," Young says, "one of the first fucking lines that's ever been drawn where pop stars really have to show their stuff, show where they're really coming from. I mean, if you're going to sing for a product, then you're singing for money. Period. That's it. Money is what you want, and this is how you get it."

Over the course of the two sessions that made up this interview—the second one was also conducted on the move, in Young's 1954 Cadillac limousine—Young, who's now forty-two, was equally emphatic about his loyalty to the Bluenotes and even indicated that the gut-wrenching rock & roll he's played with Crazy Horse may be a thing of the past.

But Young has never been a one-band man, and he's already recording a new Crosby, Stills, Nash and Young album up at his ranch. That LP is expected to be released this fall, and in the meantime Young and the Bluenotes will be hitting the road for an extended U.S. tour. As for the distant future, Young will no doubt keep everyone guessing—just as he has for the past two decades.

What prompted you to get back together with Crosby, Stills and Nash?

Well, there's a certain energy you get from singing with people you've known for twenty-five years. People who have been through all these changes with you. Gone up and down with you. Seen you do things that are wrong and seen you do things that are brilliant. Seen you fucked up to the max, you know? And you've seen them do all these things. And yet we're still here. Just to hear what it sounds like when we sing together after all these years—I was curious. I've wanted to do it for the last two or three years. And now it's possible.

I think that CSNY has a lot to say. Especially Crosby. His presence is very strong. Him being strong and surviving and writing great songs and being part of a winner is really a good role model for a lot of people in the same boat.

So he's really cleaned up?

He's doing fine. His emotions are slightly shattered, because he's just abused his emotions for so long by not letting them out. But now that he's pure and can let his emotions out, his highs are real high, and his lows are real low. Those are just the extremes of his personality. But he pulls out of his lows, and they don't turn him toward any problem areas or anything.

How about Stills?

He's definitely the rowdiest of the four of us, as far as abuses and things like that. But he's at a time in his life when things are real important. He's just been married, and his wife's pregnant. There are a lot of new things happening. And he and I playing together is a nice resurgence.

He didn't seem so together when they profiled CSN on "West 57th."

The thing that surprised me was the fact that CSN actually did the show. I mean, what are they gonna do next, "Geraldo"? And they obviously weren't thinking clearly, because every tour that CSN has ever done, Stephen has gone out the window. He blows out before he goes on the road. He blows out heavily. So what do they do? They set up a TV guy to be there when it happens. What kind of stupid move is that?

You two have had a stormy relationship.

We're like brothers, you know? We love each other, and we hate each other. We resent each other, but we love playing together. I see and hear so much in Stephen that I'm frustrated when it isn't on record or something. There have been a lot of frustrations through our whole lives with each other, but there's also been a lot of great music. He continuously blows my mind with the ideas that he has for my songs. He's one of the greatest musicians I've ever met in my life. Great singer. Incredible songwriter.

But what's he like as a person? He came off like a jerk on that show.

He's a tormented artist. He's the definition of the tormented artist. And he's a great fucking bluesman. But he's got a lot of monkeys on his back, and they're not letting him do his thing. I just hope he makes it.

And what's Nash like?

Nash is a very straight, very sincere kind of organized guy, dedicated to quality and very reliable. And he's an extremely good singer. Amazing pitch. He likes to be on top of it. He takes a lot of pride in being totally able to accomplish whatever it is that has to be done. Without Nash, there would be no Crosby, Stills and Nash at all. It would have been over a long time ago.

Are there plans for a CSNY tour?

They wanted to book a tour, and I said no way. I don't want to have anything to do with a tour. When the record's finished and we know what we've got, that's the time to talk about a tour.

Also, everyone needs to really get in shape if we tour. There's no way getting around the fact that a CSNY tour would be a nostalgia tour to a great degree. CSNY is Woodstock—it's that era, that whole generation. So why go out there and not be at our physical best? If people are looking at us as their brothers who they went through all these changes with, do they want to see somebody who's not together? No, they want to see someone who's superstrong, who's endured, who's a survivor and is still creative and looks better than ever.

If we go out there and fall on our ass, what are we? Dean Martin? All the alcoholics who went to see him, they didn't say, "Wow, look at Dean. He used to drink so much, but he got himself together and now he's strong, up there with Frank and Sammy." I feel sorry for the guy. He's in the fucking hospital.

That's a weird comparison, but in some ways it's very true. They're just another generation's heroes. So I think we have a responsibility, and I don't think we've lived up to it yet.

Crosby's recovered to a point. But he needs to recover his physical strength and endurance. His endurance is low because he's very big. And he moves very slowly. This is a problem that has to be solved. You can't go out there with all the spirit in the world. You have to have a physical body that can sustain the gruel of a world tour.

From time to time, there are also rumors of a Buffalo Springfield reunion. Is there any truth to them?

Well, there actually have been several Buffalo Springfield reunions in the last two years. At Stills' house. We just get together every couple of months and play. The original guys—Richie [Furay], Dewey [Martin], Bruce [Palmer], Stephen and I. We've done this three, maybe four times, and I'm sure we'll do it again.

Is there a chance you'll record with them?

It's crossed my mind, but I'm committed to CSNY, and there's no way I'm gonna do CSNY and Buffalo Springfield.

When you look back at that time—Buffalo Springfield, CSNY, the Sixties—how does it all seem now?

I had a great time. I think a lot of us had a great time back then. But

I don't see myself as being stuck in the Sixties or anything like that—except that I still have long hair.

What about the idealism of the period? In "Hippie Dream," you sang, "The wooden ships are a hippie dream, capsized in excess."

I wrote that one for Crosby. But I guess it could have been for me, or for anybody. It's really about the excesses of our whole generation. From hippie to yuppie—I mean, it's been quite an evolution.

What do you think about drugs? A lot of people have an image of you as having been a big druggie.

That's a myth. I mean, how would I have kept this together for so long if I was on drugs? It'd be impossible. You could not do what I have done if you were into drugs. I mean, I used a few drugs. I smoked a lot of grass in the Sixties, continued to smoke grass into the Seventies and dabbled around in other drugs. But I never got hooked on . . . you know, never got out of hand with the harder drugs. I experimented, but I think I'm basically a survivor. I've never been an alcoholic. Never used heroin.

There must have been a lot of heroin around you. Two of your friends—Danny Whitten, a guitarist with Crazy Horse, and Bruce Berry, a roadie—died of over-doses. And of course there was Crosby.

There was never any heroin directly around me, 'cause people knew how I felt about it. Anything that killed people, I didn't want to have. Anything that you had to have, that was bigger than you, I'm not for that.

"The Needle and the Damage Done," from Harvest, *was one of the first antidrug songs.*

I wrote that about Danny Whitten. He'd gotten so wasted, so strung out, that he OD'ed and almost died.

He finally did OD and die shortly after Harvest *was released. Had he known the song was about him?*

He must have. I never sat down with him and said, "Danny, listen to this." I don't believe that a song should be for one person. I just tried to make something that everyone could relate to.

What about cocaine? At the Last Waltz, you came onstage with a lump of cocaine under your nose.

I was fried for the Last Waltz. I was on my way out, falling onstage, and someone said, "Here, have some of this." I'd been up for two days, so I had some. And I was gone, you know? I'm not proud of it; I don't think people should see that and think, "Wow, that's cool."

When they were editing the film, they asked me if I wanted to have that removed. And Robbie Robertson said, "The way you are is kinda like what the whole movie's about—if you keep on doin' this, you're just gonna die, so we're going to stop doing it." They just caught me at a bad time. I had been on the road for forty-five days, and I'd done two shows the night before in Atlanta, and I just got carried away, and we just blew it out the window. So I was still up.

But I don't do that anymore. I'm one of the lucky ones who was able to do that and able to stop. But it wasn't that easy to stop that lifestyle. I had to spend some time. The monster kept coming back every once in a while. I could stop for three or four weeks or a couple of months, then I'd get back into it, just for one or two nights, then I'd stop again. It took a long time. I don't even know if it's over now.

Do you still smoke grass?

I haven't smoked any since October 7. The main reason is that on October 7, Elliot Roberts, my manager, called and told me that it looked like I was going to get off Geffen Records. And I had just smoked this big bomber, and I almost had a heart attack. I was so happy, but I was too high to enjoy it. So I stopped. I just didn't have my senses, my faculties together enough to enjoy the moment.

You'd been trying to get off Geffen for a long time.

They had a very negative viewpoint of anything that I wanted to do, other than straight pop records that were exactly what they wanted to hear. They saw me as a product that was not living up to their expectations. They didn't see me as an artist.

Geffen actually sued you for not making commercial records around the time of Old Ways.

There was a whole other record, the original *Old Ways*, which Geffen rejected. It was like *Harvest II*. It was a combination of the musicians from *Harvest* and *Comes a Time*. It was done in Nashville in only a few days, basically the same way *Harvest* was done, and it was coproduced by Elliot Mazer, who produced *Harvest*.

There's *Harvest, Comes a Time* and *Old Ways I,* which is more of a Neil Young record than *Old Ways II. Old Ways II* was more of a country record—which was a direct result of being sued for playing country music. The more they tried to stop me, the more I did it. Just to let them know that no one's gonna tell me what to do.

I would have thought that Geffen would have wanted another Comes a Time *or* Harvest.

That's what we thought. I was so stoked about that record. I sent them a tape of it that had eight songs on it. I called them up a week later, 'cause I hadn't heard anything, and they said, "Well, frankly, Neil, this record scares us a lot. We don't think this is the right direction for you to be going in."

The technopop thing was happening, and they had Peter Gabriel, and they were totally into that kind of trip. I guess they just saw me as some old hippie from the Sixties still trying to make acoustic music or something. They didn't look at me as an artist; they looked at me as a product, and this product didn't fit in with their marketing scheme.

When you look back at the five albums you made for Geffen, how do you think they stand up?

It's hard for me to disassociate the frustrations that I had during that period from the actual works I was able to create. I really tried to do my best during that period, but I felt that I was working under duress.

In all my time at Warner Bros., they never canceled a session. For any reason. And it happened several times at Geffen. It was blatant manipulation. It was just so different from anything I'd ever experienced.

They buried *Everybody's Rockin'*. They did less than nothing. They decided, "That record's not gonna get noticed. We're gonna press as few of those as possible and not do anything."

There was another record of mine, called *Island in the Sun,* which will probably never be heard. It was the first record I made for Geffen. The three acoustic songs on *Trans* are from it. But they advised me not to put it out. Because it was my first record for Geffen, I thought, Well, this is a fresh, new thing. He's got some new ideas. It didn't really register to me that I was being manipulated. Until the second record. Then I realized this is the way it is all the time. Whatever I do, it's not what they want.

I'm gonna try and expose those things that I tried to do on *Decade II,* which should come out next year. Now that I'm back on Reprise, I can do whatever I want. So I can do *Decade II.* On Geffen, *Decade II* would have been impossible, 'cause it's a three-record set, and they would never do that. There's no way they could make the money they want to make out of it.

Trans surprised *a lot of people. I don't think anyone expected you to make an album with synthesizers.*

Trans resulted from a fascination with machines and computers taking over our lives. This image of elevators with digital numbers changing and people going up and down the floors—you know, people changing levels all under the control of a machine. And drum machines, the whole thing. And here I was, like an old hippie out in the woods, with all this electronic equipment. I mean, I was astonished.

I had a whole video thing in mind for that record. I had characters and images of beings that went with all the voices. There was one guy I called Tabulon, who sang on "Computer Age." He had a big speaker in his chest, and his face was a keypad, and he kept hitting his face. [*He demonstrates, with a quick blow to his face.*] But I could never get anybody to make the videos. I could never get anybody to believe that the fucking idea was any good.

What about 1986's Landing on Water? *That album holds up pretty well.*

That album was like a rebirth, just me coming back to L.A. after having been secluded for so long. I was finding my rock & roll roots again. And my vibrancy as a musician. Something came alive; it was like a bear waking up.

What had you been doing during hibernation?

I had just been up here in the woods. And I'd been working on a program with my son Ben, who has cerebral palsy. It just kind of took me away for a while, made me think about other things. I never really lost interest in music, but there were other things in my life that were real important. My real soul was taken up with things I didn't want to sing about.

Although if you listen to *Trans,* if you listen to the words to "Transformer Man" and "Computer Age" and "We R in Control," you'll hear a lot of references to my son and to people trying to live a life by pressing buttons, trying to control the things around them, and talking with people who can't talk, using computer voices and things like that.

It's a subtle thing, but it's right there. But it has to do with a part of my life that practically no one can relate to. So my music, which is a reflection of my inner self, became something that nobody could relate to. And then I started hiding in styles, just putting little clues in there as to what was really on my mind. I just didn't want to openly share all this stuff in songs that said exactly what I wanted to say in a voice so loud everyone could hear it.

Both of your sons have cerebral palsy. How badly handicapped are they?

Well, Ben, who's nine, is a great little guy, a wonderful little human being. He's got a really beautiful little face, and he's got a great heart, and he's a lot of fun to play with. We've got a really great train set that we play with, a huge train set that he controls with buttons and stuff.

He's learning how to communicate and play games and solve problems using a computer. And he is handicapped inasmuch as he has severe cerebral palsy, and he is a quadriplegic, and he's a nonoral child. So he has a lot of handicaps. Cerebral palsy is a condition of life, not a disease. It's the way he is, the condition he's in. He was brought into the world in this form, and this is the way he is. A lot of the things that we take for granted, that we can do, he can't do. But his soul is there, and I'm sure that he has an outlook on the world that we don't have because of the disabilities.

My son Zeke has very mild cerebral palsy. He's a wonderful boy, and he's growing up to be a strong kid. He's going to be sixteen in September, and one of the things he really wants to do now is get his driver's license. He's a great guy, a great kid, and he's got a great heart.

What causes cerebral palsy?

No one knows. That's the thing. Just why they were born with cerebral palsy is a question that Pegi [Young's wife] and I ask, and Carrie [Snodgress, Zeke's mother] and I ask. There's no way to tell. My third child, Amber, is just a little flower, growing like a little flower should. It took Pegi a lot of preparation to get ready to have another kid because it was really hard for us to face the chance that things might not work out right. But so many doctors told us that it had nothing to do with anything. I went and got myself checked, because I was the father of both kids. And the doctors said, "It may be hard for you to believe this, but you had two kids, and there's no connection between them at all. It's a fluke that both have cerebral palsy."

Often in my life I've felt that I was singled out for one reason or another for extreme things to happen. This was hard to deal with. We've been dealing with it, and we've learned to turn it around into a positive thing and to keep on going. It was something that brought Pegi and I really close together, just having the strength to have another child and having her be such a beautiful little girl and having everything work out. Just believing. Coming around to believing that it's okay for us to try again.

In 1986 you put on a concert to raise money for a school for the handicapped.

The Bridge School. We've got it going now. Ben goes there. Learning how to communicate, basically, is what the school is all about.

We spent two years in another program. It was an almost Nazi kind of program. They had us doing these things that didn't help our child, but they had us convinced that if we didn't do the program, we were not doing the right thing for the kid. And it kept us busy all the waking hours of the day, seven days a week, forever—until the kid was better.

We had no time to ourselves. Can you imagine what that's like? We couldn't leave the house. We had to be there doing this program, and it was an excruciatingly difficult thing for the kid to go through, because he was crying almost all day, it was so hard. We lasted a couple of years before we just couldn't do it anymore.

When we left that, we went to a simpler type of program, and we decided to stop concentrating on the physical side so much and start trying to get the kid to communicate. It's our life's work almost now.

It was the most difficult thing I think I've ever done. That's why when someone says they can't do something because it's too hard, it makes me mad. I get upset about that.

How much has your kids' condition affected your political outlook?

I think it's affected it quite a bit. I became much more involved in family, taking care of the family, making sure the family was secure. And I related to Reagan's original concept of big government and federal programs fading away so that communities could handle their own programs, like day care. That was the crux of his domestic message, and I thought the idea was good. I thought it would bring people together. But it was a real idealistic thing, and people didn't really come together.

You got a lot of flak for coming out in support of Reagan in 1984. Were there other reasons he appealed to you?

I was very disillusioned with Jimmy Carter. On a political level, I don't think we ever should have given back the Panama Canal. I just have a gut feeling that that was a huge mistake made out of guilt, not out of reasoning. He was going to make up for all the other bad things we'd done in the world by giving back the Panama Canal. I also think it was wrong to have let the armed forces deteriorate to a point where our strength was less than it had been at a time when other superpowers were growing. I just don't think it was good ball playing. I'm not a hawk. I'm not one who wants to go to war and flex muscles and everything, but I just don't believe that you can talk from a weakness. I think it is as straightforward as that. Everybody in the world is playing hardball, and if we say we're not going to play hardball anymore, we're playing powder puff, we're going to start by putting down the hardball, I don't think it's going to work. People are going to confuse that as a weakness and take advantage of it.

Mondale, as far as I was concerned, was not going to do much different from what Carter had done. So I was for Reagan, and I thought it was an important issue. Now, to be for a president doesn't mean that you agree with everything that president does. But I thought that was an important issue, and I thought that was the right way to go, and I still stand behind it.

What do you think about the way things turned out?

Well, so many things have happened. I think he really did want to do the things that he said he wanted to do. I was disappointed in many of the things that happened during his administration. But I thought that the ideas that were behind a lot of the things he tried to do were things that I could relate to. I just couldn't back away from that.

Who do you support in the current presidential race?

Well, I would not like to see George Bush as president of the United States. I don't think the former leader of the CIA should be president. We need someone with compassion, someone who has a lot of feelings and a lot of savvy. That's why I don't see one person at this point. I think that the one person I would like to see as president of the United States is Bill Bradley. But he's not going to be a candidate. Unfortunately, I don't think the Democrats have anyone who can beat Bush. I like Jackson, and I kind of like Dukakis. But I think Jackson's the best. He's the guy I would like to see just for interest's sake. I would like to see what would happen, because there would be a lot of change.

Musically, you seem to be obsessed with change. At Geffen you went through synth rock, country and rockabilly, and now your first album on Reprise is a blues record.

It's just the way I am. When I was in school, I would go for six months wearing the same kind of clothes. Then all of a sudden I'd wear all different clothes. It's change. It's always been like that.

You've taken a lot of heat for all the stylistic changes.

When people think that I'm just doing this on a whim, it discounts the music. Music is immediate to me. It's something that's happening right now, and it's a reflection of what's going on with the people who are making it. It has nothing to do with what they did or what they are going to do.

You know, I used to be pissed off at Bobby Darin because he changed styles so much. Now I look at him and I think he was a fucking genius. I mean, from "Queen of the Hop" to "Mack the Knife." Dig that. And it didn't mean that he didn't believe in "Queen of the Hop" when he turned around and did a Frank Sinatra thing.

Yet I come up against this because I experiment around and I play different kinds of music. In my eyes, it doesn't make what I'm doing any less valid. Right now I love the Bluenotes, to a point where it feels so right to me. I'll do other things, but I think I'm gonna come back to this over and over again. I mean, playing with a horn section and playing with this band is just so great.

I think it's the best support I've had for the kind of music I was into. Everything has come together at the right time for this. There's a special thing that happens when the music is right. When it's not hard to do. When things aren't a problem. And you just play, and everybody likes it, and they start grooving. That makes me write a new song every morning when I wake up, instead of thinking, Well, if I write this, are the guys gonna be able to play it, or have I got the right band, or do I know anybody who really understands who I am, who I can actually play music with?

Yet you said something similar when you did the Old Ways *record and toured with the International Harvesters—that you were happy and that country was what you'd be doing from then on.*

At the time, I really did feel good doing it. And it was a lot of fun. And then one morning I woke up and all I could hear was this massive fucking beat. And my guitar was just rising out of it. I just heard rock & roll in my head, so fucking loud that I couldn't ignore it.

And so you went back to Crazy Horse—something you've done time and again throughout your career.

That's true, and I may come back to Crazy Horse again some day, but it seems more and more doubtful to me. The kind of music I played with Crazy Horse was a younger kind of music. And I'm not younger—I'm older. And the experience that I have of playing all the different kinds of music that I've played so intensely has a place to come to in the Bluenotes. I can incorporate everything I've done in my life into this band—blues, country, rock & roll. Nothing else that I had done in the past had the kind of passion that Crazy Horse had, but the Bluenotes do. So this is what makes me wonder what's gonna happen with Crazy Horse.

You've just finished a full-length video called Muddy Track, *which is about one of your last tours with Crazy Horse.*

I had two little video-8 cameras, which I left running all the time. I would just come into rooms and put them down on the table. And the point of view is really from the camera. The camera takes on an identity—its name is Otto—and people start talking to the camera. And this camera saw a lot of things that really go down on a tour that are not cute or funsy-wunsy. It's not like the pop-band-on-the-road type of thing. There's a lot of guts in it, a lot of feeling.

The great thing about Crazy Horse is that they're not technically great players, but they have a lot of passion.

Well, that's what Crazy Horse is all about. And they bring out a part of me that's very primitive. We really put out a lot of emotion—which is easy for a kid to relate to. So it's very childlike. I've had some great times with Crazy Horse.

How do you feel about playing that kind of rock & roll when you're in your forties?

Muddy Track covers a lot of that. Covers that feeling, you know? There's some wild stuff in there where we do speed metal. A lot of the music is only the beginnings and ends of songs. The songs themselves aren't there. It's like the interviews are only the interviewer. And you hardly ever see me. You only hear questions. It's an interesting concept of your point of view. And it talks about what it's like to be forty-one, forty-two, and still be doing that kind of music.

And the question is, how long can you keep doing it? And really be doing it? Or do you become a reenactment of an earlier happening? That's a question I ask myself.

Do you think Crazy Horse started to become a reenactment?

Toward the end, it was starting to. I could feel it starting to slip away. And I never wanted to be in front of people and have them pay to see me when I'm not 100 percent there. And if you feel that energy slipping away, then you've got to fold your deck, you know, get out.

So are you saying that rock & roll is really a younger person's medium?

I'm not really sure. There's no doubt that it is a younger person's medium. The question is whether it can also be an older person's medium. That's why I love the Bluenotes. They afford me the same kind of passion and expression as rock & roll, but in a more experienced and evolved way.

So that's why I feel real good about the music I'm playing now. It's something that I believe in and that I'm comfortable with. It's real; it's what's really happening to me now in my life.

■ **RANDOM NOTES** FOREVER YOUNG (August 11, 1988)

Neil Young joined Bob Dylan onstage for the entire length of three shows on Dylan's current tour. "We're friends, and he was in my neighborhood," says Young, explaining why he showed up for the northern-California dates. "It was a lot of fun. I love playing with Bob." Young, who has his own summer tour with the Bluenotes, says he "might try and make" more of Dylan's shows.

During the first night, guitarist G.E. Smith led Young through a few of the chord changes. But by the second show—at Berkeley's Greek Theatre—Neil was much more comfortable with the material, which included "Subterranean Homesick Blues," "Tangled Up in Blue," an acoustic version of "The Times They Are A-Changin' " and "Like a Rolling Stone."

FRED GOODMAN

MTV NIXES NEIL YOUNG'S ACERBIC "THIS NOTE'S FOR YOU" VIDEO

Rocker labels music-channel executives "spineless twerps"

NEIL YOUNG'S NEW MUSIC video has hit a sour note with MTV. "This Note's for You," the title track from the veteran rocker's latest album, is a scathing indictment of artists who endorse consumer products. The video—which was directed by Julien Temple, who made the films *Absolute Beginners* and the upcoming *Earth Girls Are Easy,* as well as videos for the Rolling Stones and David Bowie—takes broad swipes at music-oriented advertising campaigns that feature Eric Clapton, Whitney Houston and Michael Jackson. An MTV spokesman says the music-video channel will not show the clip.

The video, which opens with a re-creation of Eric Clapton's television commercial for Michelob beer, shows Young heading for a late-night jam session. It then intersperses performance footage shot at the Continental Club, in Hollywood, with sendups of commercials for Budweiser and Miller beers, Pepsi, Diet Coke and Calvin Klein's Obsession.

The song's lyrics, which include the verse "Ain't singin' for Pepsi / Ain't singin' for Coke / I don't sing for nobody / Makes me look like a joke," also mention Miller beer and Budweiser's Spuds MacKenzie. The spoofs—which sometimes take a malevolent turn, as when a Michael Jackson look-alike's hair catches fire, the famed Budweiser booze hound slobbers on a trio of female models or a woman in the Obsession segment licks spilled perfume off the floor—have proved too much for MTV.

"Programming loved the video," says Barry Kluger, vice-president of press and public affairs for MTV. "But our legal department said they had problems with trademark infringement."

Young, who clearly wants nothing to do with product endorsements, isn't buying MTV's argument, either. "We thought they'd be afraid to show it, and that's turned out to be true," Young says. "It draws a line, and we knew people would have to stand on one side or the other."

Young adds that he is particularly chagrined by the decision, because

MTV executives originally said they had no problems when they were shown the video's script prior to shooting. "Then when we sent it in," Young says, "they said they wouldn't show it because it would offend their sponsors and they were worried about being sued."

In an unusual attempt to calm these fears, Young says Warner Bros.—which owns Reprise Records, the label he records for—offered to indemnify MTV against any lawsuits. MTV's Kluger confirms the offer but says it was "not good enough."

Young and director Temple then offered to reedit the video as a performance clip, taking out all the commercial sendups. "Then they came back and said, 'It's the song we're worried about,' " says Young. "It's sort of like dealing with spineless twerps."

Young, who says the song garners "more of a reaction and crowd response than anything I've ever written" when it's performed in concert, still wants to see the video aired on MTV. "We're sending it to the networks and talking with the David Letterman show. But MTV makes the difference; they're still more rock & roll than *General Hospital*. They're supposed to be rebellious but haven't got enough guts to show something that's not middle-of-the-road."

Young adds that MTV also rejected his last video, "Mideast Vacation" (a spokesman for the channel says MTV never received the clip), and that he hasn't had a video aired by MTV with any frequency since 1983's "Wonderin'." "I guess I don't fit in with them," he says.

RICK MARIN

THE 100 TOP MUSIC VIDEOS

Rolling stone EDITORS chose the 100 best rock videos of all time for a special issue. Neil Young's "This Note's for You" was ranked Number Four.

#4 "This Note's for You," Neil Young, 1988

Who else could insult Budweiser, Pepsi, Michael Jackson, Whitney Houston, Calvin Klein, the entire recording industry and MTV all in one video? "This Note's for You" is Neil Young's finest "fuck you." Banned from MTV, it went on to win big at the MTV Video Music Awards. Irony, anyone? Young's (admittedly easy) target is big stars who sell out their musical souls to hawk soft drinks and cheap brew. Director Julien Temple simulates the perfect beer-ad bar scene, then lets loose. A Michael Jackson look-alike spontaneously combusts onstage. A Spuds MacKenzie dog-alike laps a bikini-clad breast. An ersatz Whitney Houston's wig gets yanked off. Temple recalls the experience fondly: "You can do anything you want with Neil. He transcends hangups of any kind. Of course, they [MTV & Co.] freaked out. This video went for the wallet—rather than sex or violence— which is much more scary to them."

MICHAEL GOLDBERG

CSNY RELEASE *AMERICAN DREAM*

First studio album since *Déjà Vu*

EIGHTEEN YEARS AFTER the release of their classic album *Déjà Vu*, Crosby, Stills, Nash and Young have finally completed a second studio album. Titled *American Dream*, the recording was due in stores in early November.

"The theme of the album is the American dream," says Graham Nash. "And there are so many opinions of what it was or is or could be. Therefore, you get songs about falling in and out of love, about being angry, about questioning. It's CSNY in '88."

Recorded largely at Broken Arrow Ranch—Neil Young's home in northern California—between February and May of this year, *American Dream* is a potpourri of musical styles and topics. Produced by the group and Niko Bolas (who produced both Young's and Warren Zevon's latest recordings), the album contains fourteen original songs.

The title track is about the failure of some public figures to live up to the American dream ("I used to see you on every TV / Your smiling face looked back at me / Then they caught you with the girl next door / People's money piled on the floor"). But there are also love songs—Young's folkie "Feel Your Love," Stephen Stills' bluesy "Lose That Girl" and Nash's bittersweet ballad "Don't Say Goodbye"—as well as pointed social and political commentary, such as "Nighttime for the Generals," "Name of Love" and "Soldiers of Peace." Also included are a straight country song by Young, "This Old House," and two Stills-Young collaborations, "Drivin' Thunder" and "Night Song."

Young took charge of the *American Dream* sessions—described by Nash as "insanely tension free." Nash says that Young and Stills initially spent a week together at the ranch to ensure that "if it wasn't working with Stephen, Neil would have plenty of time to call it off. I think he wanted to know it was a workable situation. And fortunately it was.

"Neil was a champion," says Nash. "He's a natural leader. It's difficult to have an entire scene that has three or four madmen at your home. Neil was the quarterback—but you still need the rest of the team."

And how does Nash think *American Dream* stacks up beside *Déjà Vu*?

"I don't compare them at all," he says. *"Déjà Vu* was created by individuals recording their tracks and bringing them to the party to be sung on, taking them away to be mixed and then bringing them back to be assembled. This time we were all there all the time, singing and playing. It really is the first CSNY record."

There are no plans for a Crosby, Stills, Nash and Young tour.

DAVID FRICKE

THIS NOTE'S FOR YOU YEAR-END ALBUM REVIEW

SO YOUNG THROWS US a white-blues curve ball; it would have been a bigger shock if he'd done something utterly commercial, like release an '88 *Harvest*. In fact, the best "blues" numbers on this album are the ones closest to the real Neil—"Twilight," which sounds like a low-key "Down by the River" scored with Memphis soul horns, and the acidic "Life in the City," which has all the makings of a Crazy Horse stomper. As for the title song, it is funny and powerful in its bristling simplicity, as proven by the corporate-sponsorship ruckus it raised. It is also good to know that there's at least one great "night" song ("Tonight's the Night") you'll never hear in a Michelob ad.

ANTHONY DeCURTIS

AMERICAN DREAM ALBUM REVIEW

★ ★

A MERICAN DREAM FADES OUT on the line "Why not keep on singing anyway?"—and that lackadaisical slogan seems to sum up the spirit in which the first Crosby, Stills, Nash and Young studio album since 1970's *Déjà Vu* was made. Despite pleasant melodies, the occasional interesting song and the signature harmonies, *American Dream* is, for the most part, a snoozefest.

The enervation at the heart of this album suggests that these four veterans found themselves washed up on the shore of the late Eighties and—after endless recombinations, solo forays and, in David Crosby's case, imprisonment and brushes with death—determined to cast their lot together and see what happened. The regrouping has done none of them much good. Even Neil Young, the only member of this quartet to have made records worth discussing in the past decade, indulges his worst tendencies. His populist protests (the title track and "This Old House") substitute, in varying degrees, sappiness, sentimentality and mean-spiritedness for conviction and insight, while his ballads ("Feel Your Love" and "Name of Love") lapse into cliché and mere prettiness.

On a couple of tracks the group does manage to flash some muscle. "Drivin' Thunder"—which amounts to Stills and Young's version of "I Can't Drive 55"—works up a galloping boogie beat, and Crosby's "Nighttime for the Generals" inspires Stills and Young to shoot sparks on guitar. Stills' jaunty "Got It Made" and Nash's atmospheric "Shadowland" succeed on their own modest terms.

Unfortunately, *American Dream*'s most cringe-inducing moment occurs at its point of greatest ambition. "Compass"—Crosby's five-minute acoustic ballad of his struggle with addiction—is so strained in its effort to achieve poetry that it's more likely to generate laughter than sympathy. Gnarled lines like "I have seized death's door-handle / Like a fish out of water / Waiting for the mercy of the cat" argue the lingering effects of the drugs Crosby has so bravely kicked.

Coproduced by the band and Niko Bolas, *American Dream* is sonically lucid, though the synthesizers used to lend the album a contemporary sheen sound hokey and forced—even, oddly, a bit old-fashioned. Finally, however, the record's main failing is its banality. Beyond right-minded generalities and lazy evocations of "love," *American Dream* has nothing to say. At the end of the preachy, bombastic "Soldiers of Peace," Nash and Young scream, "No more." I second that emotion.

DAVID FRICKE

NEIL YOUNG COVERED ON TRIBUTE ALBUM

TERRY TOLKIN WAS THIRTEEN years old when he bought his first Neil Young album, *After the Gold Rush,* in 1972. "Lyrically, it really spoke to me as an adolescent," he says, "and I was hooked from there on."

Seventeen years later, Tolkin—an ardent Young devotee who also runs his own independent label, No. 6 Records—has repaid that debt of inspiration. *The Bridge: A Tribute to Neil Young* is a compilation album of Neil Young songs covered by eleven top alternative-rock acts, including Nick Cave ("Helpless"), the Pixies ("Winterlong"), Sonic Youth ("Computer Age"), guitarist Henry Kaiser ("The Needle and the Damage Done" and "Tonight's the Night") and Dinosaur Jr ("Lotta Love"). Each track (there are fourteen on the CD) was specially commissioned by Tolkin, and a portion of the proceeds will go to the Bridge School, in San Francisco, the special-education facility for which Young has done two major charity concerts. *The Bridge* will be distributed in America by Caroline Records.

Tolkin says he was inspired to do *The Bridge* by Young's 1988 ROLLING STONE Interview. "I knew two of his children had cerebral palsy," he says. "But I didn't know anything about the Bridge School, and that's where I first learned about it. Also, my own uncle and aunt have two kids with cerebral palsy. When he was speaking about Ben and Zeke in that article, I was flashing on my own cousins."

Tolkin also knew the extent of Young's influence on the postpunk generation from his own experience managing and booking underground bands. "All the bands that are on the record are big Neil fans," he says. When Tolkin contacted the Pixies about contributing to the LP, singer-guitarist Black Francis said, "Wow, that's fantastic. One of the most important songs of my life is 'Winterlong.' I woke up every day for a year listening to that song."

Deciding who would play which Neil Young song was, Tolkin says, "a feat of coordination. Several bands wanted to do songs that other bands also wanted to do. It was a matter of me deciding who would be better at what track."

Although Tolkin has not spoken directly to Young about the album, he has been in contact with Young's management company, Lookout Management, and with Young's wife, Pegi, who runs the Bridge School. "She was really open about it and receptive," Tolkin says. "I assume that Neil is very aware of the project and that there is some tacit approval."

■ **RANDOM NOTES** (October 5, 1989)

At the end of his set at L.A.'s Greek Theater, Neil Young was joined by former band mates David Crosby and Graham Nash on "Ohio," which he dedicated to "the students who just got slaughtered in China." "It's such a trip to be doing that song," said Young afterward. "But it seems to be relevant."

In October he'll release his new album, titled *Freedom*. Unlike most of his recent efforts, which have highlighted specific musical genres, *Freedom* is pure Neil Young. "I really wanted to just make a Neil Young record, per se," he says, "where there was no persona, no image, no character that was distinct like the Bluenote guy. Something that was just me."

SHEILA ROGERS

NEIL YOUNG FINDS HIS *FREEDOM*

New album is a return to his classic style

"NEIL, DON'T DO IT, DON'T accept it," mutters *Saturday Night Live* regular Nora Dunn. A few feet away, on a balcony at New York's Palladium, stands Neil Young, flanked by Daryl Hannah, Chevy Chase and Tim Hutton. Hannah is nervously clutching an MTV Video Music Award that she's supposed to present to the singer. Although the awards show is airing live from L.A.—and Young's category, Best Video of the Year, hasn't been announced yet—the MTV cameras are ready to roll when Young's video for "This Note's for You" wins. Young is willing to accept the award, but the sound monitor falters, and his acceptance speech is reduced to several seconds of dead air.

Minutes later, Young is in his backstage dressing room, shaking his head in disbelief. "It's very strange to win this," he says. (MTV once refused to air the clip for fear of offending advertisers.) "It's just something that I never thought would happen."

Young seems to be making peace with much in his life these days. Earlier that evening, he'd played the second Palladium date of his acoustic tour. His set, which opened with "Hey Hey, My My" and included such favorites as "Helpless," "Heart of Gold" and "Sugar Mountain," also featured songs from his new album, *Freedom*. The new material fit right in with the older classics: Tracks like "Rockin' in the Free World," "Crime in the City" and "Someday" mark a conscious return to Young's original solo style.

What brought him back to his roots? "Time," he says. "I really closed off a lot of emotions, a lot of things that I didn't understand in my life. And now I feel like time has healed whatever it was that was bothering me. I can't articulate it, but now I feel more open and I can write songs that are more directly involved with what I'm thinking."

Freedom went through a couple of incarnations before Young settled on the album's eleven songs. He initially began work on an album to be called *Times Square,* recording in New York. He'd also recorded some tracks at his California ranch. Both sessions were eventually combined for an LP called *Eldorado.* But when Young reached the mastering stage, he changed his mind.

"I thought it was really good, but I didn't think that people would like it," he says. "There was nothing but abrasiveness from beginning to end." The noisier tracks have been released as an EP called *Eldorado* in Australia, New Zealand and Japan.

Young then returned to the studio to complete the tracks for *Freedom*. "I just kept juggling it around until I got something that I thought was more of an album than an assault," he says. "It's the first time I've felt like doing an album like this in years. On those other albums I was more into style. But I was losing track of what I wanted to do."

DAVID FRICKE

FREEDOM AND *THE BRIDGE: A TRIBUTE TO NEIL YOUNG* ALBUM REVIEWS

Freedom ★ ★ ★ ★ ★

The Bridge ★ ★ ★ ★

Neil Young Lets Freedom Ring

THE END OF A DECADE REALLY seems to bring out the fear and loathing in Neil Young. In 1969 he bid an embittered adieu to the shaky Sixties promise of Peace and Love with the irascible guitars and confessional despair of *Everybody Knows This Is Nowhere.* Ten years later, on *Rust Never Sleeps,* he addressed the advancing arthritis and superstar complacency of Seventies rock with bristling verse and corrosive guitar violence, not to mention the deliberately provocative evocation of Elvis Presley and Johnny Rotten in the same song.

Freedom is the sound of Neil Young, another decade on, looking back again in anger and dread. The songs are populated by the walking wounded and littered with dashed hopes and drug paraphernalia. The ties that bind—faith, love, charity—are coming undone, and betrayal is the norm. Then Young throws all this hurt at you, and it hits like a bucket of ice water in the face. You register shock at first, then indignation and finally a kind of vengeful exhilaration. As with *Rust* and *Everybody Knows*—and with other contentious classics like *On the Beach, Tonight's the Night* and *Re-act-or*—Neil Young's tour of *Freedom*'s wasteland leaves you feeling both exhausted and invigorated, dismayed at what we've wrought yet determined to set it right.

It's no coincidence that "Rockin' in the Free World," the album's de facto theme song, bookends *Freedom* in separate live-acoustic and studio-electric versions. Like "My My, Hey Hey . . ."—its twin on *Rust Never Sleeps*—the song is a singalong ball spinning on an axis of deadly irony, its superficial cheerleading charm soured by Young's parade of victims: the homeless "sleepin' in their shoes," a young woman addict, her abandoned baby ("That's one more kid / That will never go to school / Never get to fall in love / Never get to be cool"). And in the acoustic take, which opens the record, Young plays it like a body-count blues, his high, lonesome countertenor ringing with plaintive desperation.

The acoustic track, however, fades before the crucial last verse, which is restored in the climactic electric version. Over a thunder-fuzz attack that sounds like *Rust* to the tenth power, Young takes dead aim at cheap inauguration rhetoric ("We got a thousand points of light / For the homeless man / We got a kinder, gentler, machine gun hand"), then whips around and takes a different pledge of allegiance. "Got a man of the people / Says keep hope alive," he howls. "Got fuel to burn / Got roads to drive."

The whole record seesaws like that, between pensive acoustic woe and embattled electric vigor. That's partially because of the varying origins of these songs. The ballads "Ways of Love" (one of two duets with Linda Ronstadt on the LP) and the achingly beautiful "Too Far Gone" date back to the late Seventies. "Don't Cry," "Eldorado" and a frenzied cover of "On Broadway" come from a recent killer EP, *Eldorado,* culled from sessions last year in New York with a basic trio and the amps cranked up to 11. The EP, alas, was only released in Japan, Australia and New Zealand. *Freedom* also includes material cut with Young's blues 'n' brass gang, the Bluenotes.

The album's checkered makeup heightens its thematic kick. While a lot of people will fall for *Freedom* because its schizo bounce between folkie ballads and high-decibel urgency bears a comforting resemblance to the gentler mood swings of his big Seventies successes—*After the Gold Rush* and *Harvest*—*Freedom*'s mixed menu of sound and sentiment has a lot more to do with the cyclical whirl of pain, pressure and pleasure in real life. Young put out an album two years ago called *Life,* but this is more like it.

It can be hard to see sunlight through the album's gathering clouds. "Crime in the City" is a chilling litany of cynicism and resignation set to a skeletal, almost jazzy gallop and laced with Ben Keith's icy steel guitar and the earthy mooing of the Bluenotes' brass. In "Don't Cry," Young echoes a gentle but decisive kiss-off involving two lovers with alternating gestures of quiet guilt and vicious firestorm guitar. "No More" is a first-person update of "The Needle and the Damage Done," the confessions of a former junkie who lapses into the same tired whisper: "No more, no more, no more."

But if this album is about the illusion of freedom, it is also about Young's refusal to accept that as the last word on the subject. He's at least determined to go down dancing in "Wrecking Ball." He's willing to believe that "smog might turn to stars" in "Someday," a wry, warm ballad with light R&B seasoning. The mega-metal cover of "On Broadway" is delightfully perverse, Young strangling his guitar with dramatic conviction. The high, Crazy Horse-like octane Young injects into the Drifters' original street-corner hymn of blues and bravado boldly captures the competing strains of agony and ecstasy running all through *Freedom*. Still, at the end, he erupts into a nasty vocal freakout, yelling, "Give me that crack / Give me some of that crack!" and screaming like he's just thrown himself onto the Times Square subway track. So much for fairy-tale endings.

What Young does to "On Broadway" is nothing compared to the garage-punk disemboweling of his own "Lotta Love" by Dinosaur Jr or the way Sonic Youth transforms "Computer Age," his ode to the digital life, into a primitivist guitar brawl. But that's why *The Bridge: A Tribute to Neil Young* is such a gas. A compilation of eleven Young covers (fourteen on CD) by an all-star team of postpunk and college-radio acts, *The Bridge* celebrates not only Young's enduring songwriting but the iconoclastic spirit and anarchic glee with which he continually challenges rock myth and defies rock convention. The best interpretations on the album overstep the songs' original musical parameters without violating their emotional premises: the Pixies' vibrant, loving "Winterlong"; Soul Asylum's hooligan bash at "Barstool Blues"; Nick Cave's version of "Helpless," slowed to a funereal German-cabaret crawl.

The brainchild of Terry Tolkin, an ardent Young fan who conceived the project, commissioned the tracks and made a commitment to donate a portion of the proceeds to Young's favorite charity (the Bridge School, for handicapped children, in northern California), *The Bridge* does have its small share of misfires, most notably Psychic TV's overlong, overwrought "Only Love Can Break Your Heart." But the breadth of the album's artist roster—which also includes Southern-gothic chanteuse Victoria Williams, avant-rock guitarist Henry Kaiser and acid-dementia specialists Flaming Lips—is testament to the extraordinary scope of Young's influence on rock in the Eighties. *Freedom*, in turn, is Young's prayer for the Nineties, a harsh reminder that everything still comes with a price. Including rockin' in a free world.

TOP 100 ALBUMS OF THE EIGHTIES

A T DECADE'S END, ROLLING STONE editors picked the best albums of the Eighties. Neil Young's *Freedom* was voted Number Eighty-five.

#85 *Freedom*, Neil Young

"I knew that I wanted to make a real album that expressed how I felt," says Neil Young of his most recent album, *Freedom*. "I just wanted to make a Neil Young record per se. Something that was just me, where there was no persona, no image, no distinctive character like the Bluenotes guy or the guy in *Everybody's Rockin'*. It's the first time I've felt like doing an album like this in years."

Freedom veers between folkie ballads ("Ways of Love," "Someday" and "Too Far Gone") and screeching rockers ("Eldorado" and a wild-eyed cover of "On Broadway"). The album is bookended by contrasting versions of the bitter, ironic "Rockin' in the Free World." The opener is live and acoustic, with the audience singing the chorus, while the finale is an angry, electric rendition with an additional verse. (Young used a similar device on *Rust Never Sleeps*.)

"It's the longest album I've ever done," says Young. "It's a real mouthful. When I listen to it, it's almost like listening to the radio—it keeps changing and going from one thing to another."

He'd originally planned to release a purely electric rock album— "Nothing but abrasiveness from beginning to end," he says—that he'd recorded in New York. (Five songs from those sessions were released on an import EP called *Eldorado*.) For the album that was eventually released, he mixed in material from some subsequent acoustic sessions, looking to strike a balance. The result is Young's most personal and unguarded set of songs in many years.

"Music can be like therapy," he says. "It's like getting parts of yourself out, which I used to do all the time. But I was at a point in my life where I really closed off my emotions about a lot of things I didn't understand. I just shut down the whole program and did things that were more on the surface level, because it was safer. Now I feel time has healed whatever was bothering me so much. I feel more open, and I can write songs that are more directly involved with what I'm thinking."

PRODUCERS: Neil Young and Niko Bolas. **RELEASED:** October 1989. **HIGHEST CHART POSITION:** Number Thirty-five. Reprise Records.

JIMMY GUTERMAN

NEIL YOUNG PULLS PLUG ON JEANS AD

NEIL YOUNG, WHO MADE HIS feelings known about corporate sponsorship of rock & roll and the willingness of rock performers to appear in commercials with the acerbic 1988 song and video for "This Note's for You," has had his music used in a European advertising campaign without his permission.

In early November, Lee Europe/U.K. began running jeans ads that used Neil Young's song "Hey Hey, My My (Into the Black)" on CNN International and MTV Europe. The ad did not use the original recording but featured a sound-alike and look-alike singer. It was never shown in the United States.

Young, whose Silver Fiddle publishing company owns the rights to the song, was never contacted for use of the song, nor was EG Music, which acts as music administrator for Silver Fiddle. In November, Young's Lookout Management responded with a cease-and-desist letter to CNN, MTV and Lee Jeans. The ad was quickly pulled.

Despite the fast action, the jeans company is distancing itself from the ad, and it's unclear exactly where the commercial originated. "Lee International is totally separate from the U.S. company," says a Lee spokesperson. "We are not responsible for our international division. We act as totally different companies. All we do is license the name out."

Even those who should be aware of the ad claim ignorance. "We don't have any commercial like that," says Jaime Moreno, head of Lee International licensing.

"I haven't seen it," says Buzz Ahrens, managing director of Lee Europe/U.K. "I'm astounded. I'm in doubt as to the source of this."

According to Ahrens, Lee Europe/U.K. has an in-house advertising department that works with outside agencies. It is unclear whether the theft of Young's song originated in house or with an outside agency. "We have been told by those who placed the ad that under no circumstances can we give out any information," says an official in CNN's traffic department.

At press time, Young's management was considering further legal action.

JEFFREY RESSNER

CSNY HONORS ITS FORMER DRUMMER

D URING A BENEFIT CONCERT for the ailing rock drummer Dallas
Taylor last month, performers took turns autographing a large
drumhead as a gift for the veteran percussionist. "Is this where the
pedal hits?" wrote Don Henley in the center of the skin, while Taylor's old
band mate Neil Young signed his message with a more personal recollection: " 'Sea of Madness' Big Sur Folk Festival. What a groove."

The mood backstage may have been festive, but the reason for the
concert was sobering: Taylor, the original drummer for Crosby, Stills, Nash
and Young, suffers from a terminal liver disease caused by years of drug and
alcohol abuse. The March 31 benefit at the Santa Monica Civic Auditorium—which featured CSNY, Henley and the Desert Rose Band—helped
raise money for a drug-education foundation and also created more awareness of the need for organ donors.

The following night, the same musicians held another fund-raiser to
benefit the California Environmental Protection Initiative, a proposed om-
nibus bill addressing pesticide use and air and water pollution. Both four-
hour-long shows were highlighted by Young's compelling solo set and
Henley's appearance with a band that featured a string section.

But the benefit for CSNY's former drummer inspired the most heartfelt
emotion. "Everybody helps everybody," Taylor said after the benefit.
"That's what being a musician is all about." Taylor, forty-two, will die
unless he undergoes a liver transplant in the near future. Despite his condition, the drummer was in fine spirits the night of his benefit and joined
CSNY for encores of "Wooden Ships" and "Teach Your Children,"
marking the first time he's played with all of them onstage in nearly twenty
years.

Taylor played with the band Clear Light in the late Sixties; he then
appeared on Crosby, Stills and Nash's 1969 debut album and on their classic
follow-up with Young, *Déjà Vu*. Considering his sideman status, Taylor
enjoyed a unique financial arrangement through his deal with CSNY,
earning royalties on every album the group sold. The deal made him a
millionaire by the time he was twenty-one, but he wound up squandering
his fortune on drugs as well as sports cars and other frivolities.

Taylor later appeared on solo albums by Stephen Stills and Graham

Nash and drummed for Stills' band Manassas. During the Seventies, Taylor recorded albums with Rolling Stones bassist Bill Wyman and rock vocalist Sammy Hagar. But in the Eighties he had trouble finding steady work, partly because of his severe alcoholism and drug addiction. He finally cleaned up for good in 1984, only to learn last November that his long-term substance abuse had destroyed his liver.

These days, Taylor waits patiently for a transplant that could increase his life span by several years. He wears a beeper to signal him when the right donor is found. Since he's been straight, Taylor has spent much of his time doing counseling work at a rehab clinic in Van Nuys, California.

Besides the effect drugs had on his drumming, Taylor says he was kicked out of CSNY because he sided with Stills during the "ongoing battle between Stephen and Neil" over the band, and the concert marked a reconciliation of sorts between Taylor and Young. Before playing "Wooden Ships," Young clasped hands with his former sideman, and they exchanged warm smiles. "Neil was really sweet," Taylor says. "He told me that he wouldn't have missed this for the world."

KURT LODER

RAGGED GLORY ALBUM REVIEW

★ ★ ★ ★ ½

Neil Young's Guitar Ecstasy

I GUESS NEIL YOUNG is the king of rock & roll. I don't see anybody else on the scene standing anywhere *near* this tall nowadays.

The title of Young's new record aptly encapsulates its charms. Nine of the ten tracks on *Ragged Glory*—an instant Young classic, by the way, go out and get it—were recorded at his ranch in northern California. I paid a brief journalistic visit to this place some years back, and it's a huge sprawl of land. At the heart of it, Young had erected a fully equipped, open-air stage upon which he and his band buddies would clamber of an evening and crank up their amps. In the middle of a spread the size of Connecticut—*and they still got complaints from the neighbors.*

This album sounds like it was recorded on that stage on a really good night. It's loose and wild, and God knows it's loud, and it soars gloriously from one raving cut to the next. There are no acoustic ballads. Everything—even the ecological hymn that concludes the record—is intensely electric. Young launches into "Country Home," the opening track, with his guitar jacked up to about thirty and leaves it nailed there for the next hour. He solos all over the place—great gouts of railing crunch and squall— and he solos at length. Two of the tracks on the album (two of the best, actually, "Love to Burn" and "Love and Only Love") clock in at more than ten minutes each. (There are also a couple of minutes' worth of long feedback fade-outs.) And booting him along throughout, for the first time on record in more than a decade, is Crazy Horse (guitarist Frank Sampedro, bassist Billy Talbot and drummer Ralph Molina), maybe the last great garage band of our time and definitely Young's greatest group.

Ragged Glory is, in fact, a monument to the spirit of the garage—to the pursuit of passion over precision, to raw power and unvarnished soul. Young and the boys even do a nuclear assault on an actual garage classic— the R&B chestnut "Farmer John," rendered in the style of the Premiers' 1964 surfer-stomp version. This is a frankly dopey song, and aware that its lumbering, bedrock-punk riff is the whole point, the band proceeds—with what might be called malicious glee—to pump it up into an awesome sonic juggernaut that's relentless and mesmerizing.

Yes, kids, here's a guy grizzled enough to be your own quaint, ex-hippie dad, and he and his equally antique pals are blasting out a tune called "Fuckin' Up" that would singe the curls of any corporate-metal act currently on the charts. It really is inspiring. But Young is no arrested adolescent. The stature of his music has always derived from his ability to use the simple forms of his root influences—folk, rock, country and R&B—as a vehicle for his emotional candor. And on *Ragged Glory,* the emotions he probes are those of a man going on forty-five years old—a man for whom rock & roll still resonates as truly as it did in his youth, but a man with a lot of mileage on his meter as well and with memories of what now seem more shining times.

In the offhandedly exquisite "Mansion on the Hill"—a country lope buried under a truckload of overamped guitars—Young looks back on the halcyon days of the Sixties as a youthful paradise frozen in time ("Psychedelic music fills the air / Peace and love live there still"). But he's no sap. He knows those days are irretrievable, at least for his generation; that "possessions and concessions" change people over the years; and that—as he sings on the track that follows (a song with a melody and tone seemingly modeled in part on Bob Dylan's "My Back Pages")—"we never had to make those deals / In the days that used to be."

Young also ponders his own latter-day political retrenchment and its apparently corrosive effect on old friendships: "Ideas that once seemed so right / Now have gotten hard to say / I wish that I could talk to you / And you could talk to me."

And in the dark, guitar-charged "Love to Burn," he presents a harrowing scene from a collapsing marriage: "Why'd you ruin my life? / Where you takin' my kid? / And they hold each other, sayin' / 'How did it come to this?' "

The album is hardly despondent. There's hope in the near-psychedelic "Love and Only Love" and the earthy "Over and Over" ("I love the way you open up when you let me in") and a sense of simple contentment in the melodious "Country Home." And the twang-fueled "White Line," a ramblin'-man toss-off with echoes of *Déjà Vu*-era Crosby, Stills, Nash and Young, is a tribute to the eternal possibilities of a few trashy chords and a heart full of high spirits.

But *Ragged Glory* reaches its peak on the blistering and supremely rueful "Fuckin' Up," with its lacerating riff and squealing, bucketful-of-eels guitar leads and Young—in his usual microtonally adventurous vocal style—wailing what must surely be a universal lament: "Why do I keep fuckin' up?"

At the end of the album, Young turns to face the future with "Mother Earth (Natural Anthem)," a stark and gorgeous number recorded live at the Farm Aid IV benefit concert, in Indiana, earlier this year, with additional harmonies recorded by the band later at Young's ranch. A straight folk-choral item in structure, this potentially dippy paean to the planet gathers grace from its stately melody and draws muscle from Young's lone, howling guitar accompaniment—stating the theme in a Hendrix-like blare, then rumbling on below the verses to the gently cautionary conclusion: "Respect Mother Earth, and her healing ways / Or trade away our children's days." It's an unexpected and stirring end to an exhilarating album of hard guitar rock. *Ragged Glory* is a great one, from one of the greats.

JAMES HENKE

BACK IN THE SADDLE AGAIN

A FEW MONTHS AGO, AROUND the time of his performance at Farm Aid IV, Neil Young summoned the members of Crazy Horse—guitarist Frank Sampedro, bassist Billy Talbot and drummer Ralph Molina—to his Broken Arrow Ranch, in northern California. There, in a matter of weeks, they recorded the bulk of *Ragged Glory*. Produced by Young and David Briggs, it's a classic Crazy Horse album, with lots of rough edges, screeching guitar and feedback. In an entirely appropriate gesture from nature, three or four earthquakes shook the area around Young's ranch on the final day of recording. "We did four tracks that day, and during the final chord of one of the songs, during the feedback, it was real loud, and you could feel everything shake," Young says. "And everybody was going, 'Oh, wow, what an ending!' But it turned out it was the earthquake. We were riding the waves, as they say. We were surfing on the earthquake."

What prompted you to make another record with Crazy Horse?

It seemed like the right time. I try to savor those times I play with Crazy Horse, and I space them out so that we don't wear ourselves out. But this time everybody had something to prove, especially the rhythm section. They're playing really aggressively. I'm really happy with it.

A couple of years ago, you said you'd never play with Crazy Horse again. What happened?

We had just come off a really rough European tour. Nothing was going well for us, and it was kind of a *Spinal Tap* syndrome—so now Nigel's back in the group, you know [*laughs*]? It's just cycles: You wear something out, and you can beat it into the ground, or you can leave it and let the rain fall on it and the sun shine on it and see if it comes back. We've always done that. We've had musical low points and musical high points throughout the last twenty years. I think this is one of the high points.

The album reminds me of Everybody Knows This Is Nowhere, *your first record with Crazy Horse.*

It's probably closer to that record than anything else I've done. I can't compare it to anything else. We did cut an acoustic track for it, but it wasn't one I wrote in the same time frame as I wrote the majority of the songs. It just didn't fit—the feeling didn't fit—so we left it off.

It's funny, I wrote seven of the songs in a week. It was two weeks before Farm Aid. Those are the last seven songs on the album. The first two, "Country Home" and "White Line," I wrote years and years ago; they were songs we were never able to get right back then. And I wrote "Fuckin' Up" around the end of the *Freedom* period, when I did *Saturday Night Live*. We used it for a warm-up song there.

What caused you to cover "Farmer John"?

That was really spontaneous. It just came about while we were practicing one day. Well, we were recording, because practicing and recording are all the same for us. We were rolling the tape and putting things down, but we'd just about finished the album and then we got this take.

Tell me about "Mother Earth." The guitar part sounds a lot like Jimi Hendrix's "Star-Spangled Banner."

"Mother Earth" was a trip. I recorded that guitar part at Farm Aid. I wrote "Mother Earth" at the same time I wrote the other songs, but I kept hearing it in a huge place—in my mind, I could only see playing it with a gigantic crowd, with the sound swirling around as loud as could be. So I focused everything on that, and the third time I played it through was the time I played it at Farm Aid.

That song is based on an old hymn. I don't know the name of it, but it's a traditional melody from years gone by. And I modified it. I used different chords and screwed around with it. The folk process. I'm just an old folkie—I can't find my acoustic guitar anymore, that's the problem [*laughs*].

One song you recorded, "Don't Spook the Horse," is being called a "special profane bonus track." What's that all about?

We're like ancient history. When we put out a single, in our heads we still see a 45. And it used to be that there was an A side and a B side. But now it's not just a B side anymore, it's a "bonus track." And on a CD, it can be as long as you want it to be. So "Don't Spook the Horse" is our special bonus track. It's over seven minutes long, and if we had put it on the album, we would have had to make it a double CD.

That song is like those things they use in school these days, where you don't read the whole book, you read the little condensed version of the book to get an idea of what the book is about. That's how they teach kids literature today [*laughs*]. Well, that's the way "Spook the Horse" is. If you buy that, you don't really have to buy the album. It's all in there. It's a condensed version of the whole album. Especially for reviewers who don't like me at all. Just listen to that one, and you'll get all you need.

Several of the other songs on the album are also over seven minutes long.

I purposely wanted to play long instrumentals because I don't hear any jamming on any other records. There's nothing spontaneous going on on records these days, except in blues and funkier music. Rock & roll used to have all that. People aren't reaching out in the instrumental passages and spontaneously letting them last as long as they can. I love to do that, but I can only really do it well with one band. I tried it a little on *Freedom*. But that style of music is better for me with Crazy Horse.

We played just like a band. It wasn't someone in a control room with a bunch of machines—a MIDI and synthesizers and a drum machine and producers and tech people. You just can't get that old-time vibrating feeling with machines. That happens with musicians who just love to play and improvise together. I knew that not many people were doing that, so I really wanted to do it.

What's happened to the CD anthology you were working on? Is that still going to come out?

Shit, that's a giant. I'm still working on it. It's ridiculous. I recorded everything I did over the years, and I also videotaped every tour. I have somewhere around a hundred unreleased tunes, and a lot of them are videotaped. There's some really funky stuff, real obscure shit. Like the Ducks in Santa Cruz, and Crazy Horse at the Catalyst in Santa Cruz in 1982, or 1984, playing a bunch of songs that we could never record. We went to New York and tried to record these songs for three weeks, and we didn't get one track. We just blew a whole bunch of time. That was when I first introduced the horns; we had a horn section with Crazy Horse. We just never could get it to gel.

I thought it was my responsibility to try to put all this stuff in order and try to get it all sorted out so that if something ever happened to me, I wouldn't have to count on anybody else to take care of it for me. Because I do know where everything fits in and where it's supposed to be.

It'll come out as a multi-CD set and a multivideo set simultaneously with books that refer to the songs and their place in time and what was going on and who was there. Little stories about each song and opinions from different people. It's going to be really interesting, and I'm really into it, but it's not something you can just knock off in a year.

I understand that you and Crazy Horse plan to tour after the first of the year.

Yeah, I'm already dreaming about how great it will be to play with the Horse. We're gonna play the arenas, the ugly shitholes that nobody would ever dream of sponsoring, because I'm tired of the sheds, the sponsored sheds. It's like you go into this big box that's got a brand name on it and play for all these people who are paying exorbitant prices. And everybody's got these big shows, because they got all this money from the sponsor. And so everything's got this inflated huge thing going on. So I want to do a straight-ahead thing and play the arenas with the echoing, thundering sound of the Horse.

DAVID FRICKE

RAGGED GLORY
YEAR-END ALBUM REVIEW

ALL ABOARD FOR FUZZTIME. With last year's dynamic, unflinching *Freedom,* Neil Young delivered perhaps the definitive State of the Eighties address. Reunited on *Ragged Glory* with his faithful garage-rock companions in Crazy Horse, Young ushers in the Nineties with a sixty-one-minute monument to the timeless, impolite charms of distortion and the enduring eloquence of the classic rock & roll lineup—two guitars, bass and drums, played *very* loud—in the hands of expert wildcats. Indeed, leave it to Neil Young, whose mutinous streak is one of his most lovable qualities, to use digital studio gear to record an album full of farting amps and fingernails-on-blackboard feedback. The words to some of Young's songs on the album seem, frankly, incidental; everything he says about passion, commitment and the tortuous path to happiness in "Love to Burn" and "Love and Only Love" is stated plainly enough in his long, fiery guitar soliloquies. "Country Home," a simple song of heart and hearth graced with sweet, shaggy vocal harmonies, sounds like Crosby, Stills, Nash and Sonic Youth; the best thing about "Fuckin' Up" isn't the title but Young's pig-squeal soloing. Even the striking save-the-planet prayer "Mother Earth (Natural Anthem)," which closes the album, gathers much of its power from the indignant cacophony of Young's solo electric guitar; it's a stirring performance, an ecological cousin of Hendrix's "Star-Spangled Banner." On *Ragged Glory,* Young makes a glorious, and poetic, racket that would scare punks half his age out of their B.V.D.'s. If this is fuckin' up, may he never stop.

MICHAEL CORCORAN

NEIL YOUNG PERFORMANCE REVIEW

Neil Young, Sonic Youth, Social Distortion
Rosemont Horizon, Rosemont, Illinois
January 29, 1991

"**M**ORE!"
The lights came up and the taped music blared, but nobody was going home. Members of the audience stood on
their chairs and screamed, while some of the more observant read the
roadies' movements to see if there would be one last encore. An amp jockey
unplugged the mikes, another hit some mixing-board switches—the pros-
pects of another song didn't look good. Since Neil Young and Crazy Horse
had played only eleven songs, the show seemed too short, but in truth,
almost two hours had passed between the opening couplet—a Hendrixian
"Star-Spangled Banner" and "Hey Hey, My My (Into the Black)"—and
the scheduled encore, "Like a Hurricane." Time seemed to stop each time
Young dove headfirst into the marrow-melting guitar solos that anchored
every song.

As is Young's custom (one of his few), the live show was mostly loyal
to the spirit of his latest album. Though previous tours by Young and the
Shocking Pinks, International Harvesters and the Bluenotes met with
mixed success, his shows with Crazy Horse, that overachieving garage band,
have always brought out Young's bravest vocals and most lethal chords.
Ragged Glory, the latest collaboration of their on-and-off relationship of
twenty years, could be subtitled *The Electric Guitar and the Damage Done;* the
album's raw intensity and feedback-drenched solid-body strokes provided
the model for a blazing guitar show. Though the band performed only three
songs from *Ragged Glory*—"Love to Burn," "Mansion on the Hill" and
"Fuckin' Up"—older songs such as "Cortez the Killer," "Cinnamon Girl"
and "Rockin' in the Free World" gained fire from the *Ragged Glory* treatment. "Crime in the City" went from sly to demonic in the hands of the
relentless quartet. Even Young's haunting version of Bob Dylan's wartime
standard "Blowin' in the Wind" received an electric jolt at the end when
Young made like his other major influence, Jimi Hendrix, and played a
rockets'-red-glare send-off of the song's melody line.

With the second-nature rhythm section of drummer Ralph Molina, bassist Billy Talbot and guitarist Frank "Poncho" Sampedro slipping easily into a groove, Young was free to indulge his own vision of guitar heaven, as he did so brilliantly on *Ragged Glory*. Though Young barely glanced at his band mates and never addressed the crowd, the big, loopy grin on his face as he took his piercing "Cinnamon Girl" lead for a walk behind huge mock Fender amps said plenty about the chemistry in the hall.

To say that music filled the air is a tired cliché, but during Young's set the notes seemed as tangible as sparks. At times the music swirled overhead; indeed, when the lights went up, people in the upper balconies responded as wildly as those who were below.

After about fifteen minutes of screeching, chanting and frenzied clapping, the auditorium suddenly went dark, and the sound of 10,000 dreams being answered rang out. Young had decided to do one more. Unprepared for this rare spontaneous encore, roadies scampered onstage like deckhands trying to patch a dozen leaks. Fans shouted out requests—"This Note's for You," "Mr. Soul," "Tonight's the Night," "Heart of Gold," "After the Gold Rush" and other favorites—but it was anyone's guess what Young would use to satiate the crowd. After a few loud guitar strums, the band launched right into . . . "Welfare Mothers." "Welfare Mothers," that throwaway cut from *Rust Never Sleeps*? It was as if Springsteen had chosen to end a three-hour show with "[Ooh Ooh, I've Got a] Crush on You."

No one could ever get rich anticipating the whims of Neil Young, who might be the idiot savant of rock & roll. His peculiar ambiguity—perhaps best exemplified by his efforts in behalf of Farm Aid while pledging support for Ronald Reagan—was in evidence on the Rosemont stage. Dominating the huge backdrop was a peace sign with doves flying over it, while Young's oversize microphone was bound with a yellow ribbon—a puzzling array of free-floating signifiers.

To his credit, Young does not break bread with the expected. If he wanted to, he could put together the ultimate three-hour retrospective concert, playing every masterpiece to deafening applause, saving his four biggest hits for the encore. But Neil Young, the eternal incorruptible hippie, has always played the music that means the most to *him*. From his everyman vocals to his other-worldly guitar work, he's always played it close to his chest.

With two bands of similar conviction—Social Distortion and Sonic Youth—opening the show, this promised to be a strong triple bill. But like so many great matchups (Tyson and Spinks, Jeff Goldblum and Geena Davis), this one looked better on paper than it was in practice. With tattooed singer Mike Ness looking like Harry Connick Jr.'s evil twin, Social

D. kicked out a blazing set at a time when most ticket holders were deciding which freeway exit to take. Sonic Youth also tried to make the most of its half-hour, playing "hits" like "Mary-Christ," "Kill Yr. Idols" and "Tunic," but the band failed to get much of a response until Thurston Moore said sarcastically, "When this is over, I'm going backstage to smoke a big bomber." The crowd cheered as much for the dope reference as for the fact that Sonic Youth would soon be off the stage.

DON MCLEESE

WELD ALBUM REVIEW

★ ★ ★ ½

THOUGH NEIL YOUNG REFERS TO IT as his garage band, Crazy Horse operates best on the open road, where it can take songs out of the studio, open 'em up, let 'em rip. For anyone who thought Young and the band drove feedback to its outer limits on last year's *Ragged Glory, Weld* opens new dimensions of sonic turbulence.

Sure, this double concert album is something of a redundancy—with most of the material coming from *Ragged Glory,* its predecessor *Freedom* and the predictable concert staples—but it's a glorious redundancy nonetheless. While "Crime in the City" pulled some punches in the studio, the live version is ferociously definitive. If "Welfare Mothers" once seemed like a goof, it's now a savage assault—black humor from the economic under-belly. Expanded beyond thirteen minutes, "Like a Hurricane" swirls to an otherworldly climax. (Want to go even further? The album is also available as a limited-edition, three-CD *Arc-Weld* set, with the *Arc* disc consisting of a thirty-five-minute, feedback-laden sound collage.)

Rather than the escapist fare of so many concert spectacles, *Weld* offers tough music for tough times. "Blowin' in the Wind" recalls the agony of Desert Storm, which was raging during Young's tour, and "Rockin' in the Free World" sounds even more prophetic than it did on *Freedom.* Crazy Horse was once reserved for Young's brutally basic music, but "Mansion on the Hill" finds the band a match for some of his most thoughtful songcraft. The sonic barrages of Young and second guitarist Frank Sampe-dro over the rhythmic bedrock of drummer Ralph Molina and bassist Billy Talbot offer a pulverizing purity, a catharsis that makes the plaintive emo-tion of "Love and Only Love" seem all the more delicate.

Not all the material renews itself in concert. Expanded to more than eight minutes, "Tonight's the Night," once a taut tragedy, moves toward turgid melodrama. And though "Cinnamon Girl" remains a live favorite, by this point it's way too familiar to warrant inclusion. As a re-creation of the Neil Young concert experience, *Weld* is weakened by its lack of the sort of surprises that invariably marked the tours before *Ragged Glory.* Still, Young has followed this swing of the pendulum about as far as it can go, which suggests that the surprises will come next time.

ALAN LIGHT

NEIL YOUNG PERFORMANCE REVIEW

Beacon Theater, New York City
February 15, 1992

WHY WOULD A SERIES OF Neil Young concerts billed as "solo acoustic evenings" draw so many fans in Hendrix and Skynyrd T-shirts yelling for "Southern Man" or other such inappropriate Young raveups? It seems absurd, but maybe Young has spent so much time confounding the expectations of his listeners over the last few decades that these classic-rock diehards are right never to give up hope that Young may switch gears, even in midshow.

Indeed, in this most traditional of settings, Young still found a new way to surprise. Twenty years to the month after the release of *Harvest,* he used these shows (and similar theater runs in a few other cities) as an opportunity to try out the unreleased songs that will presumably constitute his long-promised sequel, *Harvest Moon.*

New material made up two-thirds of the fifteen-song set this night. Young, seated and surrounded by a fleet of guitars, was in exquisite voice. Aging love and the environment were the evening's themes, and several of the melodies recaptured the grace and prettiness of *Harvest.* Unfortunately, though, the new songs seemed mostly sentimental and slight. A lengthy narrative titled "Unknown Legend" stood out, but whatever resonance it had was quashed when it was followed by a paean to "saving the baby creatures" and a silly throwaway about Young's dog.

The languid, introspective readings Young gave to the few familiar songs (including an opening "Long May You Run" and *Harvest*'s hit "Heart of Gold") only highlighted the one-dimensional impression left by the new numbers. "It's a cool scene, kinda like a club," Young said at one point. "At least from here." From the thirty-dollar seats, though, it felt more like a focus group, a test market for yet another new Neil.

GREG KOT

HARVEST MOON ALBUM REVIEW

★ ★ ★ ★

NEIL YOUNG HAS SPENT THE LAST twenty years flitting from style to style like a moth trapped in a warehouse full of light bulbs. So it should come as no surprise that after a couple of albums in which he explored the outer limits of guitar noise, Young has pulled the plug, strapped on his acoustic and wheeled in the pedal steel for *Harvest Moon*.

The title echoes *Harvest,* Young's countryish album of two decades ago, and the music recalls its gentle flavor. *Harvest* was a mellow best-seller, an uncharacteristic middle-of-the-road pit stop in a decade of deeply personal and sometimes highly eccentric releases, and *Harvest Moon* also sounds as if it was made for lazy hammock-swinging afternoons. But beneath its placid surface are the craggy scars of middle age, when holding onto and cherishing love is a lot more difficult than finding it.

When Young last explored the same subject on *Ragged Glory,* from 1990, he whipped up great funnel clouds of feedback. *Harvest Moon* sounds like the calm after the storm, with a hushed musical landscape at times populated only by a ghostly harmonica, a few spooky bass lines and Young's cracked, lonesome tenor. The opening series of songs traces a path from restlessness to reaffirmation, in which the rootless "Unknown Legend" and the doubt-filled narrator of "From Hank to Hendrix" finally find contentment beneath the "Harvest Moon."

As if to show how his perspective has changed, Young uses orchestration similar to *Harvest*'s "A Man Needs a Maid" on "Such a Woman," but the earlier song's outdated perspective has transformed into homage. On "One of These Days," which looks back fondly on lost friends (with initials C, S and N, perhaps?), and the corny "Old King," Young briefly detours toward the maudlin and trivial. But "War of Man" and the towering "Natural Beauty" bristle with the paternal anger of one who appreciates just how fragile everything on the planet is—including the planet itself.

The Stray Gators and a bevy of singers, including Linda Ronstadt and Nicolette Larson, give these melodies just the right amount of massaging. And within these spare settings, Young's search for shelter from the storm resonates like a heartbeat.

JAMES HUNTER

LUCKY THIRTEEN: EXCURSIONS INTO ALIEN TERRITORY ALBUM REVIEW

★ ★ ★ ★

T HE ALBUM TRACKS, REMIXES AND live recordings on *Lucky Thirteen* come from Neil Young's trying affiliation through the Eighties with Geffen Records, a period that found him more slagged than celebrated. In fact, that passage only clarified Young's passionate, career-long commitment to emotion over style; it offered the genre experiments of someone who countered early-Seventies Eagles-style pop, for example, with music that sounds like Sonic Youth playing country rock. *Lucky Thirteen* resequences and rethinks the imperfect but important Eighties work of an artist who recently contended that "deep inside" his acoustic pleasantries, his distorted raveups, his troubled techno, his symphonic flights, lies "the same stuff." It's an extraordinary view for a Sixties-based rock musician to take—a refusal to moralize about genre—and on this compilation, Young begins to set his artistic record straight.

Compiled by Young himself, *Lucky Thirteen* is more concerned with demonstrating the value of eclecticism than showing off Young's finest Geffen copyrights; many memorable songs don't appear. Instead, Young tries to show how the emotional impulses behind his songwriting, performing and recording methods remain constant as his styles vary. Beginning with a spectacular remix, firm and echoing, of "Sample and Hold" (*Trans,* 1982), followed by the blend of romantic yearning and technological severity in "Transformer Man," from the same album, Young makes the bold transition into the analog guitar-and-harmonica vibe of the previously unreleased "Depression Blues." In context, the dramatic effect of a narrative shot through with worries and hope that mourns the loss of "magic" in today's world is impossible to overstate. These songs alone make Young's point extremely well: that when you're not married to one particular style, your music can then be free to develop itself totally, without fear of too much attention to what Young calls "surface."

On the rest of *Lucky Thirteen,* Young further wins his case not with theory but with music: In a live, gnarly, previously unreleased version of

"Don't Take Your Love Away From Me," he stretches out words in a George Jones kind of way. On "Hippie Dream" and "Pressure" (*Landing on Water,* 1986) he sings country aches into songs governed by involved, gritty electric guitar. And in a patch of his famous indigestibility, he tells the tale of "Mideast Vacation" (*Life,* 1987), rolling out that metal-sired "Like a Hurricane" float that could be, in the end, Young's greatest musical contribution.

A longer retrospective called *Neil Young Archives* eventually will follow *Lucky Thirteen*. Meantime, there is this extraordinary album, which lays out the crucial reasons why Neil Young perseveres and triumphs.

BURL GILYARD

UNPLUGGED ALBUM REVIEW

★ ★ ★

Reviewed in Conjunction with Warren Zevon's
Learning to Flinch

NEIL YOUNG AND Warren Zevon share a deeper kinship than might be immediately obvious. Although both men are approaching fifty, they remain defiant originals, mainstream exiles, amiable cynics. After being adrift (Young) or absent (Zevon) for much of the Eighties, both are now basking in midlife renaissances. But if you're going to peddle new versions of songs your fans already own, you should try to transcend the increasingly empty "unplugged" trend.

Even within the spare context of his appearance on *Unplugged,* Young flashes both sides of his musical personality: the earnest folkie and the edgy heretic. Young's set is neatly divided into halves: The first seven tunes are strictly solo, tapping darker material like his Buffalo Springfield touchstone "Mr. Soul" and the plaintive "Stringman," a previously unreleased gem. For the last seven songs he's backed by the current incarnation of the Stray Gators (bolstered by Nils Lofgren) and leans on softer folk, ranging from "Helpless" to three repeats from *Harvest Moon.* A beguiling acoustic re-working of "Transformer Man" and a pipe-organ take on "Like a Hurri-cane" are both revelations. Yet overall, it feels like Young's coasting. The music has the relaxed aura of a friendly fireside folk sing that could use a shot of ragged glory.

Zevon's set, culled from his 1992 solo tour, sports a better sense of humor and a stronger sense of irony but still reeks of recycling. Alternating between keyboards and crisp twelve-string guitar, Zevon delivers acoustic renderings of everything from smartass anthems like "Lawyers, Guns and Money" to the unsettling "Boom Boom Mancini." Although most of the fresh instrumental flourishes click, thirteen minutes of "Roland the Head-less Thompson Gunner" is simply exhausting. Of three new songs, only "The Indifference of Heaven" matches his most compelling work. Al-though *Learning to Flinch* is easily Zevon's sharpest since his *Sentimen-*

tal Hygiene (1987), its finest moments are drawn from his oldest material.

While Young's *Unplugged* is essentially another episode of "Neil, the Enigmatic Folkie," Zevon's collection functions more purely as a career overview. Both albums make fine mementos for fans, but they're the sonic equivalent of souvenir T-shirts: perfectly comfortable, destined to fade.

ALAN LIGHT

FOREVER YOUNG

Driven, Open, Restless—Neil Young Is Simply So
Anachronistic that in the 1990s He's Cutting Edge

"**D**ID YOU SEE *DRACULA*?" Neil Young breaks into a wide grin
over a bowl of postconcert fruit salad. "Man, they got some
wind in *Dracula* that's scary," he says. "It's *beautiful*."
Later that night, on his vintage 1970 tour bus parked outside a Chicago
hotel, a discussion about growing up in Canada quickly leads back, somehow, to thoughts of Transylvania. "I can't get it out of my mind!" Young
exclaims, shaking his shaggy head. "I got to go back and see it again."

Though his hair and the massive mutton chops might seem to indicate
more of an affinity for the Wolf Man, Neil Young and Count Dracula
actually have a surprising amount in common. Both spend much of their
time underground, occasionally surfacing with surprising, even shocking
results. Both can change style and persona to get their work done. And—
most significantly—both seem not to grow older as the years go by.

At forty-seven, Young has turned the clock back a full twenty years
with his new album, *Harvest Moon.* Recapturing the sweeping melodies and
lush harmonies of 1972's *Harvest,* still his most popular release, *Harvest Moon*
represents Young's first appearance in the Top Twenty in almost ten years.

But *Harvest Moon* is more complicated than a simple nostalgia trip or a
remake. Beneath the pedal steels and dulcet tones of *Harvest,* the twenty-
six-year-old Young sounded wizened beyond his years as he first con-
fronted aging and mortality. "As the days fly past, will we lose our grasp?"
he asked in his eerie, pinched voice on the title track; on "Are You Ready
for the Country?" he sang, "I ran into the hangman, and he said, 'It's time
to die.'" Even "Heart of Gold," Young's only Number-One single, ended
each verse with the tag "and I'm getting old."

Harvest Moon, on the other hand, is a chronicle of survival, focusing on
loss and compromise and the ultimate triumphs of being a married father
approaching fifty. It's full of bittersweet tributes to lost friends, dead hounds
and love grown old. "What this album is about is this feeling, this ability
to survive and continue and grow and get higher than you were before,"
says Young. "Not just maintain, not just feel well. Not just 'I'm still alive
at forty-five.' You can be *more* alive."

It hasn't been an easy ride these two decades for Young. He has suffered through the deaths of several musicians close to him, from Danny Whitten (guitarist in Crazy Horse, Young's frequent garage-rock collaborator) in 1972 to the passing in 1991 of Steve Lawrence, saxophonist in his bluesy big-band project the Bluenotes. Young went through a controversial, contentious period artistically throughout the 1980s, ending up in a surreal court battle with Geffen Records, his label at the time, for making what the company called "unrepresentative" albums—for making albums that didn't sound like Neil Young albums, whatever that could possibly mean. Most harrowing, he has two sons, by two different women, both of whom were born with cerebral palsy (he also has an eight-year-old daughter who does not have the condition).

Yet Young has managed to produce the most consistently compelling body of work of any musician of his generation. Who else has remained so relevant, so vital, so influential in so many musical genres? The last few years in particular—beginning with *Freedom,* in 1989, through the cataclysmic *Ragged Glory* (1990) and his subsequent tour with Crazy Horse, and continuing with his soaring, show-stealing performance at the Bob Dylan tribute last October and the release of *Harvest Moon*—have seen Young at an artistic peak, following his own muse as always and resolutely refusing to fall into the "oldies act" category that has beset virtually all of his contemporaries.

"If you're charged up and have all this experience, what else is there?" Young says of his amazingly graceful rock & roll maturation. "When you're young, you don't have any experience—you're charged up, but you're out of control. And if you're old and you're not charged up, then all you have is memories. But if you're charged and stimulated by what's going on around you and you also have experience, you know what to appreciate and what to pass by. And then you're really cruising."

THE HEAD OF CORPORATE marketing for WTTW-TV, Chicago's PBS affiliate, strides to the front of the room in the station's studios. Neil Young is about to tape the first installment of *Center Stage,* a new series coproduced by WTTW and VH-1. The station rep welcomes the small crowd, filled with industry weasels and local music-biz types, and makes one request of the 200 or so invited guests.

"Anybody who's got a tie on or is looking too corporate," he says, "could you please take them off? It's important that this look like a Neil Young crowd."

The next night, though, at an actual Neil Young concert in front of actual Neil Young fans, there are quite a few ties in the house. Their owners are seated next to kids in frayed flannel shirts, next to preppie types in

Docksiders, next to rockers in leather jackets. Garth Brooks listeners mingle with Nirvana-heads. Woodstock meets Lollapalooza. An aging hipster in a linen jacket shares a joint in the men's room with a fresh-scrubbed teen.

"Can we get it together, can we still stand side by side?" Young sings in *Harvest Moon*'s "From Hank to Hendrix." With the continuing fragmentation of the pop-music audience, a Neil Young solo concert is as close to a rock & roll consensus as you're going to find.

"They come from everywhere for the acoustic thing," Young says. "They won't meet anywhere else. But once I define it with a band, I lose half of them and bring in a bunch more extremists from one place or another."

The acoustic thing. Young has been touring off and on for the past year with just a fleet of guitars, a couple of pianos and a banjo or two, hitting two or three cities at a time and then retreating—vampirelike—to his ranch in California for a few weeks. The one consistent element in these shows is his refusal to use a set list at any time—much to the chagrin of the *Center Stage* film crew, which scrambles to shoot Young as he wanders from instrument to instrument, scratching his head and figuring out what he wants to play next.

"There's a lot I get out of doing this acoustic thing that I don't get any other way," Young says. "It opens up the music and the songs and what they're about. Being able to pick things out and change them around. A band can cover that stuff up. There's nothing worse than walking out and knowing exactly what you're going to do. At this time of my life, I don't need that."

The flip side of that, of course, is not knowing what the audience is going to make of any given Neil Young show. The *Center Stage* taping is spectacular, with Young compensating for his concerns about the bright lights of TV by delving even deeper into the songs. He ends up playing twenty songs, almost two hours, for a show that will run only a half-hour (an hour-long version will appear on PBS next summer). A painfully intense rendition of 1977's "Like a Hurricane" on the pipe organ is the highlight—Young would later refer to it as "the Transylvania version," though it actually felt closer to *Phantom of the Opera*. (Too lunatic for VH-1, apparently: The song didn't make the cut for the show.)

The following night's concert at the gorgeously restored, turn-of-the-century Chicago Theater, however, is not such a pretty sight. The crowd is boisterous and vocal from the opening minutes. Several times, Young starts to play a song only to cut it short, claiming that he can't hear himself. "Don't think I'm fucking with you, okay?" he pleads from the stage. "But some of you guys who drink a lot of beer, you know how loud you can be compared to this."

Finally, Young delivers a brief, good-natured greatest-hits set, cutting off after about seventy-five minutes. "Tonight was the opposite of what I like to do on a musical level—tonight was survival," he says after the show. "But you have to be able to read it and roll with it. I don't have to play a sensitive song while people are yelling. I play the songs for myself, and if I'm distracted by the audience, I'll just stop."

Young bears no malice for this segment of his following, the beer-swilling guys in ALLMAN BROTHERS T-shirts who turned last winter's performances at New York's Beacon Theater into a nasty, heated battle between his desire to play unreleased new songs and their calls for his familiar rock & roll raveups. "Don't you have a lot of friends like that?" he asks. "Big outgoing guys who have a few drinks and just get blown out, but if they aren't drinking, their soulful side comes out and they're actually real sensitive? They just get so high, they feel it so much, that they think they're alone in their van listening to the songs."

Harvest Moon might seem like the ultimate concession to Young's old fans, but he sees it as a valid, even experimental enterprise. "People had been asking me to do it for twenty years, and I never could figure out what it was in the first place," he says. But when he wrote a batch of new songs and finished some old ones last summer in Colorado, the *Harvest* sound was what he heard in his head. "That's when I discovered what the hell I was doing, but only because the songs made me do it," he says. "It just happened again, whatever it was that happened back then."

The track "You and Me," a quiet paean to domesticity that quotes from the *Harvest* hit "Old Man," is the musical link between the albums, according to Young: "That song was started in 1975, but I never finished it. In 1976, [bassist] Tim Drummond heard it and said: 'You've got to finish that, man. That's like *Harvest* stuff, let's do that.' And that kinda freaked me out, I got spooked by it, because it was like someone said what it was before we did it. I don't want to feel like I'm just filling in the numbers." But along with this new batch of compositions came a new intro and last verse, and the twenty-year-long jump was completed.

In the notes to his 1978 anthology *Decade,* Young wrote: " 'Heart of Gold' put me in the middle of the road. Traveling there soon became a bore so I headed for the ditch." He still expresses ambivalence about *Harvest:* "When people start asking you to do the same thing over and over again, that's when you know you're way too close to something that you don't want to be near. I can't hold that against [*Harvest*], which I did; it's certainly got the depth of the other records. But it took a while to get to that. I just didn't want to do the obvious thing, because it didn't feel right."

Obviousness or predictability would be the last things of which Neil Young could be accused. Young asserts that all the disparate styles he has explored—from his Sixties work with folk-rock pioneer Buffalo Springfield to the altered electro-vocals of *Trans* (1982) to the rockabilly of *Everybody's Rockin'* (1983)—are related, that the relevance his listeners find in the more accessible records is of a piece with the weirder, sometimes patently incomprehensible stuff. "Deep inside [the *Rockin'* band] the Shocking Pinks or *Trans* is the same stuff that people are hearing now," he says. "It's just buried; it's not on the surface. And some of it is more intense than what people are hearing now."

Nor has Young ever turned his back on any part of his musical past. His tour bus, after all, still has BUFFALO SPRINGFIELD emblazoned on the back (making it hard to miss parked outside the stage door after a show). He doesn't even rule out another go-round with his cohorts Crosby, Stills and Nash. "I'm good friends with all of them, and we could literally be making music together anytime," Young says. "If we had the songs and the circumstances were right, we could do something great. I think the potential's still there."

Driven, open, restless (he even named the band he took to Europe after *Freedom* Young and the Restless), Young's primitive guitar screech and yowling voice have served as lasting inspiration for wandering souls and fuck-ups of several generations now. In the 1990s, Neil Young is simply so anachronistic that he's cutting edge.

"I like to walk," he says when asked what he does during a typical day on tour after a lifetime in the rock & roll business. "A lot of times, I'll stop the bus and walk for three or four miles and then let the bus catch up with me on the road."

NEIL YOUNG DOESN'T listen to records. "I'm more interested in what the music of the times is," he explains over juice and coffee in the café of his Chicago hotel, still wearing the same CHICAGO BLACKHAWKS T-shirt he put on after the preceding night's show. "If it's on the radio or somebody else is playing a tape, that's how I hear music. It's what I hear in the environment." He must travel in a wide-open environment indeed, for he casually drops references to artists ranging from Trisha Yearwood to Pearl Jam, from R.E.M. to Patty Smyth. He flashes a goofy grin on the *Harvest Moon* inner sleeve bedecked in a FISHBONE T-shirt.

Young discusses music—any music—with unabashed love; it's incredible to hear anyone talk about bands without a shred of attitude or exclusion. As one who helped popularize country rock in the Seventies, for instance, he maintains that today's country boom is the result of listeners losing interest in singer/songwriters like himself.

"I drove a lot of people away by singing so loud and abrasive and the feedback and all, and I'm not the only one who's done that to them," Young says. "A lot of people turned to country because it's more like Seventies rock & roll. Pop and rock have just changed their name to country. Garth Brooks—he's a pop star, like what's his name, Bryan Adams. But he sings about things that are more rural, more country values. People like to hear about things they can relate to, not just some posey kind of antilifestyle attitude or whatever."

As for rap, the bane of many of his peers' musical existence, Young practically jumps out of his chair with enthusiasm. "I love rap!" he declares with a sparkle in those familiar, piercing eyes, professing a particular fondness for Ice-T. "It's speaking to the people on the streets. It's a whole new way of communicating that's so open to saying exactly what the hell's on people's minds in a clever way, a way that you can listen to and move your body to. Similar to, like, 'Subterranean Homesick Blues.' Dylan is early rap. What the hell's the difference?" To those who resist rap's charms, he adds, "This is the shit that's going to keep music alive—don't close it off because you don't understand it."

The new music with the clearest links to Young's work is grungy guitar rock. His turbulent instrumental squalls and Crazy Horse's thunderous backing—not to mention his flannel-centric wardrobe—echo through the work of Seattle's rising stars and a range of alternative artists from Dinosaur Jr to the Jayhawks to Matthew Sweet. Many of today's postpunk college guitar bands claim him as a spiritual godfather; some of them—including Soul Asylum and the Pixies—covered Young songs on *The Bridge,* a 1989 tribute album.

Young is loath, however, to take credit as an influence on anyone. "It's not me, it's just the music," he says wearily. "I play it, and they play it. Link Wray was doing it a long time ago. Then Hendrix, now we've got all the grungers and the distortion thing. It's just going farther and farther, which it should. It's being developed."

Not since Young put Johnny Rotten and Elvis in the same song on *Rust Never Sleeps* in 1979, however, did he embrace the next wave as he did when he took Sonic Youth on the road with Crazy Horse in 1991. "They've got this thing happening that I enjoy," he says of the art-punk superheroes. "It's soothing to me; it was very soothing before I went onstage to hear that feedback through the cement walls."

The summit of noisy icons from two generations took its toll on Young, however. Playing in the center of a jacked-up guitar blitzkrieg for six months damaged his ears. "I had hyperacoustis," he says. "I heard everything very loudly. Now it's back to normal, but I still don't like going into loud places. I had to rest for a long time and get everything together.

"Those shows were really fucking loud," Young continues. "Loud in the way a crashing plane is loud, amped up for that war sound, that kind of thing. That's what we were going for."

The entire tour was shot through with the spirit of war, which started while Young and Crazy Horse were in rehearsals. Most overtly, Young put a huge microphone stand tied with a yellow ribbon at center stage and added a blistering version of "Blowin' in the Wind" to the set. "That war really left a mark on me," he whispers back in the bus. "We were playing so raucously, so violently, really like a bombardment. It was like we were there. It was very military sounding at times—big machinery, unbelievable power and destruction. That was our sound."

Young's bitterness over the Gulf war, which lies behind a track on *Harvest Moon* titled "War of Man," has given way to excitement, tinged with skepticism, about Washington's new administration. "It has its comedic side," he says of the Clinton regime, "but it's cool that you go to places and a lot of working people are happy. They think that if things don't change right away, at least they've got somebody who knows who they are.

"But," Young adds, "I always try to get behind the guy steering the ship. That's the kind of guy I am."

It was a similar attitude that resulted in Young's most notorious political statements when he spoke out in support of Ronald Reagan in the early Eighties. Despite his ultimate dissatisfaction with the past twelve years of Republican rule, though, he has no wish to recant those opinions.

"I feel exactly the same as I did when that was going down," Young says, narrowing his formidable eyebrows. "There were some things Reagan liked that I liked. The main component of it was that people have got to talk to each other and help themselves and that government can't completely take care of them by making a bunch of promises and programs. It can't be done that way to the exclusion of working together on things like child care. That was his point—get together, people. Organize your communities.

"I agreed with that," Young says. "But because I agreed with that one thing and similar types of points, then I was a Reagan backer. It was a shock for some people that I could agree with anything that that man would say. But I'm not into this judgmental, religious-right kind of thing. My ideals don't run along those lines."

Onstage he may resemble an affable gas-station attendant or a psychopathic lumberjack, while in conversation he looks more like your burned-out ex-hippie uncle. Somewhere along the way, though, Neil Young has become the very model of all that "family values" should really mean. "My family is a unit that's behind my music and doesn't inhibit it," he says. "The most beautiful thing about my wife, Pegi, is that she never gets in the way of my music. She doesn't have an attitude about certain kinds of music. For her to have an attitude about this or that, then if I go into that kind of music, I'm thinking, 'Right here in the house we have someone who doesn't like this at all.' I never have that with her; there's no restrictions that way."

His marriage, his life on the ranch with his kids and the cars and antique train sets he collects serve as the truest metaphor for Young's work. "The real music of my life is my family," he says. "I didn't keep this marriage together just by doing the same thing over again that I was doing when I got married. I didn't get pigeonholed into having only one personality, like a lot of people do. They kind of become someone that they're not. And in music, if you do that, you've had it."

On "Unknown Legend," *Harvest Moon*'s opening track, Young sings, "You know it ain't easy / You got to hold on," and the rewards of persevering through difficult, even tragic times are evident when he speaks of his home life. He spent much of the Eighties struggling to come to terms with his sons' disabilities, and he has said that his anger and frustration and his family's experience with various rehabilitation programs inspired the impenetrable, tortured work of that era. These days, though, his craggy face looks as thoughtful and peaceful as his voice sounds on the new album. After helping to found the Bridge School, outside of San Francisco, for physically challenged kids like his sons, he now stages an all-star benefit each year to raise funds. It is his involvement with his children that now seems to keep Young happier and fresher than anything else.

"Every year now for my birthday party we do the same thing," Young says, beaming. "I build a fire, set up all the logs and build it myself. Then after dark, Pegi comes out and lights it. Then the kids come home from school, and we have all their little-kid friends and their parents over. The people that come to my party are chosen because they're the parents of my children's friends. They all come down to the fire, and we roast hamburgers and hot dogs and stuff and sit around the fire. After we have dinner, they come down with marshmallows and they all roast marshmallows. So every year at my party, the kids all come. They can't wait. It's like a big day for them. I don't know what that means, but that's us."

THE SOLO ACOUSTIC SHOWS THAT started when he wrote the songs for *Harvest Moon* are all over, at least for now, or so Young says. *"Harvest Moon* is almost a year old now," he says. "I'm almost finished doing this." Of course, in 1988 he said he probably wouldn't work with Crazy Horse again, calling their sound "a younger kind of music," only to record the majestic *Ragged Glory* with them the next year; "Yeah, well, that's typical," he says of that particular change of plans. Meanwhile, he continues to work on a long-anticipated multivolume retrospective of his career (the plans now call for different configurations "depending on how deep you want to get into it") and an autobiography.

Most immediately, though, Young is starting to hear the next sound in his head. He doesn't know what it is yet. He sure had fun playing the electric guitar again at the Dylan tribute, but maybe there's another band, new or old, to work with. The only sure thing is that it's time to move on.

"We're on the edge," Young says, nodding dreamily. "I can feel it coming. It won't be long."

DISCOGRAPHY

NEIL YOUNG

NEIL YOUNG
　Reprise, 1969

EVERYBODY KNOWS THIS IS NOWHERE (with Crazy Horse)
　Reprise, 1969

AFTER THE GOLD RUSH (with Crazy Horse)
　Reprise, 1970

HARVEST
　Reprise, 1972

JOURNEY THROUGH THE PAST
　Reprise, 1972

TIME FADES AWAY
　Reprise, 1973

ON THE BEACH
　Reprise, 1974

TONIGHT'S THE NIGHT (with Crazy Horse)
　Reprise, 1975

ZUMA (with Crazy Horse)
　Reprise, 1975

LONG MAY YOU RUN (as the Stills/Young Band)
　Reprise, 1976

AMERICAN STARS 'N BARS
　Reprise, 1977

DECADE
　Reprise, 1978

COMES A TIME
Reprise, 1978

RUST NEVER SLEEPS (with Crazy Horse)
Reprise, 1979

LIVE RUST (with Crazy Horse)
Reprise, 1979

HAWKS & DOVES
Reprise, 1980

RE-AC-TOR (with Crazy Horse)
Reprise, 1981

TRANS
Geffen, 1982

EVERYBODY'S ROCKIN' (with the Shocking Pinks)*
Geffen, 1983

OLD WAYS*
Geffen, 1985

LANDING ON WATER
Geffen, 1986

LIFE*
Geffen, 1987

THIS NOTE'S FOR YOU (with the Bluenotes)
Reprise, 1987

FREEDOM
Reprise, 1989

RAGGED GLORY (with Crazy Horse)
Reprise, 1990

WELD (with Crazy Horse)
Reprise, 1991

ARC
Reprise, 1991

*Out of print

HARVEST MOON
Reprise, 1992

LUCKY THIRTEEN: EXCURSIONS INTO ALIEN TERRITORY
Geffen, 1993

UNPLUGGED
Reprise, 1993

SLEEPS WITH ANGELS
Reprise, 1994

BUFFALO SPRINGFIELD

BUFFALO SPRINGFIELD
Atco/Atlantic, 1966

BUFFALO SPRINGFIELD AGAIN
Atco/Atlantic, 1967

LAST TIME AROUND
Atco/Atlantic, 1968

RETROSPECTIVE
Atco/Atlantic, 1969

BUFFALO SPRINGFIELD
Atco/Atlantic, 1973

CROSBY, STILLS, NASH AND YOUNG

DÉJÀ VU
Atlantic, 1970

4 WAY STREET
Atlantic, 1971

SO FAR
Atlantic, 1974

AMERICAN DREAM
Atlantic, 1988

SELECTIVE VIDEOGRAPHY

SINGLE-SONG VIDEOS

"Cry, Cry, Cry"
Release date: July 1983
Director: Tim Pope

"Wonderin' "
Release date: July 1983
Director: Tim Pope

"Are There Any More Real Cowboys?"
(with Willie Nelson)
Release date: September 1985
Director: Lana Nelson

"Weight of the World"
Release date: July 1986
Director: Tim Pope

"Touch the Night"
Release date: July 1986
Director: Tim Pope

"People of the Street"
Release date: November 1986
Director: Tim Pope

"This Note's for You"
Release date: June 1988
Director: Julien Temple

"Hey Hey"
Release date: August 1988
Director: Julien Temple

"Rockin' in the Free World"
Release date: October 1989
Director: Julien Temple

"Fuckin' Up"
Release date: September 1990
Director: Rusty Cundieff

"Over and Over"
Release date: November 1990
Director: Julien Temple

"Mansion on the Hill"
Release date: 1990
Director: Rusty Cundieff

"Farmer John"
Release date: 1990
Director: Rusty Cundieff

"No More"
Release date: 1990
Director: Julien Temple

"Harvest Moon"
Release date: November 1992
Director: Julien Temple

"Unknown Legend"
Release date: February 1993
Director: Julien Temple

LONG-FORM VIDEOS

Rust Never Sleeps
Released theatrically: 1979
Released on video: 1993
Director: Bernard Shakey

Trans
Release date: 1986
Director: Hal Ashby

Neil Young in Berlin
Release date: 1986
Director: Michael Lindsay-Hogg

Weld
Release date: November 1991
Director: Bernard Shakey

MTV "Unplugged"
Release date: April 1993
Directors: Milton Lage, Beth McCarthy

ABOUT THE CONTRIBUTORS

David Browne is the music critic of *Entertainment Weekly*. He has written for the *New York Times*, ROLLING STONE and *Musician*, and was the pop critic at the New York *Daily News*. His one experience in a "band" was playing a twenty-minute version of "Down by the River" with college roommates.

Tim Cahill is the author of five books, the most recent of which is *Pecked to Death by Ducks*. He is a contributing editor to ROLLING STONE and the editor-at-large for *Outside* magazine.

Tom Carson has written for *L.A. Weekly*, the *Village Voice*, ROLLING STONE and other publications.

Michael Corcoran is an arts and entertainment critic for the *Dallas Morning News*.

Cameron Crowe, who has written for ROLLING STONE since he was fifteen, is a writer-director of such films as *Say Anything* and *Singles*. His biography of Neil Young, a collaboration with photographer Joel Bernstein, is planned for release "sometime in the Nineties."

Anthony DeCurtis is a writer and editor at ROLLING STONE, where he oversees the record review section. He is the editor of *Present Tense: Rock & Roll and Culture* and co-editor of *The ROLLING STONE Illustrated History of Rock & Roll* and *The ROLLING STONE Album Guide*. He won a Grammy for his liner notes for the Eric Clapton retrospective *Crossroads* and has twice won the ASCAP Deems Taylor Award for excellence in writing about music. He holds a Ph.D. in American literature from Indiana University and lectures frequently on cultural matters.

Janelle Ellis's entrée to ROLLING STONE was the piece she wrote on Neil Young's *Journey Through the Past* premiere in Dallas, Texas. She is now an English professor at El Centro College.

Jim Farber is the pop music critic of the New York *Daily News*. His work has appeared in ROLLING STONE, the *Village Voice, Entertainment Weekly, New York* magazine and many other publications.

Ben Fong-Torres began writing for ROLLING STONE in 1968 and served as senior editor until 1981. He has written for numerous magazines, including *Esquire, GQ, Playboy* and *American Film,* and his books include *The Motown Album: The Sound of Young America, Hickory Wind: The Life and Times of Gram Parsons* and his memoirs, *The Rice Room* (Hyperion, 1994).

David Fricke is the music editor of ROLLING STONE. He joined the magazine in 1985 as a senior writer. He is also the American correspondent for the English weekly *Melody Maker* and has written about music for *Musician, People* and the *New York Times.* He is the author of *Animal Instinct,* a biography of Def Leppard, and wrote the liner notes for the box set *The Byrds,* released in 1990.

Holly George-Warren is the co-author of *Musicians in Tune,* co-editor of *The* ROLLING STONE *Album Guide* and *The* ROLLING STONE *Illustrated History of Rock & Roll,* third edition, and contributor to *Country on Compact Disc.* She also has written for a variety of publications, including ROLLING STONE, *Option, Men's Journal* and the *New York Times,* and currently is the editor of Rolling Stone Press.

Barry Gifford is a novelist, screenwriter, poet and librettist. His novels include *Arise and Walk, Night People, Sailor's Holiday* and *Wild at Heart,* which was made into an award-winning film by David Lynch. He is currently writing the libretto for an opera composed by Toru Takemitsu.

Burl Gilyard lives and writes in Minneapolis, Minnesota, his hometown and final resting place. He won the 1991 ROLLING STONE College Journalism Competition in the Entertainment Reporting category. He currently writes, reports, and attempts to animate news, features, and arts for the *Twin Cities Reader,* a local alternative weekly. He dwells in domestic bliss with his bride, Nicole Cina, and two cats from a previous marriage.

Michael Goldberg is a contributing editor at ROLLING STONE. He has also written about rock & roll, the music business and new technology for *Esquire, Wired, Mirabella, Musician* and other publications.

Fred Goodman is a contributing editor to ROLLING STONE. He is also the author of a forthcoming history of the rock & roll business to be published by Times Books.

Jimmy Guterman has written five books, produced many reissue CDs, and served as editor in chief of *CD Review*. He is an editor for Delphi Internet Services.

James Henke was on the editorial staff of ROLLING STONE from 1977 to 1992. During that time, he held a variety of positions, including managing editor, music editor and Los Angeles bureau chief. Co-editor of *The* ROLLING STONE *Illustrated History of Rock & Roll,* third edition, and *The* ROLLING STONE *Album Guide,* he is now chief curator of the Rock & Roll Hall of Fame and Museum.

Steve Hochman writes about pop music for the *Los Angeles Times,* ROLLING STONE, and a variety of other publications. His ears are still ringing from Neil Young's 1978 *Rust Never Sleeps* concert at the Forum in L.A.

Stephen Holden is a music, theater and film critic for the *New York Times.*

James Hunter writes about music for ROLLING STONE, the *Village Voice,* the *New York Times, Musician* and other publications.

Marshall Kilduff is an assignment editor for the *San Francisco Chronicle.* In addition to writing for the *Chronicle* for over twenty years, he has contributed to ROLLING STONE, *California* and *New West* magazines. He is also the co-author of *Suicide Cult,* a book on Jim Jones and the People's Temple, published in 1979.

George Kimball is a sports columnist for the *Boston Herald* where he has won numerous awards.

Greg Kot is the rock critic for the *Chicago Tribune.*

Jon Landau is the author of *It's Too Late to Stop Now.* He has written extensively about rock in the *Boston Phoenix, Crawdaddy* and ROLLING

STONE, where he was an associate editor for many years. More recently, he has been working as a record producer and artist's manager.

Alan Light is editor of *Vibe* magazine and a former senior writer at ROLLING STONE. His writing appears in *The* ROLLING STONE *Illustrated History of Rock & Roll,* third edition, and in *Present Tense: Rock & Roll Culture.* He has also contributed to *Vogue,* the *South Atlantic Quarterly,* the *World Book Encyclopedia* and various other publications.

Kurt Loder was an editor at ROLLING STONE from 1979 to 1988 and is still a contributing editor. He is the author of *I, Tina,* a best-selling biography of Tina Turner. He is currently an anchor of *MTV News.*

Greil Marcus is a contributing editor of ROLLING STONE. His books include *Mystery Train, Lipstick Traces, Dead Elvis* and *Ranters & Crowd Pleasers.* His favorite Neil Young song is "Surfer Joe and Moe the Sleaze."

Dave Marsh edits *Rock & Roll Confidential* and has written and edited many books on popular music, including *Louie, Louie* and best-selling biographies of Bruce Springsteen and the Who. A *Playboy* music critic, he frequently lectures and writes about the relationship of music, politics and censorship.

Don McLeese is the pop music critic for the Austin *American-Statesman,* and a frequent contributor to ROLLING STONE and other music publications. *The* ROLLING STONE *Illustrated History of Rock & Roll,* third edition, includes his chapter on Neil Young.

Shortly after the publication of **John Mendelssohn**'s review of *Harvest,* Neil Young attended John Mendelssohn's own group's debut at Holly-wood's Whisky-A-Go-Go with the express purpose of humiliating John Mendelssohn. If John Mendelssohn's group was anything, though, it was loud, and John Mendelssohn became aware of the great artist's sneering presence only in retrospect.

Jim Miller edited the first two editions of *The* ROLLING STONE *Illustrated History of Rock & Roll* and is the author of *Democracy Is in the Streets: From Port Huron to the Siege of Chicago* (Simon & Schuster, 1987).

John Morthland is a freelance writer who lives in Austin, Texas. He is the author of *The Best of Country Music* (Doubleday, 1984).

Paul Nelson has written about music for ROLLING STONE, the *Village Voice*, the *New York Times, Circus, Penthouse, Creem,* the *Real Paper* and the *Little Sandy Review,* which he co-founded in 1961.

Steve Pond is a ROLLING STONE contributing editor. His work also appears in the *New York Times, Premiere, Playboy, GQ* and the *Washington Post.*

Parke Puterbaugh is a longtime contributing editor and former senior editor for ROLLING STONE. He writes about music, travel and the environment for a number of other publications and is co-author of a series of travel books. He lives in Greensboro, North Carolina.

Jeffrey Ressner covers the entertainment business as a correspondent for *Time* magazine in Los Angeles. He previously served as a senior writer for ROLLING STONE and the West Coast bureau chief for *Us* magazine. His work has also appeared in the *New York Times, Empire, Men's Journal* and *Spy.*

John Rockwell is a cultural correspondent, critic at large and principal classical recordings reviewer for the *New York Times;* from 1974 to 1980 he was also chief rock critic. Between early 1992 and mid-1994 he was based in Paris as European cultural correspondent. He has published two books, *All American Music,* a study of American composition from classical to experimental to Broadway to jazz to rock, and *Sinatra: An American Classic,* and has contributed widely to magazines, anthologies and encyclopedias. *All American Music* includes a chapter on Neil Young.

Sheila Rogers is a former senior writer for ROLLING STONE. She now books the music for *Late Show with David Letterman* and works as a freelance writer in New York.

Bud Scoppa made the transition from English teacher to rock critic in 1969. During the Seventies and early Eighties, he enthused in print about Gram Parsons, Big Star and Brinsley Schwarz while at the same time working as a label weasel at Mercury, A&M and Arista with such other faves as the N.Y. Dolls, the Tubes and the Bus Boys, respectively. He's now vice president of A&R at L.A.-based Zoo Entertainment, where he gets worked up about the Odds and Matthew Sweet.

Judith Sims is an editor at *Los Angeles Times Magazine.* She is working on a mystery novel set in Los Angeles.

Ken Tucker is critic-at-large for *Entertainment Weekly*. A co-author of *Rock of Ages: The* ROLLING STONE *History of Rock & Roll* (Summit), he has written about music for ROLLING STONE, the *New York Times,* the *Village Voice,* the *Philadelphia Inquirer* and *Vogue.* His weekly music reviews are heard on National Public Radio's *Fresh Air.*

Ed Ward was the record review editor for ROLLING STONE in 1970. He is currently the music and food columnist for *Checkpoint,* an English publication in Berlin.

Langdon Winner is a political theorist who specializes in social and political issues generated by modern technological change. He is the author of *Autonomous Technology.* He has written rock criticism for the *Atlantic Monthly,* ROLLING STONE and other publications.